DATE DUE

Bonnie Bergin's
Guide to Bringing Out the Best in Your Dog

Bonnie Bergin's
Guide to Bringing Out the Best in Your Dog

Bonnie Bergin

with

Robert Aquinas McNally

Selected photographs by Art Rogers

T 19688

Little, Brown and Company

Boston   New York   Toronto   London

First Edition

The author is grateful for permission to include the following previously copyrighted material: Excerpt from "Her Grave" from *New and Selected Poems* by Mary Oliver. Copyright © 1992 by Mary Oliver. Reprinted by permission of Beacon Press.

Concepts from Social Styles by the Wilson Learning Corporation. Copyright © 1976, 1994 by Wilson Learning Corporation. By permission of the publisher.

Photo Credits
Photographs courtesy of Art Rogers: p. 32 (right); p. 47; p. 64; p. 77; p. 81; p. 82 (top); p. 90; p. 142; p. 143; p. 145; p. 153; p. 156; p. 184; p. 201; p. 203; p. 205; p. 207; p. 215. Photographs used courtesy of Liane Enkelis: opposite title page; p. 228. Photographs used courtesy of Roy Crockett: p. 28; p. 29 (left); p. 52; p. 61 (right); p. 122; p. 123; p. 125; p. 126; p. 128; p. 176; p. 180; p. 185; p. 186; p. 188; p. 190; p. 191. Photographs used courtesy of Dan Hess: p. 29 (right). Photographs used courtesy of Liaison International: p. 6; p. 12; p. 14; p. 16; p. 23; p. 25; p. 28 (upper left); p. 32 (left); p. 43; p. 60; p. 61 (left); p. 82 (bottom); p. 94; p. 214; p. 237. Photograph used courtesy of Gay Currier: dedication.

Library of Congress Cataloging-in-Publication Data
Bergin, Bonnie.
   [Guide to bringing out the best in your dog]
   Bonnie Bergin's guide to bringing out the best in your dog /
Bonnie Bergin with Robert Aquinas McNally. — 1st ed.
   p. cm.
Includes index.
ISBN 0-316-09284-3
   1. Dogs — Training. 2. Dogs — Behavior. 3. Dogs — Social aspects.
I. McNally, Robert Aquinas. II. Title. III. Title: Guide to
bringing out the best in your dog.
SF431.B4335 1995
636.7'0887 — dc20   94-45880

10 9 8 7 6 5 4 3 2 1

HAD

Designed by Barbara Werden
Illustrations by Patty Bratsberg

Published simultaneously in Canada by Little, Brown & Company (Canada) Limited

Printed in the United States of America

To Gravity

*who taught me what true
canine companionship is, a
shared love that reaches
beyond the heart into
the soul.*

Acknowledgments

N O BOOK happens only because of its author. A number of people and dogs played important roles in helping bring this work to fruition.

Janet Herring-Sherman did the original research and wrote the first draft. Colleen Mohyde of the Doe Coover Agency helped redefine the project and found it a home at Little, Brown and Company. She also connected me with Robert Aquinas McNally, who gave my ideas the shape and grace of words. Patty Bratsberg brought a special love of animals to her illustrations for the mastheads, and Art Rogers, Roy Crockett, and Liane Enkelis produced wonderful photographs. Nella Banwarth, Susan Bass, Eileen Bohn, Jeannie Brock, Elisabeth Farbinger, Linda Hams, Sabina Hower, Helen McCain, and Mike St. Louis, all students from my Service Dog Training Seminar, generously offered their time as models. Family, Assistance Dog Institute staff and board members, assistance dog users, and numerous others helped with and participated in the photo sessions, including Lisa Amaroli-Strifler, Camilla Gray-Nelson, Bob Trowbridge, Juliana Bratsberg, Steve Sweeney, and Jenny Holland. The dogs who generously provided significant instructive photo opportunities but who cannot read their names in print are in my thoughts. I also want to thank Liaison International for archive photographs and Wilson Learning for a conceptual framework on personality I adapted to my own purposes.

A number of Little, Brown people

merit special mention: Mary Tondorf-Dick, for her insightful editorial guidance; Barbara Werden, for creating the design; and Mike Mattil, for his sure eye in copyediting.

Most of all I want to thank my husband, Jim Bergin. He has this way of being there for me, with this book and everything else.

Rohnert Park, California
February 1995

Contents

Introduction

IN TRUTH, this book didn't begin with dogs. It started with my own search for a solution to some of life's most painful problems. That odyssey, which originated in a desire to help people, brought me to a new and deeper understanding of dogs — and the remarkable gift they are to us humans.

This book actually began one spring afternoon in 1974, while I was having lunch in an upstairs restaurant in the business district of Ankara, Turkey. Looking down upon the hurrying pedestrians and honking cars, I spotted a quadriplegic man across the street. He was dragging himself along the sidewalk and across six lanes of traffic, propelling his body with elbows, hips, and shoulders. The sight stunned me, but when I glanced around at the other diners in the restaurant, I noticed that not one of them was paying him any attention. In the Third World, people with disabilities must make do for themselves, just like everybody else.

I had come to Turkey by way of a teaching post in Australia, where my husband, Jim, and I had gone in 1971. When our contract was up, we spent a year traveling across Asia and Europe, later accepting teaching positions in Turkey. In the course of our travels I often saw people with disabilities, and always, like that quadriplegic on the streets of Ankara, they had to make do for themselves. Often, they made do with animals. In Nepal and elsewhere, I saw burros and donkeys helping people with disabilities accomplish common daily tasks. These men and women got around by leaning on the animals, which also carried the pots, pans, and other wares their owners hawked by the roadside to make a living. Here, where poverty threw people back on their own resources, animals and humans cooperated in ways I had never imagined possible.

These revelations about disability, independence, and animals gained new salience when I returned to the United States in the summer of 1974 and entered a master's degree program in special education the following year. The conventional wisdom of the time held that improving the lot of people with disabilities meant bettering the institutions where they were kept. Emphasis was laid on what professionals could do for people with disabilities, not what the people could do for themselves. This seemed wrong to me; institutionalization and professionalization undercut the basic human need for self-sufficiency. Animals, like the ones I had seen in Asia, could be the key to independent living for people with disabilities. Burros, I realized, would be unworkable in urban America, because of our public-health laws and general unfamiliarity with the animals. But what about dogs? Could they be trained to do what I had seen the burros and donkeys of Asia doing — helping people with physical limitations get around, carrying the necessities of daily life, assisting them in making a living, providing emotional connection and companionship?

The idea appealed to me, but I didn't know enough about dogs to be sure it would work. I was teaching full-time in the Santa Rosa, California, public school system at that point, so I quit to take a job in a kennel — at an unappealing two dollars an hour — to learn about dogs firsthand. And I talked to veterinarians, dog trainers, and other experts, asking the big question on my mind: Why not train dogs to help people with disabilities, just as they guide the blind? Couldn't dogs pull wheelchairs, turn light switches on and off, retrieve dropped keys, open the refrigerator door, and do similar chores for individuals who couldn't do these things for themselves? The answer I got was always the same: It won't work. Dogs require physical mastery, I was told, and people with disabilities, because of their physical limitations, cannot handle dogs.

But this conventional wisdom didn't convince me. I had a dream, and I was too determined — perhaps too naïve and ignorant as well — to admit defeat. I kept on trying, in large measure because I had a deep faith and absolute belief in the special relationship between dogs and humans. It seemed to me that there could be no better or more fulfilling role for a dog than helping a person with disabilities live independently. But I had to figure out how to train a dog to take on that demanding role. Since I had no background in dog training, I fell back on my education as a teacher, using the techniques I had learned for classroom work. Clearly, training via physical control and correction was impractical for people with physical limitations. So I went the way my own background in education pointed, building learning on top of learning rather than emphasizing rote memory, and incorporating the dog's mind and emotions into the learning process rather than relying on physical correction. It seemed to me that *how* a dog was led mattered less than *that* it was led. I set out to find out if I was right.

With a leash on Abdul, a Labrador–golden retriever cross I considered the canine most likely to succeed, I approached Kerry Knaus and asked her to be my first student. Knaus, quadriplegic from a neuromuscular disorder, told me later she thought I was a crackpot. Still, she decided to give the experiment a try. For the next two years, Kerry, Abdul, and I worked together in regular training sessions to determine how dogs could provide independence for people with disabilities.

In the course of those two years, I learned a great deal. I found out that Kerry herself was critical to the training. It wasn't enough that she simply learn and give the commands. She had to present them in such a manner that Abdul would perceive her as a powerful leader and be willing to carry out her requests. This was a tall order for Kerry, who could barely move her arms and had a soft voice to boot. The relationship between Kerry and Abdul proved to be the key to success. Building the leader-follower connection linking human and dog and cementing the emotional bond between them was as important a focus of the training work as the commands. And I learned, too, what I had long suspected: Abdul wanted to help, he lived to work. He took great joy in handling all sorts of daily tasks for Kerry — from turning off the lights at night to helping her buy a pack of gum at the drugstore, passing the purchase one way and the money the other. And mastery — the conventional bugaboo supposedly preventing people with disabilities from handling dogs — proved to be more psychological than physical. Here was Kerry, a tiny woman able to move only her hands and forearms, handling a big muscular retriever, all by means of tone of voice, a powerful emotional bond with the animal, and well-trained commands.

What's more, the relationship with Abdul paid enormous psychological dividends for Kerry. She discovered that as Abdul could do more for her, she could do more for herself. No longer was life a long list of can't-do's; now she saw every day as an opportunity to venture farther and farther on her own. She could get around in previously inaccessible buildings because Abdul operated the elevator buttons. He accompanied her to college classes with pencils, notebooks, and texts in his backpack, where she could reach them. He turned on the heater in the van she acquired and learned to drive, and he helped her operate the wheelchair lift to get in and out of the vehicle. With Abdul, Kerry achieved an independence she had never thought possible.

Based on the success of the relationship between Kerry and Abdul, I set out to expand my concept of what I was calling a *service dog* — an assistance animal trained to help people with disabilities other than blindness or deafness. Working from my home in Santa Rosa, I began training and placing more service dogs. I was also training social/ therapy dogs, which are used in work with people who are, for example, autistic or elderly infirm and also with individuals in such settings as children's centers, physical and substance-abuse rehabilitation centers, juvenile detention facilities, adult day-care centers, and group homes. At one point, Jim and I had eighteen dogs sharing our still-uncompleted house and I was financing the operation entirely out of my own pocket. By 1978, the program grew to the point where I founded Canine Companions for Independence (CCI) as a nonprofit organization. By 1981, the service dog had proved its worth and I secured a foundation grant large enough to allow me to move CCI out of my home. What a relief — no longer would business calls jangle me awake at 3 A.M.!

Over the next decade, CCI grew enormously, benefiting in part from a growing national awareness of the needs of people with disabilities and a new willingness to meet them. By 1990, the organization had expanded to include a national office, four centers for training assistance dogs, three satellite centers for raising puppies, a paid staff of sixty-five, and a $3 million annual budget. My approach traveled overseas, through programs I helped start in Canada, Holland, France, and Israel. My work also spawned imitators; about forty similar programs are now in operation.

As CCI grew through the 1980s, I perfected my original training approach. Litters were bred from dogs with the desired traits, then placed in homes in the community that agreed to raise the puppies according to my standards. At sixteen months of age, the dogs came back to the training center for six months of advanced training, where they learned a total of eighty-nine commands to prepare them to work in a variety of situations.

Equally important was the training given the candidates, who guided the evolution of what became a rigorous two-week training they themselves named — with the dark humor of the overworked — Boot Camp. In this dawn-to-bedtime intensive program, candidates discovered what it meant to live and work with a service dog. They had to learn all about dogs — their biological and psychological evolution, the social world they inhabit, their intricate emotional needs. They needed to learn how to give the eighty-nine commands and link them in order to accomplish complex tasks — like making a deposit at the bank, with the dog moving all the paperwork between the teller behind the counter and the handler in a wheelchair. And, most important, they had to learn how to be leaders and how to respond to, and bond with, the animal from an internal intimacy with their own noncognitive, animal selves. They learned they couldn't simply give orders; they had to build, foster, and manage an instinctive emotional relationship, between one animal and another.

This approach has proved to be a distinct success, from both dog and human perspectives, with over seven hundred CCI service dogs placed during the 1980s. But given the many ways that dogs can help humans, seven hundred dogs amount to but a tiny drop in a bottomless bucket. Today, the waiting period for service dogs is often five years long. With current methods, we simply cannot breed and train enough animals to fill this crying need. While the many assistance dog programs around the world have amassed a great deal of knowledge about canines and their interactions with humans, that information has never been assembled in a systematic way for analysis and dissemination. Until that happens, until a scientific base of information and methodology about training and breeding is developed and shared, we will always fall short of solving the many problems dogs can help us with.

This line of thinking led me to leave CCI in order to found the Assistance Dog Institute. My objective has been to move away from the day-to-day demands of raising and training assistance dogs in order to focus on developing new and better methods, as well as assembling, analyzing, and disseminating information to the many people interested in dogs in general and assistance dogs in particular. It is my goal to build a campus setting in Sonoma County, California, where interested people can learn the best approaches to breeding and training animals.

My approach to dog training has expanded the boundaries of what was considered possible between human and dog. It has shown that much more can happen than we let ourselves imagine. In fact, the first thing we have to do is overturn many of our cherished assumptions about canines. Most people take it for granted that dogs can be mastered by learning the right "technique" of training, that they are fluffy love machines eager to fawn upon every human who offers them the least kindness, and that they like to be pampered and hate to work.

Dogs, in fact, love to work; they long to be useful. Nor are they lovers without boundaries or good taste. In actuality, dogs are highly capable, discriminating creatures who understand what leadership is and seek it in their relationships, with humans as well as with other dogs. They are emotionally complex, displaying almost every feeling we humans know, with very much the same depth and intensity. Finally, basing mastery on physical control alone is frank nonsense. The most important connection between dog and human is emotional, between the animal in the dog and the animal in the owner — that is, the feeling, intuitive, and affective core of both beings. This attachment is the basis of the leader-follower dynamic that forms the relationship between human and dog and determines who does what for whom when.

This approach to training is revolutionary. It is also eminently successful, and not simply in terms of the total number of service dogs now at work. Countless times over the twenty years of my career, I have seen delight and joy shine in the eyes of dogs as they learned how to be of assistance to their masters, the supreme beings in their lives. And I have seen that same happiness, wonder, and awe bloom in people as they discover that they can command a dog and, equally important, that they have achieved a deep and nurturing connection with an animal.

In the course of my work, I have been asked many times whether my approach applies not only to service dogs for people with disabilities, but also to the millions of pet, sporting, and working dogs in North America. It does indeed. This knowledge can benefit the "typical" dog owner — the suburban family with a golden retriever in the station wagon, the avid upland-game hunter with an equally avid pointer, the solitary elderly woman with a mixed-breed companion dog, the professional couple with an urban condominium and a Yorkshire terrier to come home to. This book is my way of making twenty years of experience and insight available to those who would like to improve both their own lives and the lives of their dogs.

IN my experience with training both dogs and humans, I have never ceased to marvel at the dog's willingness to please, to adapt, to try a difficult task again and again until it has it right. I want you to share that same sense of wonder.

Sadly, we humans tend to misread the dog's need to feel useful, pampering our pets until their behavior becomes a problem and we discard them. Various humane societies and animal protection groups report that approximately 60 percent of the dogs adopted annually are given up yet again — many ultimately to be euthanized as unwanted. This is a numbing and unnecessary toll, and it tells about the failure not of dogs, but of humans. Every dog dumped on a country road to fend for itself, every animal surrendered to an animal shelter, every pet relegated to solitary confinement on a tether in the backyard is evidence of yet one more human who failed to understand that the dog's misbehavior was a plea. "Hey, tell me what to do," the dog was saying. "Be my leader. Just give me the rules and I'll do it your way. Your wish, master, is my command."

When your dog chews up your couch or favorite slippers or it defecates on that heirloom Samarkand rug, it is telling you that it has not received the guidance it needs. The dog's acting-out is a reaction to the unsettled question of who and how strong the pack leader is. No dog is a calculating avenger; canines do not plot elaborate vendettas to get even. Instead, left without rules, they create their own — which, such as chewing couches and defecating on Oriental rugs, may thoroughly disrupt or inconvenience your life.

A pack animal from its earliest origins in distant time, the dog is biologically predisposed to follow, work with, defer to, and please its leader — and to challenge that leader, be it another dog or a human, whenever he or she appears weak. If you want your dog to live in accordance with your house rules — which will not only protect your couch and rug but also induce your dog to obey you when you give commands — then you must become your dog's master. It is your job to take on the role of leader of the pack.

This is not at all a matter of naked power or physical abuse. Leadership is instead a matter of communicating with and directing your dog. In elementary school, teachers work with children in a language kids can understand. It is much the same with dogs. You need to work with an understanding of who and what the dog is and with a technique that transforms your understanding into methods the dog can recognize and follow.

In teaching humans how to handle service dogs, I learned early on to discourage the cognitive thought process. A dog is not a problem in mathematics or physics; it is another being. The key to success is to get the human in touch with his or her own emotional awareness. It is there — within the affective domain, *at the gut level of emotional response and reaction* — that dogs and humans connect and communicate.

One of the important differences between humans and dogs is that our basic animal instincts toward survival have been muted by culture. We tend to act from thinking, which is intellectual process, more than from feeling, which is emotional process. This is one of the reasons why therapy has become such a frequent fact of modern life; many people are cut off from their emotional lives and need counseling to help them reconnect. In a similar way, this book undertakes a similar task. It aims to guide you beyond the conventional thinking process familiar to you into this long-forgotten and oft-repressed territory of the emotional, reactive, feeling mind. There, and only there, can you truly handle your dog.

Natalie Goldberg, a marvelous writer and poet, takes a similar point of view, naming this deep portion of ourselves "wild mind."

> Western psychology calls wild mind *the unconscious*, but I think *the unconscious* is a limiting term. If it is true that we are all interpenetrated and interconnected, then wild mind includes mountains, rivers, Cadillacs, humidity, plains, emeralds, poverty, old streets in London, snow, and moon. A river and a tree are not unconscious. They are part of wild mind. I do not consider even a dream unconscious. A dream is a being that travels from wild mind into the . . . conscious self to wake us up.*

In my training work with dogs and people, I try to get humans in touch with their "wild minds." In training a dog, you need to rely not only on your intellectual knowledge of the animal, but also on this intuitive awareness. The intellect plays an important role in working with a dog. It helps, for example, to understand in a factual cognitive way the biological similarities and differences between humans and dogs. But all by itself intellect won't cut it. For one thing, thinking takes too much time. When something pops up in training — say, for example, the dog challenges your authority — and you rely on intellect to puzzle out the event, the dog, who relies on emotion and instinct, will already be far beyond you. It will have reacted before you even begin to figure out what just happened. But if you gain awareness of your instinctive emotional reactions, you can respond quickly and immediately — just as the dog does — and remain in connection and communication with the animal as its leader.

MY approach to working with dogs builds on the common ground between our two species. Humans and dogs are alike in important ways, and this is the beginning point of this book — a look into the similarities between humans and dogs in the ways we think, react, and interact. Dogs and humans are both

---

*Natalie Goldberg, *Wild Mind: Living the Writer's Life* (New York: Bantam Books, 1990), p. 32.

mammals, who need food, shelter, warmth, and security. Both species experience strong emotions, like love, fear, resentment, jealousy, and happiness. Dogs and humans are both social animals who need companionship in order to thrive. As you come to understand these similarities, you will begin to recognize them in yourself and you will slowly become aware of how and why your dog reacts in its own particular way. This is the first step toward using instinct to communicate with your dog. As this understanding deepens in you, the book will move on to a specific program of training based on my twenty years' experience with assistance dogs. The book concludes with practical guidance on maintaining your dog's good health as a way of cultivating the relationship with your pet.

In the final analysis, learning to communicate in a dog's language requires you to be extraordinarily honest with yourself. This book is not only an invitation to learn how better to handle your dog; it is also an opportunity to learn more deeply who you are.

$\mathcal{P}art\ One$
The Dog and You

*A*LL my work with dogs and humans over the past twenty years comes down to two fundamental principles.

First, to communicate with and train your dog, you must accept your own animal nature and trust your affective and instinctive awareness of the emotions in you and in your dog. *Training your dog, and benefiting from your relationship with your pet, has little to do with intellect. Working with your dog is not about superior IQ. It is about connecting, at the level of emotional awareness, with the animal reality in both you and your pet.*

At first, you may recoil from this idea and say, "But I'm not an animal, I'm a human. That makes me different." In a way, of course, you are right; only humans read books, fly airplanes, and train dogs. But in a way, you are also mistaken, holding on to a worn-out idea that the human and the animal

are distinct and separate. In fact, our understanding of evolutionary processes and the fascinating discoveries of modern cellular and molecular biology show that all life is one. Humans, dogs, and all other creatures make up one seamless fabric of being. In connecting with your dog, you are really connecting with your own deepest self.

Second, to be in a successful relationship with your pet, you need to understand that the dog is a complex individual who must be handled from a realistic and accurate appreciation of its complexity and individuality. *Dogs are not animated bits of technology that respond like computers or video games to A-B-C commands. Nor are they "just animals." Dogs are remarkably intricate, highly developed, and very subtle creatures who demand our full attention. And when we give it, we are rewarded greatly and our lives are deepened.*

Chapter One

Dogs Are People, Too

*The Common and Differing
Ground between Humans
and Canines*

*J*ANET, a friend of mine, told me
about this incident with Juba,
her five-month-old golden retriever. Janet had taken Juba out for
a romp among the rolling hills here
in Sonoma County, and she let her
pet off the leash. It was a beautiful
day, and Juba, in the first springtime
of her life, was having a ball, bolting
through the soft green grass and
following the many scent trails of
skunks, raccoons, pheasants, quail,
gophers, and other animals. Locked
onto one of those scent trails, Juba
took off on her own without a second thought, scrambling under a
nearby fence into an oak grove and
leaving Janet behind.

She went off so silently, oblivious
to all else but the line of smell she
was following, that Janet at first
didn't even notice she was gone.

When she did, she nearly panicked, afraid she had lost her dog. She called Juba's name again and again, but Juba was engrossed in the pursuit of intriguing scent and never heard her. Only when she had followed the trail to her heart's content did she turn back toward Janet, who was still calling her. Retriever that she is, she picked up a good-sized fallen branch and headed back under the fence and over the pasture to Janet, dropping the find at her feet. Janet alternated between anger at the pup for running off and relief over her return. Afraid to make the wrong choice between her conflicting emotions, she did nothing. Juba was confused by her handler's inaction. She expected praise for bringing the branch back, but she received only an unemotional silence.

Probably every dog owner has experienced an incident like Janet and Juba's, one where humans and canines encounter conflict and bewilderment because of our varying — and similar — natures. Juba desired interaction and appreciation from Janet, the leader of her pack, for bringing back the retrieved branch. Hers was a doggy way of asking for approval. She was like a subordinate wolf bringing a fresh-killed rabbit to the lead wolf to curry favor for her accomplishment. Janet, though, failed to perceive the branch for the prize that it was and didn't give Juba the response she anticipated. Janet had misread the emotional reality of her dog. And instead of acting from her own instinctive and affective awareness of feelings within her own body, she did nothing, leaving both herself and her pet confused.

THE story of Janet and Juba shows how dogs are much more connected to their instincts than humans are. I mean *instinct* in a specific way here, one somewhat different from everyday perceptions of the word. Commonly, *instinct* denotes behaviors hardwired into a creature at birth, like the honeybee's dance and the cicada's song, for example. That is one meaning of the word. But *instinct* also refers to any powerful drive or feeling in the body beneath the level of intellect. Put yourself in Janet's shoes for a moment. When she feared that Juba was lost, her body pulsed with feeling. Her stomach clenched, her blood pressure went up, her palms began to sweat. This physical response is instinctive. But Janet also began to think about her feelings — that is, to process consciously what was happening to her physically and to make judgments and assessments. This is something we humans do well because we have the large brains that make such emotional processing possible.

What I often call the affective domain has the two elements we see in Janet's reactions. One is gut-level feeling, which occurs in the autonomic nervous system — the clenching stomach, rising blood pressure, and sweaty palms. The other is conscious processing of the feeling, which occurs in the cerebral cortex of the brain. Both humans and dogs operate in the affective domain, but we divide our emotional time differently. Dogs live principally at the gut level. We humans, with our larger brains, spend more time involved in the conscious processing of feelings. In fact, we often ignore or override our gut feelings in order to follow what consciousness decides — sometimes in conflict with instinctive emotional responses.

When Juba came back to her with that stick in her mouth, Janet spent more time thinking than feeling. Torn between relief and anger and worried about making a mistake, she chose to do nothing while she thought the problem through. Janet's conscious process triumphed over her instinctive feeling process, and she used intellect to mask her emotional confusion.

Perhaps you're wondering whether Janet should have given in to her anger and scolded Juba for running off. The answer is no. Dogs live in the present, building associations with what is going on right now, not a few minutes ago. Juba would have connected the negative experience of Janet's anger with coming to her, not with running off earlier. An angry outburst from Janet would have had the undesirable effect of making Juba less likely to come when called.

Janet's indecision, and the bewilderment this caused in Juba, high-

lights the importance of developing a relationship with your dog grounded in the affective domain. To be in successful relationship with our pets, we humans need to reacquaint ourselves with our animal selves. We need to learn about the instinctive, feeling nature of dogs. And that learning begins with understanding our own affective domains and realizing how similar we are to our dogs.

I invite you to open to the animal reality of yourself — the instinctual, feeling, affective core of your being. In twenty years of training dogs and humans, I have found this to be the fastest and truest route to working effectively with pets.

A great deal of training a dog is reshaping its instincts into desired patterns. German shepherds, for example, have an instinctive desire to herd and protect. That very instinct, reshaped through careful training, makes the shepherd a fine guard and work dog. Training, therefore, begins in understanding the instinctual nature of the dog and in learning how to connect your own instinctual nature with that of your dog.

The Tribe and the Pack

The social likeness between humans and dogs is striking. Both species live in group settings with remarkably similar dynamics. Dogs are creatures of their packs; humans are members of their families, tribes, clans — and corporations, religious

The social likeness between humans and dogs is striking.

denominations, and nation-states.

The importance of interaction and approval to both dogs and humans shows the social basics of both species. When Juba came to Janet with the fallen branch in her mouth, she was seeking approval. She wanted a pat on the head from the leader of her pack for a job well done. Janet is no different. When she closes a deal with a big account at work, she wants her boss to praise her.

Approval depends on leadership: The follower comes to the leader and requests recognition and praise.

Asking for and giving approval reinforces the relationship between the leader and the follower and thus strengthens the fundamental bond of the social group.

Long ago, dogs and humans formed groups for security and safety. The team effort of the tribe or the pack ensured continued existence for all its members. And that effort required leadership — the alpha animal of the wild canid pack, or the chief of a tribe of hunter-gatherers — along with a strong sense of teamwork among the members of the tribe or pack.

Don't confuse leadership with brute force. The leader is by no means the dog with the biggest teeth and shortest temper or the hunter with the heaviest club and nastiest disposition. Leadership results from well-rounded ability across a spectrum of important areas, including physical and emotional attributes. Often, in fact, leadership and the qualities that contribute to it are subtle, and leadership roles may shift from one area of life to another.

Because of their long-evolved nature as pack animals, dogs want, seek, and defer to leadership, and they constantly seek reassurance that their leaders remain capable of leading them. This is why dogs challenge each other repeatedly. The challenge is a reality check on who is in control, and it can come at any time. One dog may try to take another's food or steal its favorite toy or push through a narrow door first. If the challenged dog backs down, the challenger's position is reinforced. But if the challenger doesn't back down, a fight will erupt.

Humans do much the same. Growing children repeatedly push against the rules of the household. Told to snack only in the kitchen, kids will occasionally plunk down right in front of the living room TV with a peanut butter sandwich in hand, just to see what Mom or Dad will do. If the parent enforces the rule and makes the child take the sandwich back into the kitchen, the challenge has reinforced the leadership relationship between child and parent. But if the parent lets the child stay put, then the leadership dynamic in the family has shifted in favor of the child.

Challenges do not end with childhood. They continue all through adult life — among friends and neighbors, between spouses, within the complex interactions of corporate management teams.

Similar dynamics are involved in challenges, whether in dogs or humans. For one thing, the closer in power that the two individuals are, the more often challenges will occur. When power is more or less equal, victory in a challenge is usually less than clear-cut, and another challenge is likely to occur soon, as another test of where things stand. Also, challenges are mounted against the leader's weakest point. Among dogs, a challenge is most likely when the leader is tired, not when he or she is fully rested and feeling strong. The same timing holds true for humans. Practically every parent has had the experience of sitting down to dinner, tired and hungry at the end of long day, only to have a food fight erupt between siblings. The children are mounting the challenge right when the parent is most vulnerable and least able to respond.

The purpose of any challenge is to seek reassurance that the leader still has the right stuff to lead. And this common ground between humans and dogs leads to conflicts. Just as dogs challenge other dogs, and humans challenge other humans, so also do dogs and humans challenge each other. Over the long course of time, dogs have come to regard humans as they would the other members of a canine pack. If humans fail to act in a manner appropriate to this reality, conflict and confusion can result — and more and more challenges will arise.

Take the commonplace situation in which you give your dog a familiar command — say, "sit" — and it seems to ignore you. This is a challenge; the dog is testing your leadership. If you fail to act as the leader of the pack, the dog will, quite naturally, assume that you are no longer capable of leading and that it must assume leadership itself and create its own rules of behavior. The dog will do as it pleases, and quickly it is labeled a "bad" dog. In fact, there is nothing bad about this dog. It has simply done what its instinctive nature tells it to. The real failure in this situation is the human who doesn't notice the challenge or responds to it inappropriately.

Dogs prefer following to leading, and so they will give their humans repeated opportunity to reassume leadership. The dog might refuse to come when called or to sit when told to, or it might dig up the camellia you just planted. Humans, though, tend to react to such goings-on as revenge taken against objects they prize. Revenge is not the point at all. The dog is once again presenting a challenge, giving you a further opportunity to assert authority, and it is making sure you pay attention by involving an object you value. If you respond by letting the dog know that its behavior is unacceptable, then you have taken the leadership role and given the dog the emotional security of the pack that it wanted in the first place. We will discuss challenges and how to respond to them in greater detail at a number of points in this book.

We often get into trouble around this point because humans, like dogs, prefer following to leading. That's something we often don't even think about; another human asserts leadership and we defer without a second thought. This can happen as well with your dog. It mounts a challenge because it senses in you some doubt, insecurity, or uncertainty, and you unwittingly defer to the dog, allowing it to assume leadership. But the challenges won't stop there. The dog, still seeking to defer to leadership, will continue to challenge you, presenting again and again an opportunity for you to become the leader of the pack once more and thus allow it to follow you.

Keep it in mind that equality has no existence among dogs. Canines are not democrats; they want leaders. Dogs, though, do understand teaming, and it is on a relationship of teamwork — human and dog together, with the human the leader — that positive work with your dog will be built.

Emotions: Where Dogs and Humans Are One

We humans like to see ourselves as different, distinct, and — usually — better than the other creatures with whom we share this planet. We describe ourselves as the dominant species and place ourselves at the pinnacle of evolution, citing such supposed advantages as opposable thumb, upright posture, and highly developed brain for our claimed status as earth's number one. This view of ourselves obscures something fundamental. While humans do differ from the other animals, we are also much like them — and we are particularly similar to dogs.

Aside from physical differences, such as four-legged versus two-legged stance, the most important difference between humans and dogs is the size and complexity of the brain. The human brain provides us with a highly developed cognitive ability. We can reason, strategize, and think our way into tomorrow, next week, maybe even a decade from now. Dogs cannot; they lack the extensive and highly convoluted cerebral cortex that makes such thinking possible. Dogs do have cognitive ability, but its capacity is more modest than ours.

Subtract cognitive ability, however, and a fascinating fact emerges. In the emotional realm, dogs and humans are strikingly, even hauntingly similar. Both species experience very much the same range of emotions: anger, resentment, jealousy, happiness, fear, grief, excitement, and so forth. Also, dogs feel their emotions every bit as intensely and deeply as we humans do. Emotionally, we humans have nothing over our pets.

We humans constantly use our cognitive ability to mask or conceal emotions or to deceive others — and also ourselves — about our feelings. Dogs cannot do this. Their emotions are obvious and immediate. In fact, dogs live their lives within immediate emotion and feeling. Something happens, and a dog reacts — just like that, without thinking. As a result, dogs are much quicker than we are. We stop and think and then do something; a dog just reacts, typically in less time than it takes us even to start thinking.

Say you are walking down a darkened alleyway and a man steps out of the shadows into your path. He is big and menacing, and in his hand something metallic flashes, perhaps a gun or knife. You are, of course, deeply afraid. Your blood pressure shoots up, your stomach tightens and twists, your muscles tense. Then you think about what to do. You can run or you can fight. "How big is this guy?" you ask yourself, "What if it's a knife instead of a gun? Can I get it away from him before he hurts me?" You assess the situation, and from that assessment, coupled with your feelings of fear, you decide what to do: advance on the threat to remove it, or back away toward the main street and what you hope is safety.

Now imagine yourself a dog walking down that the same alleyway, also facing a threat. In this case, though, it's not a man with a weapon, but a bigger dog, growling and snarling. Exactly like you, the dog will feel its entire body tense and its stomach twist. But it won't stop to think. It will react to the situation immediately, choosing fight or flight based on the emotional makeup of that particular dog.

Notice that in these examples, the gut-level emotions in dog and human are the same. The difference is the presence or absence of reflection upon emotions. Dogs reflect little on their feelings. Where we stop and ponder how we feel, dogs simply react.

Emotions are not only individual events. They are also social tools for dogs and humans; both species use them to influence the behavior of others. We humans learn early in life that crying evokes particular responses in others. Dogs likewise learn in puppyhood that signs of happiness, like tail wagging, will draw affection from humans. When humans are angry, they often hear what they want to hear. When a dog is angry or resisting, it too seems to have suddenly gone deaf. It will pretend it didn't hear what it was told and do something entirely different. You say, "Sit," and the dog instead lies down and rolls over, inviting you to rub its exposed belly. The dog is acting emotionally much like a child who tries to avoid chores or homework by teasing the parent or changing the subject when it comes up. Both the resisting dog and the diverting child are using emotions to get what they want.

Dogs, again like humans, crave any emotion over no emotion. For example, a spouse who feels left out of his or her mate's life may start a fight just to get some feelings, any feelings, flowing between them. Dogs will do the same thing. If they find themselves in an emotional desert, they may get some feeling of their own going — any feeling will do, just so long as it is a feeling. Thus are couches and slippers chewed and new-planted camellia bushes dug up by dogs seeking emotional interaction with their masters.

It is important for us to realize how dependent dogs are on us emotionally, and how responsible we must be for their emotional security. Dogs need us to satisfy all their needs, from basic physical wants like food and shelter to complex emotional requirements for interaction

and approval. A dog who feels secure in its relationship is a happy animal that will willingly follow your lead. But a canine who fears that it has been rejected is an insecure creature far too anxious over its life to learn. Your first requirement as a dog owner is to ensure your pet's sense of security by meeting its needs, both physical and emotional.

Adaptability

The humans who today run corporations, spaceships, nuclear power plants, and major league baseball teams are the direct descendants of skin-clad hunters who chased mammoths across the frozen landscape of the last Ice Age. And the dogs to whom today's humans come home are likewise descended from the loping canines that hunted alongside those Ice Age spearmen. Both species have made this dramatic shift from the cave to the city because they are inherently adaptable.

The physical aspects of adaptability are readily apparent. Look at all the many shapes, sizes, and colors of the different races, nations, and tribes of humans. Dogs are equally adaptable, representing more than four hundred official breeds as well as the practically endless variety of cross-bred dogs.

In humans, physical differences have arisen partly in response to environmental conditions. The stocky short-limbed Eskimo or Chukchi, for example, is better adapted to Arctic cold than the tall, lean, long-legged

East African savanna dweller, whose physique suits tropical heat. Similar influences have given rise to differences among dogs. Big muscular heavy-coated dogs like Samoyeds and huskies are well made for their northern habitats, and the small, nearly hairless Chihuahua of Mexico is at home in the tropics.

An important difference, though, is that humans have shaped the adaptability of the dog by choice and intention. To a great extent, we humans have made dogs what they are today, by breeding animals for specific desired characteristics. The Samoyed, the husky, the Chihuahua, and the other four hundred breeds are largely human creations from the original stock of dogs.

We have also shaped our dogs' behaviors, by breeding for particular traits, to better suit them for roles within human society. Wild dogs and wolves are monogamous; they usually take but one mate for life. Monogamy makes selective breeding difficult, so humans have bred dogs to accept more than one mate. Not only has this created more breeding possibilities; it has also made modern dogs more likely to accept several masters. Likewise, the ability of wolves and wild dogs to kill with their teeth has been bred out of most domestic dogs, which like to chase and hunt but often have little or no capacity to kill.

Curiously, our selective breeding of dogs has made them like us in another way — neoteny. *Neoteny* is a technical term from biology that refers to the retention of juvenile traits into adulthood. We humans have been neotinizing forces toward dogs. Selective breeding has favored juvenile characteristics like the domed head, smaller jaw muscles, and floppy or unpricked ears. Juvenile behavior, like play, has been favored, too. Domestic dogs typically love to play even when they grow old and gray about the muzzle, which is less true of wolves and other wild canids.

Learning How to Learn

Dogs and humans learn in many of the same ways. In fact, dogs are much better at learning and have a higher level of intelligence than we conventionally give them credit for.

Learning by observation begins as soon as the eyes open, whether they are the blue eyes of an infant child or the dark eyes of a young puppy. Human and canine youngsters watch their mothers' every move and imitate what they see. In the wild, wolf parents use instruction by imitation to teach their young to hunt. Following an instinctive timetable, the adults show the puppies step-by-step how to find and catch prey. Human babies similarly learn how to smile, drink from a cup, and hold a spoon after being shown how by a parent. Later this watchfulness encompasses more than just parents, for both dogs and humans. In the course of my work with service dogs, I had the training rooms encircled by the kennels, which faced

Learning by observation begins as soon as the eyes open, whether they are the blue eyes of an infant child or the dark eyes of a young puppy.

inward so the dogs could watch — and learn — while their peers were being trained. As we will see later, one of my training approaches is to show the dog what to do by modeling — that is, by physically moving the dog's body the way you want it to go. As the dog gets the idea of what you want, you then encourage it to repeat the action.

Dogs learn by making connections; these connections, or associations, build on themselves. Humans do the same. The letters x and y are first learned as parts of the alphabet,

often in a rhyming song. Next the letters become parts of words, and later symbols in algebra. Simple connections widen and gain complexity. As is the case with humans, the more connections a dog makes, the more it can learn. Making the connection between performing a simple "sit" command and receiving praise is one of the first human-directed associations a puppy learns. This kind of connection is the cornerstone that allows the growing pup to build more complex associations and accomplish more difficult tasks, like tracking someone lost in the snow.

You can also see the principle of delayed gratification at work here. Humans will engage in activities, like writing a book or learning calculus, that earn them praise and other rewards at some future time. Dogs will too. They work hard for hours, both for the pure joy of the work and for the praise and approval they know is coming after they complete a task.

Dogs and humans both learn through trial and error. "Once burned, twice shy," the folk saying goes; a child who reaches for a hot stove and singes his fingers won't do the same thing again. He will steer clear of the source of the pain or figure out how to use a potholder. You can see the same process in dogs. A pet who tries to get out of the yard and fails to clear the fence will next attempt to dig under it. If a dog wants to play with its master and accomplishes nothing by wagging its tail, it will likely try a new approach, like getting a favorite toy and dropping it at the human's feet.

As you can see, both dogs and humans learn through repetition accompanied by positive and negative reinforcement. Children learn their ABC's much as dogs learn to sit — by repeating the same sequence, through rounds of praise and correction from parents and teachers, until they have it right. Successful dog training works in much the same way, via repetition and reinforcement.

Dogs are not intellectual; they don't do theoretical physics or write novels. But they are rational; that is, they reason, but only into the near future. Reason here means the ability to calculate, to think ahead, to intend some objective and do what is necessary to achieve it. Dogs learn that certain actions get certain results, and they then select their actions to get the results they want. If a dog needs to go outside to urinate, it calculates how to make that happen, perhaps by scratching the back door or whining. If it wants to be fed, it may stand by its food bowl and stare at you longingly until you get the message and go for the kibble.

This immediate reasoning ability reaches well back into the evolutionary ancestry of dogs and is highly developed in them and their wild cousins. Wolves and coyotes chase prey in relay teams, for example, and wolves set ambushes and chase prey into them. Coyotes in winter follow elk through the snow, knowing that the elk's pawing uncovers mice and other small rodents. If a dog wants to dig out of its yard, it figures out that it has to dig at the fenceline, not in the middle of the lawn. And it also realizes that it must dig out as well as down. Obviously the dog has an intention and it has determined a way to achieve that intention. This is reason.

Dogs also think, but their thinking is limited by the way their memories work. Both humans and dogs think in visual images, but

Dogs vastly exceed humans in their ability to remember smells.

back to a park or a lake it hasn't visited for a while. I suspect the excitement is less the visual memory of a game of Frisbee or a long swim on a hot day than the dog's highly developed recall of the park's smells. Humans, of course, have a memory of smells. An apple pie baking in the oven may take you back to your grandmother's kitchen in childhood. The difference is that in dogs this capacity is much more highly developed and a great deal more sophisticated.

A Manner of Speaking

Dogs and humans communicate, among themselves and with each other. Communication here means simply the sending of clear signals from one being to another, and it can be as elementary as a wag of the tail or as complex as a spoken sentence. Language is a highly developed system for communication, one that entails conventional and mutually understood signs, sounds, gestures, or symbols. We humans, obviously, have language. What many of us don't realize is that, though dogs lack true language, they do have an elaborate system of communication.

Humans can think forward and backward in time, shaping the past and imagining the future, in large part because we have language. Dogs lack language and thus cannot reason far into the future nor journey into the deep past; they are focused on this moment and what lies just

dogs retain images for only a few hours, a much shorter period of time than holds true for humans. However, dogs and other canids vastly exceed humans in their ability to remember smells. They possess an indexing memory of scents that is extremely accurate and apparently lasts throughout their lives. Once a dog or a wolf has encountered a smell, it remembers that odor in exquisite detail. Possibly you have seen a dog get very excited when taken ahead. Also, without language, dogs cannot communicate intellectual substance. Humans can have a meaningful conversation around a statement as abstract as Einstein's $E = mc^2$. Dogs cannot. Living as they do in the realm of feeling and emotion, their communications come from and pertain to the affective domain.

Dogs have a great many ways of communicating how they are feeling and of picking up how you are feeling. They make a variety of noises — barks, growls, whines, yelps, yips, howls, snarls, among others — each of which tells other dogs, and humans who know what to listen for, how the dog is feeling. Canine communication entails many tactile cues as well, such as licking, mouthing, and jumping up on you. And dogs also communicate visually, particularly with facial expression and in the ways they hold their bodies and tails.

Dogs are highly adept at picking up human communications, particularly emotional signals. Your own pet learns how to determine your mood by observing your facial expression, body posture, tone of voice, smell, and other cues. Often pet owners will say their dogs can read their minds. They can't. Instead, canines pay close attention to a range of emotional communication we humans often ignore.

To communicate effectively with dogs, we humans must use the signals dogs do. Talk as you will at your dog, it will never understand what

you are saying. Yes, it can learn the meaning of certain words, typically as auditory cues for an action or experience it knows. But your dog will never understand language as you understand it. Instead, you can communicate with your dog by means of words as cues (commands like "down," "sit," "stay," and so forth), your tone of voice (which is extremely important), touch (petting, rubbing, scratching the chest), and body posture, physical motions, and facial expressions.

Growing up

Given that humans and dogs learn in very similar ways, it is hardly surprising to realize that both species go through remarkably similar developmental stages. In fact, the training method I developed with service dogs incorporates stages based on the social development of human children. A puppy of eight to twenty weeks of age equates to a child in nursery school, so the dogs are called Nurserypups. Puppies twenty-one to thirty-three weeks of age are Kinderpups, and as they age, they move on to Grammarpups through Juniorpups to Seniorpups.

In infancy, both puppies and babies determine whether their world is a satisfying place. Both species develop trust if — and this is a big if — their physical needs for nourishment, sleep, and warmth are met, as well as their psychological needs for response, contact, and affection. If these needs are unmet,

Human and canine babies need play in order to grow into well-adjusted adults.

through abuse or neglect, both puppies and babies either fail to thrive, and may even die, or they develop a lifelong pattern of distrust and suspicion.

Like human infants between seven and twelve months of age, puppies display a fear of the unknown at about eight weeks of age. A stressful trip to the kennel or the veterinarian can leave a lasting and detrimental impression. Puppies need to be socialized to people before they are twelve weeks of age, or they grow up to be shy of humans. Likewise, they must be exposed to a variety of sights, sounds, and places between three and five months of age in order to fully develop their awareness and versatility, or they are apt to cower fearfully in public places.

Both dogs and humans are in some major measure the outgrowth of their family settings. Family interactions instill a sense of right and wrong in puppies and children, who learn it's right to do what you're told and wrong to disobey. Babies, both human and canine, first learn about discipline from their mothers, who scold them for nursing too hard, wandering too far, or throwing food on the floor.

Humans and dogs share a similar sense of responsibility and duty to family, a common ground that serves as the basis of the powerful bonding between pet and master. And it is part and parcel of the pack nature of humans and dogs that siblings in both species take sides in family squabbles.

Play in early life is more than a lark. Human and canine babies need play in order to grow into well-adjusted adults. Wrestling with siblings teaches both humans and dogs how to abide by rules and inhibit aggression. It also provides the opportunity to experiment with the roles of leader and follower as well as winner and loser. A long infancy and childhood full of play increases the chances of a productive and well-adjusted adulthood. When children are playing hide-and-seek, or puppies are ambushing and attacking a slipper as if it were prey, they are perfecting instinctive and necessary social skills.

More Social Mores

When humans greet each other, they smile and may kiss. So do dogs, although their kissing might better be called face-licking. Dogs often lift a paw to solicit interaction with another dog or a human, just as we reach out and touch someone.

Humans of different cultures have different personal distances. East Africans talk animatedly separated by only about sixteen or eighteen inches of space, a distance most Americans find much too close for comfort. Dog breeds likewise vary in their personal distances. Terriers in particular tend to be intolerant of other dogs coming close.

Dogs and humans need privacy and solitude. When humans have been through a social whirl of parties, family gatherings, and evenings out, they typically feel a need for quiet private time, perhaps to rest overstimulated senses. Dogs do much the same, retreating to a peaceful denlike place to rest after a frenzy of play or the commotion of a dog show. This need for protected privacy, plus their natural instinct to nest in a cave or den, explains why dogs like crates.

Dogs are well known for their proclivity to roll in odoriferous materials, including such pungent smellies as rotting animal carcasses, horse and cow dung, and skunk spray. Some biologists think this is a camouflage technique whereby the dog obscures its natural scent from prey. But others say it is more like the human desire for perfumes, aftershaves, and colognes, a way of carrying about a signature smell and telling everyone who sniffs who you are.

Born into Different Bodies

Some of the most important differences between dogs and humans are physical. The human body has evolved in a manner that lets it do what the brain is capable of thinking up — like rubbing two sticks together to make a fire, or fashioning flint, wood, and sinew into a bow and arrow. These accomplishments are as much the work of the opposable thumb as of the cerebral cortex. Without our thumbs, we humans would never have been able to make tools, create instruments to write language, play musical instruments, eat with knives and forks, or design the space shuttle — all activities for which dogs are neither physically nor mentally equipped.

Dogs' paws are designed for covering long distances at a lope or a run, tearing at prey carcasses, and digging dens. Without thumbs or flexible fingers, a dog cannot grasp objects, except to balance them between the paws when it is lying on its back. Typically dogs carry things in their mouths.

In their evolution, dogs have retained the features required by a fight-or-flight mode of survival — a four-legged body structure with powerful haunches and thin legs for stamina and speed, colors easily camouflaged in the wild (there are, you will notice, no pink or turquoise dogs), and facial expressions and tails for communicating emotion. Human evolution has followed a different path, relying less on speed and strength than on brain capacity and the advantage of upright stance for a wider visual field. Dogs run their prey to ground, where humans use stealth and ambush. And where humans are omnivorous, eating both other animals and plants, dogs are largely carnivorous hunters and scavengers.

There are important differences in our reproductive realities, too. In human females, ovulation is not readily apparent, but in dogs heat, or estrus, is obvious. The genitals of the canine female swell and bleed in estrus, giving off a smell that prompts a powerful desire in intact male dogs to get to the female and copulate with her. This drive is so compelling that the males often jump, dig under, or otherwise get around all sorts of barriers humans erect to keep them away from the female. Human reproductive behavior is a good deal different.

Dogs see in black and white and their primary visual response is to movement. Humans see in color, with greater detail and acuity than dogs. At night, though, dogs can see much better than humans because their eyes contain a special reflective layer called the tapetum lucidum that gives them superior vision in the dark. Dogs and humans see from different perspectives. We humans look out from eyes five to six feet off the ground. Dogs, even the largest breeds, are closer to ground level, and therefore more sensitive to visual stimuli lower down. Also, dogs have a wider field of vision than humans.

Dogs hear much higher pitches

than we can. Both species are born blind, but dogs are also born deaf. In humans, eyesight and hearing develop before the motor system is in place, but in dogs the senses and locomotor ability develop simultaneously.

The sense of smell is perhaps a million times more acute in dogs than in humans, and dogs use smell much as humans use vision to gather a great deal of information about their environment. Breeds do vary in their sensitivity to smell, however. Afghan hounds, one of the so-called sight hounds, have less keen noses than scent hounds such as the bloodhound and the beagle. Still, even in the sight hound breeds, smell is highly developed. If you watch carefully how a dog explores its world, you'll notice that smell is key to its explorations and that the dog discovers much more through its nose than you might think possible. It is in fact humbling, as poet Mary Oliver writes, "A dog can never tell you what she knows from the / smells of the world, but you know watching her, that you know / almost nothing."*

Touch is probably less acute in dogs than in humans. Still, dogs do love to have their bodies stroked, much as humans do, and they touch each other and humans as a form of social contact and caregiving. Where we humans mostly use our hands to touch, dogs use their mouths.

Dogs don't cry; humans do. It isn't that dogs don't experience feeling as deeply as we do. It is that tears are, for some unknown reason arising in the mystery of our evolution, a solely human attribute.

The differences between dogs and humans are important, yet the similarities between us are even more remarkable. And that points to an overriding and central reality — in our cores, under our skins, both we humans and our dogs are animals. There, on that common ground, our relationship with them begins, grows, and flourishes.

---

*Mary Oliver, *New and Selected Poems* (Boston: Beacon Press, 1992), p. 15.

Chapter Two

Making a Companion

How the Modern Dog Came to Be

*T*HE pet who sits at your feet while you watch TV or who runs in pure joy across the lawn after a Frisbee is heir to a long legacy as both wild and domesticated animal. Its evolutionary heritage begins with *Miacis*, a frankly catlike and ferret-sized creature with a long tail, four short legs, and five toes, of the Paleocene era of some forty million years ago. This, according to our current understanding of the fossil record, is the earliest known ancestor of the dog. *Miacis* shared the warm, mild Paleocene forests with many still-extant bird species as well as with early versions of modern horses, pigs, and rodents.

Miacis gave rise to more than dogs. Over the next twenty-five million years of evolutionary change, it branched off into lines ancestral to cats, pinnipeds (seals and walruses), and possibly bears as well as dogs, wolves, jackals, and their congeners. The first obviously canine descendant of *Miacis* is *Hesperocyon,* a foxlike animal that roamed North America during the Oligocene, some thirty-seven to twenty-nine million years ago. It was a time when the first grasslands were appearing and over them wandered horses, pigs, elephants, and rhinoceroses. Over millennia *Hesperocyon* gave way to the fox-sized and hyena-looking *Messocyon*, which appears to have died out by the end of the Oligocene.

Simultaneously, Europe was home to *Cynodictis*, a fox-sized animal with five toes and retractile claws, which could be drawn in like a cat's and indicate *Cynodictis* probably lived in trees. One line of descent from *Cynodictis* is considered a possible ancestor to the wild dogs of Africa and India; the other, a hyena-like form known as *Cynodesmus*, became extinct.

Before *Cynodesmus* disappeared, however, it gave rise to *Tomarctus,* which some paleontologists hold to be the direct ancestor of wolves, foxes, and domestic dogs. Originally, *Tomarctus* was unimpressive — a small, omnivorous, slow-moving animal preyed upon by other carnivores. But, remolded over time through natural selection, *Tomarctus* became a strong distance runner, with good sight, hearing, and smell. As its legs lengthened and its feet became more compact,

allowing greater speed and stamina, the fifth toe became useless and moved from the paw up the leg to become the dewclaw.

The evolutionary heirs of *Tomarctus* were varied in appearance, but it is likely they evolved into primitive dogs and wolves. There is a gap in the record here, a lost chapter in the story. It is clear only that large, fast, strong wolflike canids — that is, members of the dog family, or *Canidae* — were hunting the earth about the time early humans first fashioned tools, some two million years ago. And then, about fifteen thousand years ago, hunter-gatherer peoples, who were genetically identical to you and me, began living and working together with wolves.

We have no idea exactly how this cooperation began. It is possible that humans first learned to hunt in teams, using ambush and relay, by watching how wolves downed big game. Wolves may also have followed human hunting bands, scavenging abandoned carcasses and other leftovers. Over time, wolves and humans could have developed a working relationship, with wolves helping humans hunt and humans feeding the wolves in return. Interestingly, just such a relationship between wild animals and humans is known in both Australia and Africa, where fishermen and dolphins fish together and share the take. Wolves and humans probably got together in a similar way, and then the relationship between the two species became closer and closer over time.

The wolf, and the dog it would become, was the first animal domesticated by humans. And it was different. Whereas other domesticated animals — cattle, horses, goats, pigs, chickens, ducks, and so forth — were taken by force from the wild, the dog apparently moved in among humans on its own. Dogs joined with us because they wanted to.

Domestication of canines is one of the earliest human cultural activities, predating herding and agriculture and preceded only by hunting and gathering, toolmaking, storytelling, and fire-making. And from those earliest days, we humans have prized our dogs highly. A twelve-thousand-year-old artifact from what is now Israel shows the form of a human touching a puppy, as if to protect it. And an architectural dig at a Basketmaker Indian site in Arizona dating to about the first century A.D. yielded two canine mummies along with the preserved bodies of humans. The dogs who had been prized companions in this life were being sent along to stand by their masters in the next.

DOMESTIC dogs seem to have appeared all over the world at about the same time. Remains that are eight thousand to twelve thousand years old have been uncovered in England, Switzerland, Denmark, Turkey, Israel, Iraq, China, and North America. Did the dog arise in one locale and then disperse across the face of the earth? Or were canines domesticated and bred in different places simultaneously? Scientists argue both sides of the question. Some hold out for parallel evolution at various sites, and others say the modern dog had but one original birthplace — perhaps the Middle East's Fertile Crescent, perhaps northern Europe, perhaps China, perhaps North America. The issue remains unsettled.

There also continues to be debate about exactly which canid animal is the true ancestor of the modern domestic dog. The *Canidae* family contains over thirty species, including the dholes (wild pack-hunting dogs of India), coyotes, foxes, jackals, wild dogs, hunting dogs, and wolves as well as the domestic dog (whose scientific name, *Canis familiaris*, means "the intimate canine"). All the canids bear strong resemblance to one another; each has seventy-eight chromosomes and can breed with the others to produce fertile offspring. Dogs, for example, can be crossed with wolves or coyotes to yield young who can themselves breed with other canids.

Konrad Lorenz, the Nobel Prize–winning student of animal behavior and a dedicated dog fancier, proposed that four subspecies of wolf, not one, were the forebears of dogs, each type being bred into distinctly different groups of domesticated canines. In Lorenz's view, the woolly-coated wolf of Asia yielded such breeds as the mastiffs, retrievers, pointers, scent hounds, and span-

The Canidae *family contains over thirty species: coyote (top left), red fox (top right), gray wolf (lower left), and the black-backed jackal (lower right).*

iels — typically large sporting dogs with keen noses who like water and stand up well to cold. The European northern gray wolf was the progenitor of malamutes, chow chows, collies, huskies, Norwegian elkhounds, and similar breeds, the pricked-ear dogs that are fervently tenacious hunters and herding dogs. The pale-footed wolf of Asia was the ancestor of the basenji, Rhodesian ridgeback, pariah dog, dingo, and Canaan dog, which are breeds with both keen noses and outstanding vision. Finally, the long-legged desert wolf of Arabia led to the Afghan hound, borzoi, greyhound, Irish wolfhound, whippet, and saluki, all sight hounds capable of great speed.

In the end, we may never know exactly which animal was the ultimate ancestor of the dog nor where the domestic dog first arose. The fossil record is by nature fragmentary, and its evidence more suggestive than conclusive. But we do understand the central theme of the story: that the dog arose from a wild ancestor who moved in voluntarily among us humans. Ever since then, we have been reshaping the dog to make it what we want.

How Breeds Came to Be

Cave paintings, pottery decoration, and the literature of ancient cultures tell us that humans of long ago were already refining dogs to better suit the tasks they were assigned. Successive generations of dogs were bred into shapes, sizes, and behaviors in keeping with their emerging roles. Hunters became bigger and stronger, trackers developed heightened smell, herders grew quicker and more agile, pets became ever smaller and more childlike in temperament. Overall, dogs became less wild and more reliable, and increasingly they bonded with humans.

These changes, of course, didn't happen by accident. They were instead the result of purposeful breeding by humans, who selectively crossed dogs to achieve the qualities they wanted. Humans became very adept at this purposeful evolution of dogs well before the appearance of what we would currently recognize as written languages. Hunting dogs with massive shoulders and strong jaws were present in Neolithic England, and in ancient Mesopotamia, two distinct dog breeds — one small and wolflike, the other huge, with the appearance of a mastiff — were apparently developed as war dogs to attack enemies in battle. In Egypt, between 4000 and 3000 b.c., both heavy greyhound-type dogs with erect ears and long-eared saluki-like hounds were used to chase game. Evidence of selective breeding can also be seen in the miniature Chinese lapdog breeds, which had appeared by 2000 b.c.

Typically, dog breeds arose in particular areas, then traveled with humans to other regions where they might be crossed with local breeds, yielding yet more types of dogs and more possibilities for selective breeding. In isolated parts of the world, like distant islands well off the trade routes, dogs were more likely to remain purebred and similar to their origins. This is one explanation for the Australian dingo, the only type of *Canis familiaris* that lives in the wild. The theory is that it arose from domestic dogs brought from Asia about 9000 b.c. and left behind. Since there were no local canids to breed with, the dingo remained similar to that original Asian dog until Europeans colonized Australia in the nineteenth century.

As selective breeding progressed, humans became more and more specific in the qualities they bred for, developing not only body types and colors but distinct behaviors. In the beginning, for example, there were hunting dogs. Then there were dogs who hunted by sight, dogs who hunted by scent, dogs who chased game in hot pursuit, dogs who merely pointed to its presence, and yet other dogs who retrieved downed birds and small animals. A similar process occurred with herding dogs, companion dogs, working dogs, and so forth. As humans discovered, many significant characteristics in dogs can be bred in or out.

Many of the behavior patterns in dogs are inherited. For example, some breeds, most notably the retrievers, like water and love to swim; others, like some of the terriers, dislike anything to do with water. Love

Some breeds, most notably the retrievers, like the water and love to swim.

of, and aversion to, water are inherited behaviors. Likewise, how a dog hunts — by sight or by scent — is inherited. Some dogs dig for prey, others won't, again because of inheritance. Herding is also inherited, as is willingness to carry objects in the mouth.

Over the centuries, mixing and matching characteristics of behavior and physique has resulted in the wide variety of dogs known today, represented by some four hundred breeds worldwide. Even if you don't care about breeding, it still pays to know where your own dog fits in.

Breed origins can tell you a great deal about what you can expect from your pet and the kinds of behaviors it is likely to exhibit.

Dogs' Worthy Work

From the beginning, dogs have been involved with humans as workers, handling particular tasks because they do them better than we do. Early on, dogs were hunters and guardians, then they became herders, retrievers, and playmates to children and adults alike. As breeding became more and more sophisticated, dogs were developed to fill ever new and more unusual roles — sleeping with kings and queens to warm the royal nights in drafty castles, helping in the kitchen, chasing rats from peasant hovels, guiding travelers through the snow, and leading the blind along city streets.

HELPING humans pursue game is very likely the oldest of all canine professions. Selective breeding has produced a great many specialized hunting breeds, each developed to focus its hunting energies on a particular type of game animal. The Irish wolfhound and the borzoi, both big and fast breeds, coursed wolves with the noble hunters of their respective countries. The Irish were so good at this sport, and their island so small, that the wolf was eventually exterminated from Ireland. In Germany, Airedale terriers preyed on otter, as did otter hounds in Great Britain. In southern Africa, the fearless Rhodesian ridgeback hunted lions. In England, where hunters pursued foxes on horseback, two kinds of specialized dogs were created: foxhounds to range out in front of the hunters, and border terriers to trail along behind. The English, among whom poaching is a high art, trained terriers to poach game from their neighbors' fields and likewise used them to kill snakes — a clear case of reptilophobia, since Britain lacks poisonous serpents. The Karelian bear dog sniffs out hibernating bears in the pine and birch forests of its Nordic homeland. The Norwegian puffin dog hunts for birds' eggs on steep seaside cliffs and fetches them back unbroken. The Portuguese water dog may have the most unusual hunting role of all. It retrieves lost nets and tackle for fishermen, and even pursues fish that try to get away.

DOGS have been used to keep horses or oxen turning a grist mill or thresher by nipping at their heels. Boring as this job must have been, it was probably easy compared to the monotonous task entrusted to the turnspit dog until the 1870s. This small dog ran inside a kind of giant hamster wheel attached to a spit over a fire, which turned as the dog ran. The turnspit dog had to keep running until the meat was cooked, which could take hours.

DOGS have long helped humans fill their leisure hours, in ways both appealing and appalling. The most horrific form of putative entertainment involving canines is dogfighting, which is a modern form of medieval European bullbaiting, a barbaric spectacle in which a bull was tied to a post and set upon by dogs trained to seize it by the nose and throw it to the ground. Eventually, bullbaiting was banned and fights were staged instead between bull terriers, bulldogs, and other fierce breeds. This "sport" came to

America with European immigrants and was highly popular in the California gold fields from the 1840s through the 1880s. Although now illegal throughout the United States, dogfighting continues as an underground and particularly vicious spectacle.

Dogs are also raced like horses. In the United States, strong regulations have been adopted in the states that allow racing in order to promote humane handling of the animals.

Dogs have long been entertainers in carnivals and circuses, riding horses and doing all sorts of outlandish tricks, and they have played similar roles in movies and television. Rin-Tin-Tin, Lassie, Benji, Beethoven, and Toto are dog media stars loved and admired by adults and children alike. The demand for canine actors in movies and TV has grown so great that animals have their own professional guild and even a version of the Oscar called the Patsy — the Performing Animals Top Star of the Year, presented annually by the American Humane Society. Acting has also launched dogs into advertising careers, like the Basset hound touting Hush Puppies shoes and the fox terrier listening attentively to RCA records.

You can find dogs in newspaper comic strips too. Snoopy is central to the cast of "Peanuts," Odie plays daily comic foil to "Garfield," and Gary Larsen didn't let a week of "The Far Side" go by without slipping in another of his deliciously bizarre sidesplitters about dogs and their various misadventures — rolling in garbage, scratching fleas, chasing cats, and swallowing unmentionables.

THE name *assistance dog* refers to any canine who helps people do what they are physically unable to do for themselves. Dog guides for the blind are probably the best-known assistance dogs. They first made formal appearance in Europe during World War I, but medieval woodcuts show dogs leading people without sight. German shepherds were the original dog guides, but since then other breeds have been recruited. Labrador and golden retrievers are popular in this country, and Airedale terriers, collies, and Newfoundlands have been used in Russia. Dog guides act as the blind person's eyes, stopping at curbs and stairs, avoiding low-hanging tree branches, maneuvering through traffic and crowded sidewalks. Highly responsive and obedient, they are also trained in "intelligent disobedience" — refusing to obey a command if it will lead the dog or its master into danger.

Hearing dogs alert deaf or hearing-impaired individuals to crucial sounds — the ring of the phone, the blare of a smoke alarm, the baby's cry, a knock on the door. Hearing dogs serves as deaf people's ears, helping them negotiate the world of sound. The most successful hearing dogs are active breeds highly sensitive to sound, like Pembroke Welsh

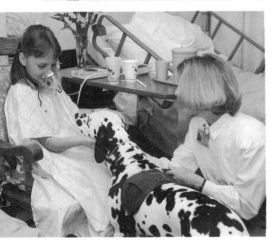

Assistance dogs open many doors otherwise unavailable to individuals with disabilities: guide dog (top left), hearing dog (top right), service dog (center and bottom right, opposite left), and social/therapy dog (bottom left, opposite right).

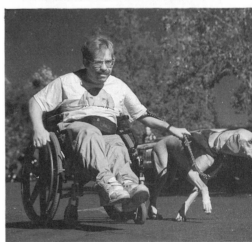

corgis, border collies, and terrier-poodle mixes.

Service dogs, the concept I pioneered over twenty years ago, help people who experience mobility limitations because of polio, spina bifida, spinal cord trauma, muscular dystrophy, cerebral palsy, and similar disorders. Service dogs do what the human cannot — push elevator buttons, flip light switches, retrieve dropped or needed items, even pull wheelchairs. Labrador and golden retrievers and crosses of these two breeds have proved particularly successful as service dogs.

So-called specialty dogs are specifically trained for individuals with multiple disabilities, such as paraplegia combined with deafness. Cross-training is used to develop in the dog the particular mix of skills needed to help a given individual.

Social/therapy dogs may also work with people with disabilities as well as individuals who are institutionalized. The difference between a social/therapy dog and other assistance dogs is that the social/therapy dog's handler facilitates interaction with the individual who is disabled or institutionalized. Often the social/therapy dog is owned by its handler, who volunteers his or her dog and then undergoes special training along with the dog to learn the needed skills. Social/therapy work is a good way for many companion-dog owners and their pets to help others in a way that is rewarding to both human and animal.

IN some cultures and places, dogs have helped humans keep themselves and their surroundings clean. In the days when fleas and lice were a constant annoyance to humans, small dogs were allowed to sit on the master's lap so that insect pests could migrate onto the dog and then be removed. In Mexican California, where the principal economic activity was raising huge herds of nearly wild cattle for their hides, great packs of dogs were kept on the rancheros to eat cast-off carcasses, offal, and leather trimmings at slaughter time. Canines play a similar role today in impoverished parts of North Africa, the Middle East, and Asia, where feral dogs clean up all sorts of waste.

BLOODHOUNDS are the detectives of the canine world. With their exceptionally keen noses, they can track escaped criminals or lost children through city or country, even when the trail is old. Never used as attack or protection dogs, bloodhounds have such an unerring sense of smell that evidence they uncover on the trail of miscreants is legally admissible in court.

These days bloodhounds and other scent hounds are using their noses for tasks besides pursuing road-gang escapees through steaming swamplands. These dogs can be trained to sniff out caches of smuggled drugs or to uncover bombs deftly concealed by terrorists. Searching for explosives is a particularly demanding task. The dog must learn to find the bomb, but not re-

trieve it as its instinct would lead it to do, since the least touch might set off the device. Canines are so good at this task that practically every bomb squad in North America and Europe has its dog.

True police dogs, which pursue and apprehend lawbreakers, were first used in Germany in the late 1800s. The German shepherd was the breed of choice, followed later by the Airedale terrier and the Doberman pinscher. Since then, in various parts of the world, other breeds have been used. A well-trained police dog can make patrol work much more efficient and effective, and sometimes the very sight of a dog will deter crime. When commanded to pursue a suspect, a police dog is trained to seize and hold the person, not to inflict injury.

Dogs make excellent sentries. The German spitz has been a traditional vineyard guard in Germany, the Dutch smoushond protects stables, and the keeshonden is the breed of choice to watch over houseboats in the inland waterways of Belgium and Holland. Today, guard dogs, many of them also trained to detect bombs, work in all sorts of places — prisons, nuclear energy plants, military installations, museums, and historical sites, including the Statue of Liberty.

Dogs also help with search-and-rescue work. Newfoundlands are well known for their willingness to pull drowning people out of the water. They swim in circles around the victim, buoying the distressed person up until he or she can grasp the big, strong dog and be pulled to safety. If the victim is unconscious, the Newfoundland takes gentle hold with its mouth and swims ashore.

The Saint Bernard is also known as the Good Samaritan dog for its feats of rescue. Saint Bernards are particularly adept at finding people lost in snow. Though depicted with a brandy cask about their necks, Saint Bernards usually carry a fog lamp to light the way of the human rescue team following behind.

Search-and-rescue dogs are used in snow country in time of avalanche and in the back woods to find lost hikers, fishermen, and hunters. They are also brought in to locate children who have wandered away or been kidnapped and to locate people trapped in the remains of buildings brought down by earthquake, explosion, or bombardment.

Folktales and newspaper accounts document the many dogs who have gone out of their way to rescue a trapped human or bring help — the Irish setter who saved a child from quicksand, the mutt who raced alongside a train to signal that its master lay unconscious across the tracks just ahead, the hunting dog who brought help to a master badly wounded in a gun accident. All such incidents are powerful evidence of the bond that exists between our two kinds.

DOGS have aided humans since ancient times in our organized efforts to kill and maim one another, which are known as wars. In twentieth-century conflicts, dogs have performed a variety of tasks besides sentry and patrol duty — carrying messages and munitions to and from units trapped behind enemy lines, leading medics to the wounded, sniffing out buried mines, providing companionship to lonely soldiers, parachuting with their military masters in airborne assaults, trailing and locating enemy units.

Wars have helped boost the popularity of certain breeds, usually by exposing foreign soldiers to dogs they have never seen before. The German shepherd first became popular in England, Canada, and the United States when Allied soldiers brought the dogs back from Germany after World War I. (Because of anti-German sentiment at the time, the breed was commonly renamed the Alsatian, which gave it a falsely French flavor.) Likewise, in World War II, returning Americans brought Akitas back from Japan, and the vizsla first appeared outside its native Hungary following the Russian takeover of that country. But sometimes war has the same lethal effect on dogs that it does on humans. The Bouvier des Flandres nearly became extinct when its native Flanders was ravaged by Nazi blitzkrieg.

SOME dogs guard livestock, some herd them, and others do both. After helping the shepherd or cowherd

Dogs can be trained to protect in wartime or in peacetime.

drive the sheep or cattle up from low-lying winter pasture into mountain meadows, livestock-guarding dogs remain behind to watch the flock and protect it against wolves. These dogs, of which the Anatolian shepherd is a prime example, are big tough fighters who patrol the edges of the flock, and they are fully willing to challenge and drive off a wolf, bear, or lion. Anatolians were even equipped with sharp-spiked collars to prevent wolves from seizing the vulnerable throat in the event of an outright fight. These big, protective dogs have cream-colored coats that look much like sheep's wool, and they spend all their time with the sheep, as if they too were members of the flock. In the United States, ranchers who have found that guns,

traps, and poison don't stop coyotes are using guardian dogs to protect their stock, with successful results. Usually coyotes steer well clear of any flock protected by a guardian dog.

Some herding dogs excel at rounding up strays. Others control a herd by running circles around it. Still others attain mastery by challenging the biggest ram or bull with a steely stare. The Hungarian pulik has the most creative approach of all. It walks across the backs of livestock or rides them, as if it were a jockey in the saddle.

BEAGLES sniff out termite infestations in houses and commercial buildings, scratching at the floor when they find a nest of these wood-eaters. Since beagles are small, they can fit into tight places where humans cannot. Similarly, dogs have been trained to locate the eggs of the gypsy moth and may be used to find other harmful insects in the future. In France, where truffles are a delicacy, dogs (and pigs!) are used to locate these underground fungi. The newest innovation among scent dogs is the animal trained to detect the odor of a cow in estrus and signal to the cattle farmer that breeding time has arrived.

DOGS have long been used to carry things from one place to another. In North America, before Indians domesticated horses, dogs pulled the Plains tribes' travois, a kind of stretcher made of two shafts lashed together with a platform for holding loads. It is reported that the Pueblo Indians — who also used dog manure in their kilns to give pottery a black cast — hitched drayage dogs together in a kind of pack train. Crow Indians on the warpath used dogs to carry baskets of spare moccasins. In the mid-1800s, when the fur trade flourished, dogs kept trappers and mountain men company, then hauled the winter's catch of pelts back to the trading post.

In both Asian Siberia and American Alaska, dogs pulled sleds, often with extraordinarily heavy loads, at speeds of up to twelve miles per hour for short stretches. Arctic breeds were key to the exploration of both North and South poles by Americans and Europeans, and they became the first link between the civilized world and the Arctic. In 1925 a team of Siberian huskies covered 560 miles of ice and snow in only 127 hours — for an average speed of 4.4 miles per hour — to bring serum to a remote settlement beset by a diphtheria epidemic. The annual Iditarod race celebrates this sled dog tradition every March, as hundreds of teams cross Alaska from Anchorage to Nome, a distance of over eleven hundred frozen miles.

The Bernese mountain dog was developed in the Alps around Bern, Switzerland — a city known for its cheese-making and basket-weaving — to haul wagons of cheeses and baskets to market. Poodles were put to similar work in Russia. In the United States laws ban the use of dogs as commercial dray animals, but hobbyists enjoy dog-carting for pleasure with some of the giant breeds, like mastiffs and Saint Bernards.

FOR warmth, Australian aborigines sleep with their dogs, which are descendants of the dingo. The colder it gets, the more dogs are needed; hence the term *three-dog night*. Arctic sled dogs often sleep with their masters, sharing warmth against the subzero cold. Toy-sized canines — called pillow dogs because they sometimes rested on a pillow as footwarmers — were employed as primitive heating pads, their body heat said to alleviate abdominal pain and other maladies.

North American Indians used the hair of the Indian dog to make cloth for clothes, Pekingese hair was woven into socks for soldiers in World War I, and Samoyed hair has been spun into wool. Today, the hair of Afghan hounds, Lhasa apsos, and Great Pyrenees is occasionally used to make yarn.

Heart to Heart

The role dogs play in human society has shifted markedly over the past three hundred years, and in that shift we have rediscovered how fundamental and significant our connection to canines is.

In the old days, not really so long ago, dogs did significant economic work. They hunted game for food, helped fishermen secure their catch, kept rats and other destructive pests under control, pulled carts, protected livestock, and stood guard over cottage and farm. Dogs were useful and necessary.

But in the Industrial Revolution, all this changed. In the movement from muscle to machine, many humans were rendered unnecessary by new technology and thrown out of work. The same thing happened to dogs. Steam-driven locomotives made dog-pulled carts obsolete and merely quaint. Fewer and fewer people hunted the woods and fields for food, and, with the rapid consolidation of farms and pastures, fewer dogs were needed to guard and herd. Dogs were kept less for work than for leisure-time diversion.

The portraiture of the eighteenth and nineteenth centuries reflected this change, as dogs were shown in sentimental poses and attributed humanlike feelings. Personality became more important than work. More and more breeds were created with puppyish characteristics — dogs who were endlessly bouncy, innocent, and dependent, even into old age. At the same time the former livelihood pursuits of canines — hunting, herding, and running — became sports, in which dogs competed against one another, often with their owners betting on the outcome. Dogs were transformed from workmates into extensions of the human ego, a way for their masters to gain status, notoriety, and prestige.

Still, the basic emotional connection between humans and dogs remained, despite the change. And it was in the realm of emotion and feeling that dogs made a new mark.

The first documented use of animals in modern psychotherapy came in the 1940s at the Army Corps Convalescent Hospital in New Jersey. So-called healing-paws dogs were instrumental in helping World War II veterans recover from shell shock — a profound physical and mental collapse we would today call post-traumatic stress syndrome. Dogs helped affected soldiers recover their sense of connection, often renewing their purpose for living in a world that had literally exploded all around them.

In the 1950s, clinical psychologist

Boris M. Levinson serendipitously discovered the usefulness of dogs in individual psychotherapy. Levinson is recognized as the founder of pet-facilitated therapy — which today is known as animal-assisted activities and therapy. Ohio State University psychobiologists Samuel and Elizabeth Corson took Levinson's work further by introducing dogs into the successful treatment of hospitalized mental patients who had not responded to traditional therapies.

Meanwhile, new approaches were made in using dogs to help people with disabilities. A deaf woman whose own naturally trained hearing dog had died contacted the local humane society to find a replacement. The society asked Agnes McGrath to train such a hearing dog, and her success with the concept ballooned into the many hearing-dog programs now found around the country. At about the same time, I was training Abdul, the first service dog. Both hearing dogs and service dogs help people with physical limitations deal in a more independent and autonomous way with the world, and, in practically every case, the individual with an assistance dog gains in self-reliance and overall happiness. What I discovered — very much in line with the work of Levinson and the Corsons — was that although the relationship with the dog added to the human's psychological well-being as well as his or her physical welfare, the dog broke the ice, creating a social bridge between able-bodied individuals and the physically challenged handler.

More and more, dogs are being used in a wide variety of therapeutic and institutional settings to help humans heal. Therapists, for example, find that including the family dog often promotes the therapeutic process. When the dog is present, family members are more relaxed and more likely to expose their feelings, usually by projecting them onto the dog. "He feels angry today" is code for "I feel angry today." Observing the dog as a mirror of the family's feelings, the therapist can better determine what is happening emotionally and thus guide the healing process. Dogs are also being used with the elderly in convalescent homes, with children in cancer wards, and in prisons, where resident dogs calm tensions among inmates and reduce the level of violence.

The point of all this isn't that you have to be a special person with a special dog to benefit from canine-human interaction. Even in the middle of the mainstream, dogs do enormous good for their masters and families. In an age of overbusy lives, with stress pushing adults and children alike to the breaking point, a dog can provide welcome relief to tension and conflict. Research has even shown that having a dog helps people survive heart attack and that petting a dog lowers blood pressure.

Dogs offer a great deal to children, not only as playmates to come home to, but as teachers. For example, when a dog has had enough of playing dress-up or being pulled around the neighborhood in the little red wagon, it is teaching the child that it, too, is a being with limits who requires consideration. This is only one of the many important lessons dogs can teach kids. And dogs often serve as childhood confidantes, particularly for teenagers, who are unwilling and unable to talk to adults. The family pet will listen to their worries and fears with wide eyes, wagging tail, and a complete absence of judgment.

Adults, likewise, gain a great deal from relationships with dogs. There is companionship for single people, and working with a dog requires emotional consistency, a valuable lesson for the unmarried and the married alike. Dogs help relieve stress, and they offer solace and companionship to people in demanding careers. The elderly seem particularly to benefit from dogs, who give their lives purpose, meaning, and a felt sense of love and connection.

Stand by Me

Dogs need and love people more than anything else in the world. No other animal has allied itself so closely with humans — nor is any other animal so utterly dependent on us for its physical survival and emotional fulfillment. And we need dogs, because they remind us who we really are. We humans still think of ourselves as above and apart, when in fact we are all of piece with the animal world. It's a lesson that is brought home to me every time I work with a dog in training, or I stroke Keila, Hoja, or Timbre after a long day. I look into those dark and knowing eyes, and my human self melds with their canine selves — two animals, dog and human, wound round each other at our deepest roots. It's a special feeling.

Chapter Three

Fallacies and Falsehoods

Common and Harmful Misbeliefs about Dogs

*Y*OU'VE probably heard at least some of them — you can't teach an old dog new tricks, all dogs chase cats, and they smell bad too. These beliefs, and dozens more like them, are just plain wrong. In fact, old dogs can learn, canines can be trained not to chase, and clean dogs smell perfectly fine. Such fallacies, though, fill the popular mind and get in the way of relating clearly, truly, and instinctively with the dogs who share our homes and lives.

The Nature of Dogs

"A dog is a dog is a dog is a dog is a dog is a dog. . . ."

Easily the deepest and most destructive misbelief about dogs is that one dog is more or less the same as every other dog, as if all dogs were like, say, cars. A Chevrolet and a Mercedes appear to be distinct, but under the hood and the sheet metal they are pretty much the same. Step on the gas, and they get up and go. Commonly, people approach dogs as if they were machines. If you do A, then the dog should do B.

But this simply isn't the case. Certain obvious generalities do apply to dogs, of course. Yet every dog is distinct, different, unique. In truth, each dog is a person in the very same way that each human is a person.

Even if you know your own dog well, try this. Call the animal over and have it sit in front of you. Now take hold of its face and focus into its eyes with your own. Get close; this exercise is about intimacy. Pay attention to what you are seeing — two highly expressive eyes set in a face that shows emotion as widely and as deeply as your own. Look all the way down into those eyes, let yourself fall into them. Yes, that is an individual you see reflected there, another being, a form of life as full and round as you yourself.

Don't approach your dog with assumptions. Instead, treat its being with the wonder and freshness it deserves.

"Training a dog to work is cruel and unusual punishment."

Since some humans think the end-all of life is to sit on a beach and sip piña coladas through an eternity of sunsets, they assume dogs want to follow their own version of that fantasy — lying around in the backyard, eating garbage, chasing cats, and refusing to come when they are called. It is cruel, this line of argument goes, to train dogs to perform tasks at their masters' bidding. Teaching a dog to follow commands, whether bringing in the newspaper or lying down, violates the animal's nature by making it slavishly dependent and subservient.

This is a classic example of anthropomorphic thinking — that is, attributing human characteristics to the dog. And it is itself a form of cruel and unusual punishment, because it fails to see the dog for what it is.

The fact of the matter is that dogs love to work. They achieve fulfillment by being taught how to do jobs and then being assigned the responsibility to complete them. Remember again that the dog is a pack animal. In the pack, which hunts by teamwork, every dog plays a role on the team. Dogs have evolved over the millennia to fill those roles; their very biological natures make them task-oriented creatures who want to be told what to do and then go do it. Playing an assigned role gives the dog security within its social structure, be that a wild pack or a suburban family. To the dog, working within the framework of relationship is the primary path to self-actualization. Dogs become most who they are by doing tasks and by receiving appreciation for their efforts.

Training a dog isn't a form of slavery, nor is it cruel. In fact, failing to train your pet and give it the opportunity to a develop to its highest potential may be the most unusual punishment of all.

"Dogs have no feelings."

Canines aren't robots that respond to external inputs. They are put together very much the way we are. Emotions and feelings are as real in dogs as in humans, and they are a prime mover of behavior. Whenever something unusual and unpredictable happens with your dog, and the response is not instinctive, the likelihood is that its actions arose from feelings like anger, frustration, despair, or hope.

"Dogs respect whoever feeds them. So if you want a dog to be yours, be sure you're the one who serves up its meals and treats."

Leadership is much more the basis of relationship with a dog than food. In kenneled dogs, for example, love and devotion are saved for the trainer, not the kennel worker who brings the daily kibble. In families, the issue of who feeds the dog makes little difference. Instead, the person who feels as if he or she is the dog's owner is the one who has made an emotional alliance with the animal. It is to this person that the dog will look for leadership.

Canine Lifestyles

"Leash laws impose cruel limits on a dog's freedom."

In fact, leash laws protect dogs from dangers they are unequipped to handle. In the city, unleashed dogs cannot judge the speed of cars and are likely to dash into the street and be hit. In the country, dogs running free are prone to form packs and harass livestock. The laws of most states allow farmers and ranchers to kill any dog that threatens cattle, horses, goats, chickens, or other animals. A similar fate can befall dogs that chase or hunt wild animals on public lands.

To protect your dog from death by car or bullet, fence it securely at home. And when the two of you leave home, keep your partner on a leash at all times.

"To be happy, dogs need to roam free with their canine friends."

Dogs do need to bond, but that need can be met with humans as well as with other dogs. As for chasing and hunting, retrieving tennis balls or dumbbells fills the bill.

If you want your dog to play with other dogs, do so only in a confined and fenced area. Let the dogs off-leash to play. If left on-leash, the dogs — and you — can become seriously tangled. Leashed dogs who don't know each other are likely to get into fights, too. Dogs tend to defend the area around the owner's feet. Also the leash encumbers the dog and makes it responsive to you, preventing certain facial expressions and body postures that communicate vital social information when dogs greet each other.

Scent is one major reason why dogs like to run free. You can satisfy that need with a retractable leash, which stretches to twenty-six feet in length. The retractable leash gives the dog freedom to explore the universe of smell available to its nose, but, because it winds back to normal leash length at the touch of a button, it protects the pet against sudden dashes into danger or mischief.

"The best way to keep a dog from wandering is to tie it to a tree."

Confronted by danger, a dog has two options: fight or flight. But a dog who is tied up cannot run away. Instead, its inborn tendency to defend itself and the small territory surrounding it is heightened. Out of frustration, a tied dog is likely to bark, perhaps incessantly, which will win neither you nor your dog any fans among the neighbors.

Tethering can also pose a major risk to the dog's life. If the animal tries to hurdle a fence or other barrier, it may end up being hanged — a miserable death no dog deserves.

Simply, don't tether your dog to a stationary object. If you must secure it, use a tie-out trolley, which consists of a length of rope between two trees or posts about eight feet off the ground. The trolley line is run through the loop at the end of the dog's leash, which is then fastened to the dog's collar — NOT a choke chain. Be sure that the leash is long enough to allow the dog to lie down, and be sure the dog has access to shade, rain shelter, and water.

The issue of tethering can be avoided altogether by providing the dog with a properly confined area. This means a fence six to eight feet high, with no loose boards or holes the dog can slip through (beware: dogs can get through openings that look far too small for them!). If the dog is a digger who might try to burrow under the fence, imbed a layer of chicken wire or concrete at the bottom. Again, be sure the dog has protection from the elements and a supply of fresh water. A safe play toy (see chapter 12) won't hurt either.

"Dogs are animals, so they belong outdoors."

Dogs are pack animals who require strong social bonds. They aren't meant to live a life of solitary confinement tied up to the doghouse out back. Such dogs know their lives have no point. Without anyone to please or to love, they become powerfully insecure and sometimes dangerously aggressive.

Even in the wild, dogs had warm caves or dens to crawl into, and they slept with their fellow pack members. The same requirements hold for canine happiness within our technological civilization. Give your dog a place within your family and inside your home.

"Don't get a dog unless you live in the country and have lots of room."

First of all, it's not true that big dogs require big spaces. In fact, highly energetic terriers typically require more exercise than the huge but placid Great Dane. The truth is that no matter where you live, there is a breed suitable to those conditions — and an individual dog who would like to share your life.

While their masters may prefer rural acreage at the foot of mountains to a cramped apartment in the city center, dogs have no such preference. What a dog needs is exercise, security, and quality time with its master. That can happen anywhere.

"When you travel, it's better to leave your dog at home."

Not necessarily. A well-behaved dog can be an excellent traveling companion and is welcome in many hotels and motels. For example, state travel guides published by the American Automobile Association indicate whether pets are allowed in approved accommodations.

If you are going into the woods or wild lands, your dog is likely to enjoy the trip as much as you do. Although dogs are banned in wilderness areas of United States national parks, they are allowed in national forest backcountry, including designated wilderness, primitive, and roadless areas. The only requirement is that the dog be kept under control to prevent harm to other humans, wildlife, or grazing livestock. Also, campgrounds in many state and national parks, as well as designated campgrounds in national forests, permit dogs on leash. Check with the campground where you're headed to find out about pet rules and regulations before you arrive.

Traveling with a dog in the car is something like traveling with children. You need to make the journey comfortable and nonthreatening. Stop often to let the dog exercise, always on leash, and you can train it to urinate on command and on-leash (see chapter 9). Bring along a supply of water from home (sudden changes in source can cause diarrhea), the dog's blanket or bed, and some favorite toys, to preserve a sense of the familiar.

If you must leave your dog at home, a pet sitter can be good way to keep your animal healthy and happy while you're gone. The sitter will come by to feed and play with the dog, usually twice a day. The dog gets the attention it needs, and it is able to stay in its home surroundings. Alternatively, use a boarding kennel — but check it out in advance. Make sure that the kennel is secure, safe, and sanitary, that the dog has a good place to sleep and exercise, and that provision is made for veterinary attention and any other special care your dog may need. Your veterinarian is a good referral source for both pet sitters and boarding kennels.

Training

"There is one best way to train a dog."

Absolutely not! Training a dog is not like memorizing the manual for word-processing software. Every dog is an individual who must be trained in the method most appropriate to its learning style and ability. The same thing holds true for the trainer. You too are an individual who must find a method that works best for you and modify it to fit the dog you're working with. Usually, what makes one trainer better than another is not the specific methods he or she uses, but his or her ability to draw on a repertoire of methods to suit a particular situation. The purpose for which a dog is being trained also plays a role in selecting the right method. Police dogs, for example, are trained differently from companions.

"You can't teach an old dog new tricks."

Adult dogs, like adult humans, can and do learn, but in a manner different from puppies. Puppies are much like children: they are highly attuned to learning, and often acquire new behaviors very quickly. It helps, too, that both children and puppies are physically agile. Adult dogs, much the same as grown-up humans, may take longer to learn and be less flexible in the body, but they have longer attention spans than their youthful counterparts, can draw on past knowledge, and focus better on learning. As long as the trainer is patient and consistent, adult dogs can learn or unlearn practically anything. Age is no barrier to teaching a dog.

"Barking is just something dogs do. You can't stop them."

The wild canid language of barks, whines, howls, and growls is indeed inborn. Dogs bark instinctively to sound an alarm or get attention. Still, a dog can be taught to bark only when appropriate and to be silent on command. For example, you can readily train your dog to bark when someone approaches the front door and stop barking once you know who it is and say, "It's okay." We'll discuss training routines for barking later in the book.

"Dogs naturally hate cats. You'll never stop them from going after them — or from chasing joggers or cars, for that matter."

It is natural for dogs to give chase. Throughout their evolution in the wild, dogs caught dinner by running it down. Thus the ability to pursue smaller creatures that run away from them is very much a part of canine nature. Dogs chase cats not because they instinctively hate them but because cats run away — and give the dog something appealingly small and fast to go after. Some dogs, such as the hunting breeds, retain this an-

Dogs and cats in the same household may even become quite attached and friendly.

cient trait more than others.

Dogs and cats occupying the same household tolerate one another, and may even become quite attached and friendly. Puppies who grew up with cats learn to adapt to them as adult dogs, unless the cats of those early days habitually ran away from them. Dogs even learn from cats. A friend told me that his cats taught his dogs to use the litter box in case of emergency, and even showed them how to clean their faces in the approved feline manner.

For their own safety, dogs who are inclined to chase cats should be trained not to. A dog in hot pursuit of a feline will ignore dangers like speeding cars and can easily end up dead. And if the dog does catch the cat and corner it, it may discover most painfully how much damage those claws can do to eyes and face.

Whenever your dog indicates interest in a cat, correct it. Start with a firm and emphatic "No!" If necessary, use a choke chain (see correction instructions in chapter 9). Be sure to set up purposeful temptations for the dog, exposing it to situations where it will come into contact with cats and perhaps even be teased by them. If and when the dog wants to go after a cat, correct it. Continue the correction and the temptation trials until the dog has gotten the idea.

Chasing joggers and cars is much like pursuing cats — dogs instinctively go after creatures that run away from them. Like cat-chasing, this behavior needs to be stopped, for the dog's sake at least. Joggers who have been confronted by one too many dogs may try to drive your pet off with rocks, which can cause serious injury. And a dog who runs after cars is likely to be killed by one. To eliminate the problem, use the same techniques of correction and temptation that apply to cat-chasing.

"It is inborn in dogs to respect humans."

Actually, I wonder sometimes whether dogs distinguish us from their own kind. Obviously we smell different and look different, but we relate in similar ways. Dogs differentiate among other dogs in terms of respect and affection, and they practice the same differentiation in regard to humans. Overall, it is the responsibility of humans to teach their dogs respect for other humans and to behave themselves appropriately, not to assume that respect is our inherent birthright.

"Dogs naturally jump on people

and lick them to show affection, so it's okay to let them do it."

When a dog jumps up on a human, it is trying to make eye contact and win attention. It can be annoying, however, and sometimes dangerous. A Labrador, Great Dane, or Newfoundland lunging zealously for affection can easily bowl someone over and break bones. Instead, correct the dog against jumping up, and teach it to greet humans with all four legs on the ground and to show affection by sitting and shaking hands or giving a kiss. These commands are covered in chapter 9.

"A dog who learns quickly is smarter than one who learns slowly."

Speed of learning is one measure of intelligence, but not the only one. Different dogs, like different people, assimilate information at different rates. Often the dog who learns quickly also discards it quickly, and the dog who learns slowly retains the learning for the remainder of its life. As in other aspects of life, both human and canine, there are many trade-offs between one thing and another.

"Dogs will play when the master's away."

No doubt you've heard one of those horror stories about coming home to a house destroyed by a dog left on its own. A friend of mine told me about a friend of his who lost the entire interior of his Toyota — seats, steering wheel, sun visors, even the dashboard knobs — to his Labrador, whom he had left inside for several hours. The problem here isn't destructiveness; it's boredom.

A dog left alone for a long period with nothing to do is like a child confined at home with no toys. Pretty soon the youngster will make toys and games of its own — throwing rocks through the windows, writing on the walls with Dad's fountain pen, decorating the den with computer paper, or some other wild antic. The child is neither evil nor vengeful. It is an intelligent and resourceful creature figuring out creative ways to fill empty time. The Toyota-eating Labrador was doing much the same. Dogs who bark, eat furniture, and dig holes in the garden are entertaining themselves and expressing a natural drive to escape boredom.

You can protect home and car in your absence with a few simple measures. First of all, give your dog a job to do while you're gone. Dogs, as we will discuss in more detail in the training chapters, are highly responsible and want to be charged with tasks to accomplish. When you leave the house, say to your dog in a commanding tone, "Watch the house." Your tone tells the dog it has something to do, and it will indeed do it — which will help the animal stay out of unwitting trouble.

You can also provide the dog with sources of entertainment. Leave your dog with safe toys (see chapter 11). Tie an old rag to a tree, so the dog can play tug-of-war. Turn on the TV or radio at low volume; dogs like familiar sounds, which they find soothing.

Companionship is also a great solution to boredom. Adding a cat or a second dog to the household provides a playmate for the times when you are away.

"Training a dog takes an enormous amount of time."

A dog is a commitment, but quality time counts over quantity. Dogs actually learn best when they have short but frequent training sessions, typically of ten to twenty minutes' duration, in either morning or evening. Also, training and exercise can be combined. Unless you want to prepare a dog for shows or field trials and follow the rigorous regimen these activities entail, training can become a natural and easy part of your daily routine — and one of the best opportunities you have to spend focused time with your pet.

"My dog won't follow commands because it doesn't like me."

Whenever you start imputing negative feelings to your dog, you are assigning it emotional control over you and your life rather than recognizing that you are the animal's authority figure and the source of all good emotion. Misbehavior isn't a matter of liking or disliking on the part of the dog. It springs from the human's unwillingness to maintain leadership, poorly designed training, or both. If you lead your dog, and if you shape its training effectively, it will behave. That is the simple truth.

"If my dog loved me, it would do whatever I ask."

This complaint is the flip side of the foregoing misbelief. Yes, loving you does help make the dog responsive to your commands, but it takes more than that. You also need to have taught the dog the response you want and — even more important — not have taught it an undesirable behavior. Let me give you an example, using the common problem of a dog who does not come when called. Its delay in obeying is not the result of a lack of love. More likely, you called the dog one time and it hesitated. Then when it did come, you scolded it. What the dog learned was that coming to you would result in a scolding, not that it should come faster. As a result, it is likely to delay even more when you call, to put off the inevitable correction.

"My dog has this way of taking control of the situation and making me the victim."

Now stop a minute and give this one some thought. Fact is, your brain is much bigger than your dog's and you have capacities, such as advanced reasoning and an ability to invent, that far exceed your pet's. It is highly unlikely that your dog is making you a victim. Chances are you are misunderstanding the dog's message by assigning it a psychological complexity more in line with yourself than with canine reality. The situation is compounded if you are a person who tends to put yourself in victim roles.

Whenever you find yourself thinking that your pet is victimizing you, simplify the situation. Drop your own complex thinking, look at things from the dog's point, and act accordingly. It's a lot easier than you think.

"Dogs take deliberate revenge."

Misbehavior by your dog has nothing to do with personal slights. It does not arise because the animal cognitively devises a strategy of rebellion and then follows it. Instead, the dog's actions are immediate emotional responses to a situation — most commonly, the human's unwillingness or inability to lead. Misbehavior is one way the dog has of challenging its master to determine whether he or she still has the right stuff. Sometimes, too, a dog learns that misbehavior gets your attention and it will act up in order to elicit an emotional response from you. You need to respond to misbehavior not by punishing misperceived vengeance, but by proving you can manage and care for your dog, thereby providing the security it needs to feel content and follow the rules of the house.

"Mutts are smarter than pure-breds."

The generalization is unfair and overly simplified. Some breeds have been inbred so seriously that undesirable physical and mental characteristics now predominate. But don't mislabel a purebred who is long on energy and short on exercise and discipline as stupid. A mixed-breed dog under the same conditions will be equally unruly.

Because of their mixed breeding, mutts often enjoy hybrid vigor, which can make them quick-witted as well as strong-bodied. But it is by no means true that mixed breeds learn better or faster than purebreds. Although certain breeds and lines of dogs are better at learning certain things, few dogs, whether purebred or mixed breed, are incapable of learning.

The most common cause of stupidity in a dog is its owner. Whenever a dog's master calls the animal stupid, he or she has almost certainly failed to make the right kind of emotional commitment to training the pet. Lack of intelligence in the dog isn't the issue; lack of good training by the human is.

Mean Dogs and Mean People

"A dog with a wagging tail won't bite."

There's more than one way to wag a

Because of their mixed breeding, mutts often enjoy hybrid vigor.

tail, and the tail is just one part of the body. Instead, look at the whole dog. If it seems combative or threatening, you'll probably see that only the part of the tail close to the tip is wagging — a behavior appropriately called flagging. Slow deliberate flagging often signals resistance as well as aggression, a phenomenon we'll discuss in depth in regard to training.

"A dog who bites is mean and should be destroyed."

Biting is one of the weapons wild canids wield to defend and assert themselves. Coyotes, wolves, dholes, and other wild canids bite each other in struggles over mates, food, leadership, and territory. Now that humans make up the domesticated dog's pack, we sometimes become the target for biting, just as if we were other dogs.

Before a biting dog is branded as mean and marked for destruction, determine just what caused the bite. Practically any dog, even one of placid demeanor, may bite if its toys or food are snatched away; if it never sees any human but the person who feeds it; if it is in severe physical pain or is a female in heat (the origin of the word *bitchy*); if it is excessively shy or frightened; or if it has been physically abused — that is, punished repeatedly, painfully, and maliciously.

Because it is dangerous, biting cannot be tolerated. Even a puppy's playful nips must be corrected. Still, it can be difficult to break a dog from biting if it has inherited the tendency to bite in certain situations. Preventing a dog from biting is one of the best reasons to learn how to manage your pet consistently and effectively.

"Old dogs get mean."

Dogs of a certain age can indeed be crochety, but the passing years alone aren't the issue. Discomfort is a more common cause of the grouchies. Ailments like arthritis or hip dysplasia are typically aggravated as a dog ages, and it may snap protectively if the painful area is touched. Often the problem can be corrected with medication prescribed by a veterinarian.

"Only male dogs fight, and only with each other."

Males may fight one another. But males may also fight with females, and females may light into each other as well. Anytime one dog — male, female, or neutered — is introduced into the territory of another dog, a fight is possible, particularly if the two dogs are about equally assertive and therefore need to establish a pecking order. The tendency to fight can be minimized if the master is stronger and more assertive than the dogs, who will be content to follow the human's lead and feel less need to contend for leadership with each other.

Because territoriality often figures into dogfights, dogs who will be spending time together should be introduced on neutral ground and off-leash. The lack of established territory dilutes the dogs' need to defend their own turf, and without leashes to get in the way the dogs can get to know each other. You can expect aggression to be expressed at some point or other. Understand, though, that there is a difference between a display fight and a serious conflict. In a display fight, no blood is drawn and much of the struggle is a matter of posturing. Display fighting is a normal part of dog behavior, a way the animals have of settling social issues like pecking order.

Still, keeping your dog on a leash is a good preventive to fights during casual encounters between dogs. When two leashed dogs display aggressively toward each other, their owners can control and correct them. If a loose dog approaches your dog on-leash and acts combative — back and neck hair erect, low growling, flagging tail — stand still, or back yourself and your dog away. Moving toward the dog or turning tail to run may provoke an attack.

"Any two dogs who fight seriously should be separated from then on."

Keeping them apart does solve the problem in the short term, and it may even prove necessary as a final solution. Be aware that a serious fight may have erupted because of an extenuating circumstance, such as weak human leadership. In such situations, tension builds over time and just makes matters between the two dogs worse. It is worth trying other solutions before taking the extreme course of lifelong separation. One way is to give the dogs a chance to interact on leash, with both handlers correcting them against aggression (chapters 9 and 10 discuss correction techniques in detail). Once the dogs know that the humans are the leaders, they may lose much of their need to vie for dominance. Whenever the dogs are together, the master must correct either animal for even the slightest display of aggression, well before a fight has any chance to erupt. The lesson you want to instill is simple: Fighting is not acceptable, not now, not ever.

"The best way to break up a fight is to throw cold water on the dogs."

Cold water can work, by surprising the dogs long enough to part them without getting bitten yourself. Trouble is, a great many dogfights break out a long way from a water supply, and an empty bucket can be even harder to find when the fur is flying. A blanket or a coat thrown over one of the dog's heads works just as well, by disorienting the animals long enough to separate them. As soon as the animals are apart, restrain them securely, or the fight will immediately enter round two.

Never try to separate two fighting dogs by getting between them. Putting your hands, arms, or body into a dogfight is a sure way to get bitten. In the heat of the moment, even your own dog may take a piece out of you if you get in the way. Fighting dogs usually go for each other's throats, so if you insist on pulling two dogs apart by main force, take hold of the back of the collar.

Recognize that any excitement or anxiety you show will increase the fight's ferocity. Other dogs playing spectator have the same effect, and they often dash into the fray, turning up the volume of the conflict considerably. When you try to break up a fight, don't unwittingly make it even more intense. Be sure, too, that any fight you break up is in fact a serious conflict and not simply a display.

"Some breeds are mean by nature — pit bulls, Doberman pinschers, German shepherds, and Rottweilers, among others."

Behind almost every vicious dog there is a human who has a great deal to do with the animal's behavior. Irresponsible breeding is one cause of canine aggression; the pit bull is a classic case in point. Properly known as American Staffordshire terriers, pit bulls were bred originally to fight bulls. When bullbaiting was banned, they were turned on each other and other fighting breeds to entertain those who enjoy such cruel bloodsports. Lines of this breed have been developed that are explosively aggressive. This tendency is then enhanced by humans who reward and encourage fighting to train dogs for the pit. The responsibility for this situation belongs to humans who abuse their power to breed and train dogs, not to the dogs themselves.

On the one hand, a well-bred mentally sound pit bull — and such animals do exist — in the hands of a responsible master makes a fine pet. On the other, a dog of any breed who is purposely mishandled and praised for aggression can be turned into a fighting animal dangerous to other dogs and to humans.

German shepherds, Rottweilers, Doberman pinschers, and other breeds used for police, military, and guard work are not by nature sadistic or nasty. Instead, these inher-ently assertive and protective dogs are trained to pursue and apprehend, and they do so only on command. When highly trained and well managed, these animals are doing what they have been told and are performing worthy work for society's benefit. There is a flip side to this human-canine reality, which is that an untrained and unmanaged aggressive dog is a time bomb waiting to explode — because a human has failed to bear responsibility for channeling the dog's nature.

"Neutering a dog, male or female, is unfair and unnatural."

Frankly, there is little reason not to neuter a dog, unless you are seriously in the business of breeding canines. Neutering pays a number of benefits. By eliminating the sex drive and its frustrations, neutering helps keep the dog focused on its role in your family, rather than the cute collie down the block. Neutering prevents unwanted pregnancies, which can save you the cost of veterinary abortion or the emotional turmoil of finding good homes for the puppies. In females, neutering makes it unnecessary to confine the dog during heat or to clean up her estrus. In males, neutering prevents wandering and sexually motivated aggression. In both sexes, neutering prevents a number of common infections and cancers.

Dogs don't need to procreate to ensure the survival of the species, nor is sexuality necessary to the individual personal fulfillment of dogs in the same way that it is to humans. Neutering will do you and your dog a favor — and it will stem the tide of irresponsible breeding that puts thousands upon thousands of homeless dogs onto our mean streets every year, where they suffer needlessly. Dogs deserve better, and neutering is one way you can ensure they get it.

"Before you spay a female, it's best to let her have a litter."

Actually, waiting pays the dog no benefit and may even cause her subsequent grief. Spaying before first heat greatly reduces the likelihood of breast and uterine cancer, which are common causes of sickness and death in older female dogs. Don't wait. Spay your dog before she whelps.

"Dogs hate training. Putting them through their paces is as cruel as having a child sing the national anthem in front of the assembled aunts, uncles, and grandparents."

Years ago I lost count of the number of times I had seen a dog I was working with pick up its own leash and nuzzle the choke chain in excited anticipation of the training session about to begin. Dogs love to learn. Training meets their drive toward a deepened relationship with you, satisfies their powerful curiosity and interest in the new and novel, and gives them a job to do. Dogs are

pack animals; they live in complicated teams with roles divvied among them. A dog wants to work because when it works, it knows its place.

It is true that every dog rebels against training from time to time. This, however, isn't hatred, but resistance — a phenomenon we'll explore in chapter 8.

"The choke chain is cruel and unusual punishment."

Used properly, a choke chain is an excellent training aid that does no harm or punishment to the dog. A choke chain distributes pressure equally around the neck. A collar, on the other hand, has the exact opposite effect, focusing the pressure on only one part of the neck.

Problems can arise if a choke chain is used improperly. The chain is meant to be jerked quickly and released, in order to surprise the dog and get its attention, not held tight to punish it by slow strangulation or to drag it around by the throat (see chapter 9). That is cruel indeed. And it is cruel, too, to leave a choke chain on a dog at all times. Should the chain become entangled, the dog could strangle. Use a choke chain only for training sessions and take it off at all other times.

"A crate is even more cruel."

Watch where your puppy or dog goes when it is frightened or sick. Odds are it will hide under a bed, be-

Dogs gain a sense of security in denlike spaces.

hind a chair, or in a closet. Dogs gain a sense of security in denlike spaces, a clear holdover from their evolution in the wild, where canids seek caves or dig caverns in which to sleep and whelp. The den, enclosed on three sides and open on only one, offers protection and easy defense.

A properly constructed crate creates the same sense of security. A crate is an excellent way to transport a dog, and it makes a good sleeping area during housebreaking or travel away from home.

Don't mistake a cage — which is open on all four sides, rather than one — for a crate. In a cage, a dog feels completely exposed, with no safe retreat. Instead of safety and security, the dog experiences vulnerability and fear. Caging in an unfamiliar environment can cause severe emotional trauma.

"Leaving a dog home alone all day is mean."

A dog can handle solitude and confinement quite readily. What it requires is good exercise before and after, something to keep it occupied, a job to do (like watching the house when you're gone!), and perhaps a playmate. With dogs, as with children, quality time counts most.

Dirty Dogs

"Dogs shed hair everywhere, so it's best to keep them outside."

Long-haired breeds do shed a greater volume of hair than their short-haired cousins, and all dogs shed more in the spring, as the weather warms. That much is true. But some breeds don't shed at all — the poodle and the Bedlington terrier are prime examples — and others, particularly curly- or wire-coated breeds like the Airedale, shed very little.

Shedding is no reason to throw a dog out. Hair problems can be eliminated or reduced by grooming the dog regularly, particularly before it comes into the house. Talk to your pet store owner about the right tools for your pet's breed. If hair remains a problem, limit the dog's movement in your house to uncarpeted areas or to its own bed.

"Dogs smell."

There once was a television character named Dirty Sally who said the three most unforgettable smells in the world were an illegal still, over-cooked cabbage, and a wet dog. In point of fact, though, a dog who is bathed and groomed regularly should give off nothing more than a pleasantly animal aroma. Chapter 12 has further advice on how to groom and bathe a dog.

If a clean and well-groomed dog does smell offensive, take it as evidence of a health problem. The animal could have kidney disease, dental infection, inflamed anal glands, or ear mites, among other problems. A bad smell on a clean dog means it's time to see the veterinarian.

"Dogs spread disease to humans."

In fact, few diseases move from healthy dogs to healthy humans. As long as you follow certain commonsense practices, like picking up dog feces daily, keeping your pet's quarters clean, and washing your hands before eating, there's no reason to fear infection or contamination from a canine housemate any more than from a human.

"Dogs defecate and urinate when and where they want."

You can teach your dog to empty its bladder and bowel on the command "better go now," a simple and easy technique to be discussed in chapter 9. This command lets you control where your dog eliminates, and it can be a real time-saver and convenience. On a cold and rainy night, it's much more pleasant to have your dog relieve itself on command rather than wait while the animal takes its own sweet time, sniffing and fidgeting until the mood moves it.

Elimination on command is also a matter of good citizenship. It does no one, including canines, any good to see and smell dog feces littering sidewalks, driveways, parks, and athletic fields. Teach your dog to eliminate on command in a place well away from foot traffic, then scoop up the feces with a ten- or twelve-inch paper plate torn in half, and deposit them in an airtight bag for disposal in a refuse container.

Dogs are as much creatures of habit as we humans are. If you don't want to bother teaching your dog to eliminate on command, you can still control where it defecates and urinates simply by becoming aware of its usual schedule. As long as a dog is fed at about the same times and in the same amounts every day, it will usually eliminate on a predictable schedule. Take the dog to the place of your choosing at those times, and the problem of misplaced waste is solved.

"It's natural for dogs to sniff everything, including people's crotches."

Dogs do indeed want to investigate things with interesting smells, and that includes human bottoms, ice cream cones in toddlers' hands, fried chicken at a picnic, garbage in an open heap, and other dogs. However, what a dog sniffs can be controlled by teaching it the command "leave it." The technique is discussed in chapter 9, and you will find it useful. "Leave it" will allow you to keep your dog's nose from sniffing anywhere it's not wanted.

Sad Endings

"Dogs make great gifts."

Giving a puppy for Christmas is a prescription for disappointment — and the probable destruction of the dog. For a human to get the most enjoyment from a dog, he or she must consider his or her own wants and expectations. No one understands those feelings better than the individual, and outsiders, even close family members, shouldn't impose on the relationship between human and dog by picking out a puppy. A bad fit is all too likely, leading to behavior problems and the likelihood that the pet will be given up and possibly destroyed.

If you really want to give a dog as a gift, let the person choose his or her own pet. Everyone will be happier in the end.

"If you want a dog to love you, you must get it as a puppy."

The good thing about puppies is that you can control the animal's earliest upbringing, which influences behavior in later life. Puppies are also undeniably cute, but they entail enormous and time-consuming responsibility. In many ways, coming home with a puppy is like bringing a baby into the family. It is fun and it is also a huge amount of work. That's why many people prefer to start with a grown or nearly grown dog.

The age at which a dog meets its

owner does not determine the quality or success of the relationship. No matter how old a dog is, it will bond with you and respect you as soon as it becomes aware that you are a worthy leader. In fact, most dogs will transfer their loyalty and affection to a new owner with remarkable ease, even when they are well up in years.

"One of the best ways to teach children responsibility is to get them a puppy."

I once saw a cartoon that showed an obviously tired woman dressed in business clothes walking up to her front door. The caption read, "Working mothers know the kids will feed the dog." Next to the front door, though, lay the dried-up skeleton of the family pet, with a rolled newspaper still held faithfully in its bony mouth.

That's funny, but in a way it's not funny, because it points out something true. The needs of a puppy or dog far exceed a child's ability to meet them. While kids can be expected to help out in caring for a pet, it is unreasonable to charge them with total responsibility for the health and welfare of the animal. Laying that task on them will likely result in harm to the dog and failure for the kids. To bring a dog home, parents must be willing to take final responsibility.

"Dogs hate collars and shouldn't be made to wear them."

When a collar is first put on a dog, it reacts against it, scratching at the new sensation and trying to bite it. Soon, though, it gets used to the feeling, much as you yourself become accustomed to a watch on your wrist or a ring on your finger. As long as the collar is not so tight that it constricts the neck or so loose that it can slip over the dog's head, it is safe.

A collar is essential because it provides a good handhold in times of emergency and because it is the best place to attach a dog license and ID. Most local governments require licenses, and a lost dog without an ID may never be returned to you.

"Lost dogs almost always find their way home."

Canines have remarkable homing instincts, but that inborn ability can be easily thwarted by freeways, fences, cars, ranchers with guns, other dogs, and distractions of one sort or another. In the movie, Lassie does come home, but not all such stories have happy endings. Some lost dogs get killed; others, distracted by offerings of food and water in a backyard, wind up as somebody else's pet; still others are picked up by dognappers who sell them, often to unethical animal research facilities.

The best way to ensure that a lost dog gets home is to see that it doesn't become lost to begin with. First, be sure your dog is confined safely and securely. Second, when you take your pet away from home, keep it on a leash at all times. Third, be sure that your pet wears a collar with a license or that it is tattooed with an identification number.

If your dog is lost anyway, you may be able to find it by alerting individuals and agencies who could come across it. Get in touch with animal shelters, emergency veterinary clinics, police departments, animal rescue groups, universities and laboratories that use dogs in research, dog groomers, boarding kennels, and dog clubs. Some television and radio stations and newspapers run lost-pet announcements at little or no cost. Let the neighbors, particularly children, know the dog is lost. They may have spotted it. Posting a flyer with a full identification of the dog and its photo can also help.

Good Canine Citizenship

Many of the falsehoods and fallacies debunked in this chapter are perpetuated by dog owners who handle their pets ignorantly and irresponsibly. Loose dogs roaming the neighborhood, cat-chasing, garbage-eating, fly-specked feces in the park playground, and unwanted crotch-sniffing work to the disadvantage of dogs — and of us humans who work with and admire these animals. We can all do our part to dismiss the falsehoods and build a true image of dogs by handling them well in public and ensuring their welfare in our homes.

Here are some basic rules to follow when you take your dog out into public. They will benefit your dog, and all dogs.

- Make sure your dog is clean and well groomed.
- Keep your dog on leash.
- Never let your dog sniff people or dogs.
- Never allow your dog to initiate contact with other humans without your permission. Remember: Some people are truly afraid of dogs and others are allergic.
- Never let your dog eat food it finds on the floor or ground or that is offered by strangers.
- Never let your dog bark, whine, growl, or make other noises disturbing to people.
- Never let your dog rub against others or jump up on them.
- Never let your dog block an aisle or passageway where people are walking.
- Never tether your dog by a choke chain, and never leave a tethered dog unattended.
- Never let your dog chase cats.

Part Two
Right Fit

*M*AYBE you've seen the bumper sticker that says, "A dog is for life, not just for Christmas." The sentiment is both wise and well taken. It is altogether too easy to fall in love with that puppy in the window, only to bring it home and find six months later that it has grown into a big headstrong canine bent on destroying every piece of furniture in your house. This kind of unfortunate and unhappy outcome occurs all too often, and every time it happens, it is the fault not of the dog, but of the human — who failed to realize that a dog is a responsibility and a relationship, not a whimsical acquisition or a cute Christmas gift.

Dogs are beings and persons, every bit as unique as you or I, and their uniqueness affects the quality of the relationship between pet and master. We all know this from our experience in relationships with other humans. For ex-

ample, you can be in a certain kind of relationship with some people but not others. Most of us have a fittingly short list of possible spouses or lovers, and it is truly said that the best way to destroy a good relationship is to go into business with a friend. The same fundamental truth — that you will likely be happier with certain individuals than with others, and that different relationships have to be managed differently — holds true for dogs as well as for humans.

These chapters provides guidance about the factors involved in satisfying human-canine relationships drawn from my nearly twenty years' experience in bringing people and dogs together. You can use this approach to help you select a dog. Or, if you already have a pet, you will find insight here into why things have gone right — or wrong — between you and your animal.

Chapter Four

Physical Characteristics

HE first part of selecting the dog who is right for you is choosing an animal whose body type, physical characteristics, and instinctive behaviors fit what you want or need. Remember the central point made in chapter 2: No other animal is as dependent on humans and as needful of our emotional and physical commitment as the dog. Dogs require more than a daily bowl of kibble and a warm spot to sleep. They need emotional support and connection as well. To be happy with your dog, you must be willing to spend time with it — not simply relegate the animal to a doghouse in the backyard and expect it to take care of itself. Happiness with your dog is impossible if the dog's physical nature drives you crazy. Thus, the first aspect of connecting with your dog is having a pet who meshes well physically with your wants, needs, and lifestyle. Only when you have chosen the type of dog whose physical characteristics match your needs can you turn to the issue of matching personality, which we will discuss in chapter 5.

So Why Do You Want a Dog?

Self-knowledge applies to choosing a pet as well as to everything else in life. It may seem mundane or even trivial, but before you go out puppy shopping, take the time to reflect on what it is you're looking for. Be specific. Do you like long-haired dogs or short-haired? How do you feel about big canines? About small ones? Is a protective dog your idea of perfection, or do you want a happy-go-lucky pet who greets every guest who comes to the door? Do you have hobbies, like distance running or camping, you'd like the dog to take part in? How do you feel about male dogs versus female dogs? Do you have strong feelings about neutering either sex?

Underlying each of these questions about physical characteristics, there is a deeper and ultimately more significant issue: What do you want your dog to be? A dog isn't just a thing, like a VCR or a Lamborghini. It is someone, a being, who plays a daily role in your life. Give serious thought to the type of relationship you're after.

Do you want a watchdog? Such dogs bark a warning when someone approaches your house. They

Adventurers need a dog physically suited to their hobbies.

don't attack; they simply signal the presence of a stranger. Many terrier breeds, smaller herding dogs, and toy dogs are good watchdogs.

Do you want a guard dog? These dogs keep people out of the place they are guarding. They are fierce attackers and require heavy management when people they don't know are present on their turf.

Do you want a child substitute? Such dogs respond well to mothering and fathering, curling up in your arms and cuddling. Toy dogs and some small terriers, like the Yorkshire, are common child-substitute canines.

Do you want a working partner? These dogs engage in a hobby or pursuit with you: hunting, field trials, and dogsledding, for example.

Dogs enjoy a range of activities — and playmates.

Obedience and trainability are important, and you need to choose a dog physically suited to the pursuit, like a Chesapeake Bay retriever for duck hunting and a Siberian husky for the Iditarod dogsled race. You may also choose a dog as a companion in a pursuit like jogging or camping. Retrievers and pointers make good outdoor dogs for campers and backpackers, and joggers will do well with long-legged runners like pointers and German shepherds.

Do you want a playmate? That means a physically active dog who is more playful than gravely obedient. Spaniels, some terriers, retrievers, and other sporting breeds make fine playmates.

Do you want a playmate for your children? Apparently, dogs treat children as equals, and they are much more likely to bite kids than adults, whom they see as superior. Good dogs with kids are pets who are playful but neither aggressive nor defensive. More research is needed into this area, but from my experience I would recommend some retrievers, spaniels, and terriers.

Do you want a friend? A dog who is your companion and buddy, goes where you do, and is generally unobtrusive and accepting. Retrievers and spaniels often make excellent friends.

Do you want a showpiece? Some owners want a dog they can enjoy for its aesthetics as if it were, in a manner of speaking, an animated *objet d'art*. Tibetan terriers, poodles, and Afghan hounds are good examples. Such animals usually require special grooming and care and a major commitment of time and energy to their physical maintenance.

Do you want some combination of these roles? Perhaps a dog who plays well with you and your kids, follows you down the Appalachian Trail with your backpack, and listens to you attentively when you rant about your boss. Or maybe you want a good watchdog you can also take to sheepherding trials. If that's the case, you should seek out a type of dog that combines the two or three qualities you're after. A playful backpacking-empathic-companion sounds most like a Labrador or golden retriever. And an Australian shepherd makes an excellent watchdog and herding trial participant.

Other Considerations

A number of additional matters bear consideration in choosing the dog who's right for you.

Town and Country

Don't give up the idea of having a dog because you live in an apartment in the concrete center of the city. A dog doesn't need a twenty-acre pasture for romping. It needs exercise, which you can provide by walking it regularly, whether on city streets or country lanes. In fact, one of the worst things you can do for a dog is let it run free, whether in town or out. Dogs don't know that cars maim and kill; they don't understand that sniffing a calf or goat may get them shot by a protective farmer. For their own safety, dogs should be exercised on a leash or in a fenced area, period, whether in the city or the country.

Working away from home all day is also no reason to give up the idea of having and enjoying a dog. I have known any number of well-adjusted and happy dogs raised by equally well-adjusted and happy two-career couples living in condominiums. Dogs want time with their owners, but quality counts over quantity. Dogs will gladly wait throughout the workday for the reward of fifteen minutes of delighted play and an evening spent in your company.

The Season of the Year

It pays to consider the time of the year when you are bringing a dog into the family. If you're a student or a teacher and have summers off, or if you work in construction and go through winter slowdowns, the slack season is the ideal time to introduce a dog into your life. You'll have time to spend with the animal and get it adjusted to your lifestyle before your schedule picks up and keeps you away from home for longer periods.

Weather is another seasonal variable to keep in mind. Housebreaking a puppy outside in the dark snowy winter of the Northeast or the blistering summer of the Southwest is a nuisance.

Young, Old, or In-Between

Puppies are cute and cuddly, but puppies aren't for everyone. As a rule of thumb, the younger the puppy, the more time and supervision it requires. You will need to spend considerable time with a new dog over the first few days of its life with you for bonding to occur. This is true of all dogs, and particularly true of puppies. If you work, a three-day holiday weekend is a good time to bring a puppy home. The newcomer is likely to alternate periods of sleep with efforts to solicit attention from you as it seeks a place in its new pack.

Seven to eight weeks is the best age to acquire a pup, so you can ensure that the dog is properly socialized with people. If, between five and twelve weeks of age, puppies do not receive adequate exposure to humans, they become fearful of people. Therefore, consider only puppies under twelve weeks of age, who are still young enough to socialize properly. We will discuss the how-to's of socialization in detail in chapter 11.

Young pups are harder to housebreak than older animals. They have little or no voluntary control over their sphincter muscles and therefore lack the ability to hold urine on demand. An older pup is easier to housebreak but is more likely to be a chewer, since pups teethe between four and six months of age and are on eternal lookout for things to sink their new teeth into.

In most breeds, a year-old dog is an adolescent and very much into the same kind of rebelliousness human teenagers display. Neutering helps, particularly in males, but adolescence is adolescence nonetheless.

If you're patient and don't mind putting up with such misbehavior, it will end in time. But if you find even a temporary rebel-without-a-cause an unpleasant housemate, a dog older than eighteen months, with its longer attention span and lesser proclivity toward rebellion, is a better choice for you.

If you are thinking about a mixed-breed dog and size or coat length is an issue, a puppy poses a problem. At nine weeks, a mixed-breed puppy can appear short-haired and tiny; at eighteen months, it may have grown into a long-coated giant.

The advantage of an adult dog is that you know what you're getting in terms of size and personality. Also, young adults have longer attention spans and are therefore easier to train right from the start. They may already possess the basic social graces, such as being housebroken. The drawback is that an adult dog may exhibit problem behaviors learned in its former home. It is always a good idea to test adult dogs thoroughly, by taking them on a leash into stressful situations like crowded streets with hurrying people and honking cars or parks where other dogs are playing. Usually, problems like fear biting or submissive urination will surface, and you can determine whether the behaviors can be eliminated by your own training or whether they are intolerable and intractable. Remember: It is always better to say no to a candidate pet before you take it home, rather than after.

Lifespan may also be an issue in

Males tend to be bigger than females.

adopting an adult dog. Usually the smaller the breed, the longer the life expectancy — from seven or eight years for a Great Dane or Saint Bernard, to over fifteen for a Chihuahua.

Guys and Dolls

A dog's gender may or may not be an issue for you. In my experience with training service dogs, I have found that males and females work equally well and are equally trainable. There are, however, a number of gender-based differences that may influence your choice.

Adult female dogs can retain urine longer than males. That will be important if you plan to be away from home for long periods and leave the dog indoors. When you do let dogs out to urinate, females finish faster. Males tend to sniff around a great deal and mark their territory with semantic bursts of urine. This ritual can take a while and it will require of you a certain patience with male ways. Males tend to be bigger than females, which makes them look more threatening — an important consideration if you want a dog for protection. Females are thought to be more tolerant of small children and are less prone to be protective of territory. Males, if not neutered, are more likely than females to get out and wander.

I do recommend neutering unless

you are seriously devoted to responsible breeding of show- or work-quality animals. Neutering lessens the number of unwanted puppies who are destroyed every year, and it pays health benefits to the dog, decreasing the likelihood of various infections and cancers. Males who are neutered are also less combative and easier to train. Neutering surgery for a male costs less than for a female, which may be a consideration if your pet budget is tight. Typically, males are neutered at ten to twelve months of age, and females at five to six months, but adult dogs can be altered.

The gender differences between neutered dogs are less striking than between unneutered dogs. Still, it has been my experience that even after neutering females remain generally more affectionate than males and are easier to housebreak.

Purebred or Mutt

Registered purebred dogs, particularly ones from recognized show or trial lines, can costs hundreds and hundreds of dollars. Of course, you can find purebreds from less illustrious pairings that cost less. Still, purebreds are expensive.

The advantage to any purebred puppy is that you know what you're getting, at least within certain limits. Even though a Pembroke Welsh corgi puppy at seven weeks looks pretty generic, you know how it will look as an adult. No matter what, a corgi pup won't grow up to be a Belgian Tervuren. But there can be a drawback to purebreds, owing typi-

cally to excessive inbreeding within popular breeds. Inbreeding can cause a wide variety of physical and psychological problems, from deafness to extreme emotional sensitivity to birthing difficulties.

With mixed-breed puppies, you may not always know what you're getting, unless you can meet the parent dogs. But one of the good things about mixed breeds is their usual good health. Mixed-breed dogs benefit from a wider inheritance than purebred dogs, which gives them what geneticists call hybrid vigor — that is, potentially superior health and hardiness arising from the crossing of different genetic lines. My research into assistance dog programs all over the world revealed that Guide Dogs in England had a great deal of success with Labrador–golden retriever mixes, for example. Both breeds are popular and have sometimes suffered from inbreeding. Crossing the two made for healthy, trainable animals who were hard, reliable workers and excellent companions.

Four Different People and Four Different Dogs

Let me give you four examples to show how selecting for physical characteristics helps build a healthy relationship between human and canine. In the next chapter, which focuses on personality, these stories will be amplified to show how personality characteristics also figured into the human-canine matches.

The first example centers on a

young man I will call Tim — tough, physical, and highly involved in sports and social activities. A single man, Tim was interested in a puppy for companionship and he asked me for help in choosing the right animal. He told me he wanted a dog who would enjoy roughhousing; in other words, he wanted a dog as physical as he was. He also wanted a dog who would accept physical praise — massage, patting, and rubbing — as well as verbal.

At my suggestion, Tim looked at Labrador retriever puppies. Labradors typically have energy levels in the mid to high range, much like Tim's. They are very physical dogs who were bred to retrieve downed game even in heavy brush and cold water, so they have a high tolerance for pain and discomfort and are fundamentally cooperative. Typically, too, Labradors are neither emotionally supersensitive nor highly responsive to sound, so they are well suited to physically tough and active people like Tim. Labradors have a deserved reputation for intelligence, but their wits are displayed less in a willingness to act on new information than in general awareness and an accepting, imperturbable nature — desirable qualities in pets who live with active people. Because they have short, dense, and weather-resistant coats, Labradors require little grooming. That likewise fit well with Tim's active lifestyle. I also suggested to Tim that he look more at male pups than females because the characteristics he wanted are stronger in males than females.

Finding the right physical match for a young woman I will call Louise was a more subtle choice. A somewhat timid person who lived alone, Louise had become very skittish in the wake of two burglaries. She wasn't after a true guard dog, like a Doberman or a Rottweiler, but she did want a dog who would provide at least some protection. A fastidious person who kept her house absolutely tidy and clean, Louise disliked dirt and mess. Then, too, she collected Irish crystal as a hobby, and she had no interest in a physically rambunctious dog who might bring all that costly glassware crashing down.

At first glance, a Labrador might have seemed a good choice for Louise. Since Labradors are big and muscular, they look protective, and their imperturability makes them unafraid of things that go bump in the night. However, because she was physically shy, Louise would have had a hard time with a Labrador, since the breed's physical and emotional insensitivity can necessitate strong, authoritative, and forceful handling skills.

Instead, I pointed Louise toward adult standard poodles, whose physical characteristics matched her wants closely. Choosing an adult dog would free Louise of the bother and housebreaking accidents of a puppy, and poodles do not shed, both factors important to a housekeeper as tidy as Louise. Poodles are big, agile, and rarely accident-prone. Though generally unaggressive, poodles are one-person dogs with a strong protective sense, which would provide Louise the security she was after. In Louise's case a female made good sense. Females are generally more trainable than males and less likely to mount challenges, which timid people like her find difficult to handle.

The third human is Brian, who wanted a dog in part for companionship but also for the thrill of dog training and trial work. A young, intelligent, demanding man with a high energy level and a love of challenge and competition, I suggested he look at border collies. Brian could train a border collie and compete with it in herding or obedience trials, and that prospect excited him. There also were important physical matchups between him and the border collie breed. Like Brian, border collies are intelligent and quick-witted, highly aware, with the capacity and savvy for acting immediately. These characteristics serve them well in herding sheep or goats, which they move in the desired direction by circling the herd, crouching down, and sometimes nipping at the heels. Those same characteristics also make border collies extremely alert, sensitive to their surroundings and handlers, and highly trainable. Males tend to be tougher and more forward than females, and since Brian admired these characteristics, I proposed that he select a male. Border collies do occasionally bite children in response to their sudden movement, but this posed no problem for Brian, who was childless.

Another friend, Jane, did have children, and they figured prominently into her choice of dog. A working single parent with two elementary-school-age daughters, Jane wanted a dog who could play with the kids and also be a friend to her. Hectic as her life was, the last thing on earth she needed was another hassle. She knew she had to have a dog who would go along with the family program and require only gentle handling.

My suggestion for her was the golden retriever. Goldens are big but unprotective, and they love to romp with kids. They are sweet, highly malleable, and rarely if ever threaten or bite. Goldens also get along. They usually follow their owner's bidding with minimal challenge, and since they are more physically and emotionally sensitive than Labradors, most goldens respond well to only gentle handling. A golden retriever was likely to provide the companionship for herself and her daughters that Jane wanted, and its inherent obedience and easy disposition would make it fit easily into her family.

The Shorthand of Breeds

The dog breeds we have been discussing — golden and Labrador retrievers, poodles, and border collies — are essentially lines of inheritance within which specific physical characteristics have been selected for over a period of time. Breeds are largely artificial creations resulting from human manipulation of canine genes. If dogs were left on their own to breed at will, they wouldn't look the way they do now. Feral dog populations around the world produce remarkably similar animals, which are typically mid-sized and short-coated, something like the Australian dingo or the pariah dog. Very likely, these feral dogs are by and large similar to the original domestic dogs of ten thousand years ago. Dogs are different now because we humans have bred them to gain the physical characteristics we want.

In talking about the characteristics of different breeds, we are discussing three categories of traits. The first is body characteristics, such as size, length and color of coat, the presence or absence of shedding, and so forth.

The second is overt behavior patterns that are hardwired into the dog. Sometimes these are referred to as instincts or inborn drives, and they include behaviors that form components of such activities as herding, guarding, protection, retrieving, and pursuit.

The third category refers to general temperament. This is not the same as personality, which involves the particular and unique traits that make a particular dog an individual different from its littermates. General temperament describes the dog's overall behavioral predisposition. As an example of general temperament, German shepherds are more responsibly serious and grave in their demeanor than golden retrievers, who can be goofy, lighthearted, and childlike.

Understand two facts about breeds. If you acquire a dog of a particular breed, don't be surprised when behavior similar to that of other dogs of the same breed appears — even if you have tried to train it differently. Many breed behavioral characteristics result from genetic predisposition and are hardwired into the dog. A border collie will herd, if not sheep then maybe the neighbor's chickens. And you can't make a scent hound into a sight hound, nor expect a protective dog like a Rottweiler to become the stranger-loving welcome mat many golden retrievers are. By the same token, however, since many pedigree dogs have been bred more for appearance than behavior, and also because of unplanned backyard breeding, some individual purebreds don't exhibit all the behaviors of their breed.

In addition, not everything about breeding is positive. Certain breeds have health problems — for example, hip dysplasia in large and giant dogs, age-related retinal degeneration in Labradors, and cleft palates in pugs. You need to learn about these in advance, before acquiring a pet. And some physical characteristics come with a price tag. Curly-coated breeds such as the Airedale terrier and the poodle shed practically not at all, but they do require professional grooming as a result. Be sure you're ready to include the necessary care and maintenance, whether from groomers or veterinarians, into your financial and emotional dog budget.

All in all, it's good to know something of the characteristics of the breed of dog you choose, simply so you have an idea of how your pet is likely to behave and what arrangements you may want to make for it. Terriers, for example, love to dig and can ruin a flower bed in nothing flat. Keeping them on cement patios ends the problem. Likewise, predatory hunting dogs like coonhounds and some dogs bred for field trial work will instinctively chase small creatures rushing past, be they squirrels or cats. Fencing protects wildlife, other people's pets, and the dogs themselves.

A Dog Breed Once-Over

By current estimates, this world is home to some four hundred breeds of canines. Here I simply want to give you a look at the basic groupings of dog breeds, classified principally by the role the dog was originally bred for. Consult a handbook on breeds for more information on the types of dogs that interest you.

Herding dogs do exactly what their name implies — they herd livestock, circling the animals to hold them in one place or nipping at the heels to hurry them along. Some of the herding breeds, like the Australian shepherd and the border collie, are small-to midsized. Others, like the collie and the Bouvier des Flandres, are big.

Hounds may represent the oldest of all dog breeds, dating to the fourth millennium B.C. Hounds find and pursue game, using either sight

or scent or a combination of the two. Afghans, borzois, and greyhounds are sight hounds. Beagles, bloodhounds, and black and tan coonhounds are scent hounds. Basenjis, dachshunds, and Rhodesian ridgebacks use both eyes and nose.

The *nonsporting dogs* are something of a catch-all category of breeds with no single role or whose role has changed over the centuries. Dalmatians, for example, were originally guard dogs, but now they are prized for their appearance. Poodles, too, started out as working dogs but are now bred largely as pets.

Sporting dogs were created to hunt, principally birds and small game. Pointers locate hidden birds, then lock into position to hold the game in place and summon the hunter. Setters also locate birds, but instead of pointing they sink to the ground — or set. Spaniels flush game from cover to expose it to the hunter's gun. Retrievers fetch downed birds, particularly waterfowl, using a soft mouth to prevent damage. Dual-purpose sporting dogs can play two or more hunting roles, such as both pointing and retrieving.

Terriers originally hunted small fierce game like badgers and weasels in the burrows and tunnels where they took refuge from pursuit. Terriers love to dig and, though often small, are typically tenacious, stubborn, and courageous. A few terrier breeds like the Airedale and the American Staffordshire terrier (aka pit bull) are midsized to large.

The *toy dogs* were bred originally

to be worn stylishly by royalty. They are all small enough to fit comfortably in the lap, and they behave like antic children. Toy dogs come in long-coated (for example, Pekingese, toy poodle, and shih tzu), short-coated (for example, smooth-coated Chihuahua and toy Manchester terrier), and wirehaired (for example, affenpinscher and Brussels griffon) breeds.

Working dogs are large, physically tough, and capable of sustained labor. Some are excellent guard dogs, like the Akita, bullmastiff, Doberman pinscher, and Rottweiler. Alaskan malamutes and other sled dogs are also classed as working breeds. So are rescue breeds like the Newfoundland and the Saint Bernard.

Choosing a Breed

Once you've become clear about the role you want your dog to fill in your home and family, you can begin to investigate the breeds most likely to work best for you. There are a great many sources of information, both published and personal. Your local library contains background books on breeds plus current copies of dog magazines. You can find reams of printed material at pet stores, too. Veterinarians, breeders, and dog fanciers are also valuable sources of information. And it pays to attend a dog show or obedience trial or two. Dog shows will expose you to a great many breeds, so you can get a good idea of the appearance and physical characteristics of particular breeds. But, since show

dogs are bred for appearance alone, shows will tell you little about how a breed behaves. That's why obedience trials are important. As you watch a handler put a dog through its paces, you can get an idea of how easy — or how hard — a particular breed is to work with, its general temperament, and its instinctive behaviors.

Shows and trials are also good opportunities to meet dog owners and handlers. You'll find they are proud of their animals and willing to talk about them in detail. Ask them about their dogs, and be specific. Their answers may be surprisingly frank, and they can give you a great deal of information that will contribute to your own informed choice of a pet. Here are some suggested questions. Don't be afraid to pry and do ask for details.

- Why did you choose your breed?
- How does the dog behave around children? Around infants?
- Is the dog aggressive and dominating or submissive around other dogs? Does it get into fights readily?
- Does the dog require extensive grooming? Can you do the grooming yourself, or is a professional required? If professional attention is needed, how often and at what cost?
- Is the breed prone to health problems — for example, breathing problems in short-nosed breeds like pugs, hip dys-

plasia in large and giant breeds? Remember there is no federal "truth in dog buying" act to protect you against congenital and genetic health problems. You need to make yourself aware of them on your own.

- Does the breed require special veterinary procedures, like tail docking and ear cropping, to achieve its desired look? How much does this cost? (Ask yourself, too, whether you are willing to subject the animal to cosmetic surgery.)
- Is the dog easy to housebreak?
- How much exercise does it require?
- What kind of amusement does the dog prefer — for example, Frisbee, swimming, running, roughhousing?
- How does the breed adapt to apartment living? To the suburbs? To a rural lifestyle?
- Is there a line within the breed that is better suited to a particular task, such as protection, hunting, obedience competition, herding, and so forth?
- What is the breed's expected lifespan?

Where to Find the Dog of Your Dreams

Don't go to a pet shop. While there are reputable operations that sell well-bred and healthy dogs, too many are purveyors of mentally and physically damaged dogs churned out by mass-production facilities appropriately called puppy mills.

There are much better options.

If you are interested in acquiring a purebred dog, remember that you will be investing a considerable sum to acquire a registered animal. Your best bet is to locate a reputable professional breeder who specializes in the breed you want. Veterinarians and pet groomers can recommend breeders. The American Kennel Club will provide you with the names of breed clubs close to your home, and the clubs can refer you to breeders that members know and trust.

Buying a purebred from a breeding hobbyist — for example, a neighbor who is nuts about beagles and produces litter after adorable litter from her pet female — can be risky. Too often, hobbyists don't know how to avoid pairings that perpetuate inherited health problems like hip dysplasia. However, puppies from a hobbyist are likely to cost much less than those from a professional breeder. If you can find a healthy pup with the traits you want, this route may work for you.

Newspaper classified ads can be a way of locating adult purebreds — usually pets being given up because the owner is moving away — as well as mixed-breed dogs and puppies. Another good source of adult purebreds is rescue leagues, which are networks of dog enthusiasts dedicated to furthering the welfare of a particular breed. For example, a saluki owner who must give up her dog contacts the saluki rescue league and asks for help in finding her dog a new home. The league puts her in contact with people looking for adult salukis. You can locate rescue leagues through veterinarians, dog groomers, and breed clubs.

If you are interested in an adult dog, the local animal shelter is also a good source. It will also have puppies, usually mixed-breed but also purebred from time to time. Adult dogs from a shelter may have had at least some training and are already used to people. Also, any dog you take home from a shelter has been saved from probable euthanasia. Such dogs are by no means problem-free, however. Kenneling can disrupt housebreaking, so a shelter dog may have accidents when it first arrives in your home. Don't feel cheated; a refresher course, just like what you'd give a puppy (see chapter 9), will usually solve the problem quickly. Also, some dogs end up in the shelter because of behavior problems, so additional retraining may be needed. Other dogs find their way to the shelter because they have been abused. Past abuse complicates the task of establishing a relationship, and it may make training more difficult. Such a dog will need extra patience.

Assistance dog training programs are another source of pets. Policies vary, but such programs periodically put both young and older adult dogs up for adoption. The older animals are retirees, dogs who are no longer able to perform assistance dog duties well but who typically have several more years of life expectancy and are already well trained and highly skilled around people. The younger dogs were released from training before placement. Though they have some physical or psychological characteristic that makes them unsuitable as assistance dogs, they remain excellent candidates as pets.

And what about strays? If a dog shows up on your back step and you like it, first do the right thing: Make every effort to find the owner. Check the lost-animal ads in the paper, and place one of your own. Look for some characteristic, like a chipped tooth or a scar, only the true owner of the dog will know so you can be sure that the person who claims the animal is its legitimate owner. If no owner surfaces and you want to keep the dog, conduct a test of its temperament by taking it on a leash into stressful situations and seeing how it behaves. You should also have the dog examined by a veterinarian before you decide for sure to adopt it.

A thorough veterinary examination within forty-eight hours is a good policy for any dog who's new to you, no matter where it came from. If serious health problems surface, be honest with yourself about whether you want to deal with them. It is far easier — on both you and the dog — to say no before a relationship has developed than to be forced to walk away after it has formed.

Chapter Five

Personality

*I*T IS upon the shoals of personality, not physical characteristics, that all too many human-canine relationships run aground. In my experience with people and dogs, I've rarely ever heard anyone say that he or she got rid of a pet because it was too big, too white, or too hairy. Instead, people almost always name personality or behavior as the reason why they gave up a dog. They mention the pet's pushiness, refusal to obey, tendency to wander off, or other similar nuisances. The dog has somehow become obtrusive and obnoxious, and the owner, unable or unwilling to shape its behavior, instead takes it to the animal shelter, finds it a new home in the country, or, far worse, abandons it by the side of the road to fend for itself — and likely die miserably.

The core issue in such incidents isn't that the dog is bad; nor, for that matter, is the human evil. Instead, dog and human are incompatible. The same human matched with a different dog, and the same dog matched with a different human, could be content.

Obviously, the best way to avoid running into incompatibility with your pet is to carefully select the traits you need and want in advance. Of course, that isn't always possible, nor, even in the best of circumstances, will your selection be perfect. But don't fret. Dogs are unique in their capacity to align themselves with the moods, activity levels, and needs of their pack. If you understand the remarkable ability dogs have to synchronize with their masters, and if you understand ,too, the way that human and canine personalities can mesh and interact, you can shape your dog into a pet you can get along with well.

So let me tell you a story, one from my own life. It gets right to the heart of this matter.

Gravity and Me

I happened upon this ideal synchrony of human and canine quite by accident, during the time when I was training service dogs full-time. My work with service dogs had already made me aware that dog and human must be well matched. The dog had to serve the person's needs, yet not be overly demanding of time and energy. But I saw this match as a matter of overt behavior, not personality. The connection between the two had yet to dawn on me. That dawning began in an unlikely way, when Fidelco Guide Dogs in Connecticut offered to donate a pup for an experimental breeding program. I was to be sent an animal that looked to be the best choice on the basis of its genetic background. By chance, another pup, one who appeared on paper to be less interesting, became available about two weeks early, and she was offered to the program as well. I decided to accept this pup and place her in a breeder home, even though she looked to be less than the best.

I drove down to the San Francisco airport to pick up the new breeding prospect on a flight inbound from Connecticut early one morning. I loaded the crate with the puppy inside into my station wagon and drove off, intending to find a safe place down the road to let the pup out to urinate. But my own eagerness and a stop sign changed my plans, and I opened the crate. Out stepped an eight-week-old German shepherd, and my life changed.

I am well aware just how deeply we humans are drawn to puppies and how easily one can mistake that rush of feeling for real connection. By this time in my career I had handled hundreds upon hundreds of pups and trained myself to stand back objectively from the deep pull we feel toward these precious little beings. But the moment I saw this pup, something different happened.

We connected, she and I, at heart and soul and being's deepest core. From that first encounter, she was my dog. She stayed by my side night and day as a trusted and true companion for the next thirteen years, and through all that time it was as if the two of us were one creature.

In my life I have had many dogs, and I loved them dearly, but still I had to work with each pet to develop a positive relationship and to manage the animal well. Not so with Gravity, the name I gave her because she kept me rooted to earth. Truth be told, the only training I had to do with her was informal. She and I were so in tune that she learned by osmosis. Once she figured out what I wanted, she did it. It was that easy.

Gravity wasn't a superdog everyone loved. She was no legendary Rin-Tin-Tin or Lassie come off the silver screen to live in my house and wow the neighbors with her many wonder-deeds. My husband, Jim, liked her well enough, but without any particular enthusiasm, and my employees and friends found her an acceptable pet, but not otherwise remarkable. The perfect connection existed only between her and me. She slept alongside my bed at night, came to work with me each day, napped when I was busy, followed me while I completed some task or other, watched my every mood and action like an observant hawk, came over to be petted whenever I needed contact with her solid body and good soul, stood guard when I worked late at night. She and I were

in touch and in tune all the time. And when she died, I let her go without guilt, regret, or anger, without trying to hold on, because the thing between us had been so very good and the time had come to let go. I look now at the site of her grave, down the lane from my house on the ranch, and I know she lives still in my spirit and in the understanding of canine companionship I want to pass on to you.

Understanding Personality

Gravity and I fit together well because we were matched at the most basic levels of personality. You may find it peculiar to attach the word *personality* to a dog. The truth is, though, that humans and dogs are alike emotionally and that we share similar personality types. Personality is the reason why you will find yourself more compatible with one dog than another and why in training no two dogs and no two trainers are exactly alike.

Personality is not the same thing as the general characteristics of temperament and behavior present in a dog because of its breed background. As a rule, golden retrievers are tractable and malleable, German shepherds are businesslike, and Dandie Dinmont terriers are stubborn. Such traits are behaviors that, under specific circumstances, will appear, like it or not. If something small and furry runs past the nose of a pointer, it will pursue. The pursuit says nothing about the personality of the pointer; it tells you, instead, about the dog's ancestry as a hunter. Personality refers rather to those other traits and behaviors that go to make up the unique individuality of the given dog, the ones that differentiate a particular canine from its littermates. Personality forms from prenatal and early puphood experiences, and it refers both to learned behavior and to modifications and variations of hardwired instincts.

Gravity, for example, was much like most German shepherds, in that she was a serious, devoted pet with a strong protective instinct. But what set her apart, and what attracted me to her, was the particular way she was put together emotionally. That, not her breed's seriousness, devotion, or protectiveness, was what drew us together and bonded us deeply.

What traits in dog and human make for the best match? The answer begins with the understanding that dog-human matches work differently from successful human pairings, particularly marriages and longtime companionships.

Marriage counselors, therapists, psychologists, and psychiatrists have noted again and again that people tend to choose their opposites as life partners. An assertive woman, for example, is likely to be attracted to a soft sweet man, and vice versa. If the marriage ends, both spouses are likely to select as new partners individuals similar to their original mates. This drive toward connecting with one's opposite, per-

haps to strike a complex psychological balance, is apparently deep-seated in human nature.

Balance and compensation drive life partnerships between humans. Between humans and dogs, however, the key is similarity. The most successful connection between pet and owner occurs with two beings who are so highly matched they become almost one. The key is synchrony, not balance. If you are trying to reach the stars, you don't want your dog pulling you back to earth. And if you are content to remain on earth, you don't want your dog surging ahead into the outer cosmos.

Let me give you an example using Janet, the woman whose misadventure with her dog, Juba, we discussed in chapter 1. Janet is a low-key, gentle, and introspective person, and she rightly chose Juba, a female golden retriever who is emotionally sensitive, physically gentle, and responsive to soft-voiced commands. Had Janet selected a strong-minded, outgoing, highly physical male golden retriever, she would have found something as simple as taking her dog for a walk to be unmitigated frustration. He would have pulled at the leash, jumped up on her constantly, barked at every stimulus from a skunk scent to a child on a bicycle, and ignored her softly spoken commands. Neither human nor dog would have been happy.

Janet's husband, Alex, was affectionate and loving toward Juba during quiet moments at home in the

Between humans and dogs the key is similarity.

evening, but the dog's soft ways frustrated him. Alex is indeed Janet's opposite: exuberant, assertive, extroverted. He wanted to roughhouse with Juba, but she was too gentle and sensitive to enjoy hard physical play. Thus Alex was mismatched with Juba, but this proved to be little problem in the household because Juba was Janet's dog, not Alex's.

Typically, the relationship between human and dog works out best when it is like Juba's and Janet's — the two are highly similar, but the human is slightly more assertive than the dog and also slightly more desirous of social interaction. Whenever Janet wanted to pet Juba, Juba was available. But Juba was not so pushy that she was always asking for attention, even when Janet didn't want to give it. Had that happened, Janet would have felt put upon by Juba, and the relationship would not have worked anywhere near so well as it did.

The ideal pet is one with whom you are in natural sync, with the balance of assertiveness and desire for interaction ever so slightly weighted to the side of the human. The dog instigates nothing the human doesn't want, and it is ready and willing to go along with everything the human starts. Emotional connection is assured, and the leader-follower dynamic is maintained with little effort. That's how it was with Gravity and me. It was as if we were two halves of the same whole, yet I was the one leading the way through the world and she was right there with me.

Measuring the Match

People have been categorizing other people by personality type for at least the past 4,500 years. Many of us resent typing. Being told that you fit into one of four, five, or nine elemental personality types runs against the grain of a culture that trumpets individuality as its greatest good. Still, it has been shown repeatedly that personality traits do cluster and that groups with these clustered traits have certain overt and observable characteristics. This is as true for dogs as it is for humans. The issue surrounding personality typing, then, isn't which system is correct; in fact, all such schemes share important common ground. It is how well the system works for your purposes.

Some years ago, I came across an easy-to-use system for assessing and typing individuals that is very useful in working with dogs and humans. This system, developed originally by Wilson Learning Corporation, focuses on social style — how behavior is perceived in group or interactive settings. The system was created to help high-level salespeople determine the social styles of individual sales prospects and select the most effective marketing approach. I have adapted the Wilson system to fit human-dog relationships because it measures the two most important aspects of our interactions with canines and because it uses observable physical activity to type personality. With this system you can literally look at a dog and figure out its personality type.

The chart below will help you understand this system better. It is a grid, or two-dimensional graph, that places a given individual at a point determined by his or her rating on each of the two dimensions — the one left to right, the other up to down.

The Four Basic Social Styles

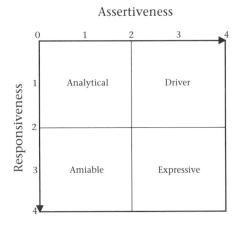

The left-right dimension measures assertiveness, an aspect of the dominance hierarchy critical to managing canines. Every book you'll ever pick up on dog training will make the same point: To manage your dog, you must be the pack leader, the alpha wolf. The first dimension assesses this quality. Assertiveness measures how likely you are to direct or lead an activity rather than defer to the leadership of others. The more assertive a human or dog is, the more likely he or she is to take control, compete, take risks, and appear assertive, tough-minded, and dynamic.

The second dimension, responsiveness, measures an individual's interest in social interaction and his or her desire for emotional and affective connection. Every human, and every dog, needs a social life, but different individuals require different amounts of interaction. Some humans get along with a minimum of socializing, spending their days in front of a computer screen or maintaining contemplative silence in a monastery, while others — say, the glad-handing politician at a Fourth of July picnic — thrive on personal contact and can't imagine a day without a huge helping of it. Dogs span a similar range, from hermits to social mavens. The higher one ranks on the responsiveness scale, the more likely that human or dog is to be sociable during a significant portion of the day, to interact readily and willingly with others, and to appear warm and approachable.

You can see how well this system applies to Janet and Juba. Janet, though quiet and restrained, is still a bit more assertive than Juba, who prefers to defer to Janet. As a result, there is little conflict around the basic dog-human issue of who is running the show. The same dynamic applies in the area of responsiveness. Janet desires social contact a little more than Juba, and so is more likely to initiate it. Janet does not have to put up with Juba's continuing insistence on interaction, that dog-in-your-face-all-the-time feeling that can become a true annoyance.

This scale comes with an important proviso: It does not account for psychosis. Both dogs and humans can be neurotic or psychotic — that is, behaving inconsistently in consistent situations, or acting in aberrant or dangerous ways that cannot be controlled or explained. The scale works only for normal individuals, both canine and human.

Even without going through formal testing, it is possible to get an idea of where you and your dog fit on the grid. These categories identify general tendencies within an individual, not hard absolutes.

The first personality group, which measures low on both assertiveness and responsiveness scales, is referred to as analytical. Humans in the analytical category often display stoic, poker faces. They are highly reserved. Analyticals speak deliberately, with obvious pauses, employing a large vocabulary and good diction. Their physical movements and gestures are controlled and restrained. In a chair, analyticals sit back but remain somewhat tense.

Their humor is wry and dry. Analyticals rarely initiate social contact, and they like work for its own sake, displaying a strong orientation to detail.

A person ranking high on assertiveness and low on responsiveness is called a driver. Drivers have intense, pressured faces, and they speak quickly, often in a monotone but with great changes in volume from soft to loud. In a chair they sit forward, on the edge of their seats, as if about to make a sudden move. They use action-oriented words and are animated, but in a directed way. Typically, drivers are socially uncomfortable and formal, often humorless. They like work for the results it delivers.

A person who ranks high in responsiveness and low in assertiveness is referred to as an amiable. Amiables have warm friendly faces, and their attitude is patient and forgiving. They seem to speak deliberately and melodiously, with pauses, in a vocabulary that evidences concern for the feelings of others. Amiables dislike controversy and conflict. Body gestures and movements are flowing; like analyticals, amiables sit back in a chair, but they look relaxed and at ease. Amiables are humorous in a safe sort of way, and more intimate in one-on-one interactions than in large groups. They do not initiate social contact, but instead invite it. They like work because it helps meet their need for personal interaction.

A high ranking on both assertiveness and responsiveness scales denotes an expressive. Expressives have highly animated faces, and they talk so fast, in widely fluctuating voices, that they seem to interrupt themselves. Their vocabulary is directed to "me, myself, and I." Expressives are socially adept, working well with groups, whether at parties or meetings. Expressives are impatient — they do poorly in grocery checkout lines or going through customs — and are humorous, often with an edge of sarcasm in their jokes and wisecracks. They gesture widely and initiate social contact. Like drivers, expressives sit forward in a chair, but they are emotionally animated. Expressives like work because it gives them the opportunity to call attention to themselves.

The same basic classifications apply to dogs, except of course that dogs exhibit their personality styles differently from humans. Dogs don't talk, nor do they gesture with hands and arms. Pay attention instead to their facial expressions (which are every bit as detailed and diagnostic as those of the human face), the way they hold and move their bodies, their attitude toward you and others, and their tail-wagging.

Analytical dogs — that is, those low on both responsiveness and assertiveness scales — wear a questioning look on stoic faces, often with softly serious eyes and creased asking brows. They are somewhat physically rigid and avoid contact more than other dogs; instead of fawning all over you, an analytical dog will sit quietly at your side. Challenges — a topic we will discuss at length in chapter 8 — take a passive form, usually freezing in place. When corrected, analytical dogs often avert their eyes. Unless reacting to a stimulus like visitors, food, or a challenge from another dog, analytical canines move slowly. They wag their tails from side to side, particularly the six inches closest to the rump, inside the body frame — that is, if you drew invisible lines paralleling the external dimensions of the dog' body, the tail would wag deliberately within those limits.

Driver dogs have serious faces that seem to say, "Let's do it." Like analyticals, they wag their tails within the body frame and their body movements are deliberate, but quicker. Such dogs are unintrusive; they initiate little physical contact as compared with other dogs in general and their own breed in particular. Drivers are assertive dogs, with some breeds completely master-oriented. Given a task, they set out to perform it promptly. When stressed, they are likely to growl or challenge actively.

Dogs who fall within the amiable category have soft sweet eyes with a limpid, liquid look. Their faces are welcoming, inviting contact. Like analyticals, their brows may crease as if they are asking tough questions, but their body movements are animated, flowing, and graceful. Their tails wag outside the body frame, but gently, without great force, unless

Analytical — serious, questioning expression.

Driver — serious, assertive expression.

some significant stimulus such as food is present. Amiables challenge passively, by going belly up, and they initiate a great deal of physical contact, usually by fawning and asking for reassurance ("Is everything okay?"). Amiable dogs make perfect followers; they do what their masters want unless they are pushed too hard, in which case, they freeze in place.

Amiable — soft, gentle, relaxed expression.

Expressive — intense, assertive expression with emotional animation.

Expressive dogs have highly animated eyes and faces, and their attitude is forceful and in-your-face. They push for physical contact with you, climbing into your lap perhaps or jumping up onto you without invitation. Their tail wags are huge helicoptering movements that fit with their generally dramatic, histrionic emotional style. Expressives are physically explosive, and are the dogs most likely to bite under only mild stress. They are not mastered easily, often rebelling. Expressives follow best when excited by the task they have to do. They like the spotlight and are prone to practical jokes.

Be aware that there is no right or wrong in all this personality typing. Being higher on a scale isn't the same thing as being better. Nor for that matter are analyticals superior to drivers, or amiables to expressives. Quite apart from right or wrong, this is just the way people and dogs are.

Finding the Balance Point

The grid shows how and why conflicts arise between dogs and humans. To begin with, dogs respond to and require a dominance hierarchy, which is represented by the assertiveness scale. As I have said repeatedly in this book, dogs look for leadership, and if they do not find it, they assume the leader's role themselves. This reality can lead to powerful turmoil if you are an analytical person with a driver dog, for example. The two of you match on the responsiveness scale, desiring contact with about the same intensity and frequency, but the mismatch on assertiveness can cause conflict. As an analytical, you tend to defer to leadership, and your driver dog is likely to try to take over in the vacuum created by your deference. Therefore, you must either practice taking a stance more directive than what feels easy and natural to you, or you will face continual challenges from your pet.

Similar discomfort will arise if you, still an analytical, are sharing your house with an expressive dog. By nature, you desire relatively little social contact, but, equally by nature, your dog wants it all the time, which puts it endlessly in your face or on your lap asking for affection. As an analytical, you're not going to like that constant intrusion one bit.

Clearly, the best human-dog relationship occurs when the human is a bit more assertive and also a bit more responsive than the dog. This was precisely the situation with Gravity and me. I remember to this day what she looked like when she emerged from the crate near the airport. She had just endured a seven-hour flight, not the most enlivening experience for an eight-week-old puppy, but she stepped out confidently, wearing a look of curiosity and interest in this new world. She didn't rush over to be petted. Instead, she checked out the situation, then came to me, not with one of those overall puppy wiggles that asks for whole-body cuddling, but with an interest in simply being close. Today, after working with canine personality issues for years, I recognize that Gravity was moderately high on the assertiveness scale — that is, self-directed but not totally dominating — and moderately low on the responsiveness scale — that is, somewhat interested in social contact, but with greater importance set on quality than

quantity. This is, in fact, much the way I am, generally assertive and selectively responsive, and just a little higher on each dimension than Gravity. Thus our match was ideal. Because she and I were so similar, we mirrored each other behaviorally and emotionally, but I was always the leader and she the follower — quite without effort.

How did I know Gravity was the dog for me? My reaction was intuitive. I saw her and I knew; it was that simple. You can do the same, trusting your gut response to a dog, even an eight-week-old puppy.

Which brings up an important point — too many people select a dog for the wrong reasons. One wrong reason is to choose solely on the basis of size, color, breed, or some similar physical characteristic. Long ago I lost count of the number of times I have heard someone say he or she is looking for a Labrador or a golden retriever or maybe an English bulldog or a shi tzu or whatever. Breeds do have certain important behavioral characteristics, as elaborated in chapter 4, but within a given breed all four basic personality types can be found. The point isn't only to get a dog of the desired breed, but to choose the individual dog who most closely matches your personality.

A variant of this particular fallacy is selecting a dog who mirrors a particular personal characteristic of the owner, but not the whole personality. Macho dogs fall into this category. A great many Dobermans,

German shepherds, Rottweilers, pit bulls, and similar breeds are purchased because, like a fast car, they tell the world something about their owners' self-perceptions. These dogs are possessions, toys even, but not individual beings in a relationship. Likewise, women particularly — and I myself have done this — choose the weakest and most dependent puppy in a litter because we females have been culturally conditioned to mother and rescue. Sadly, neither macho nor motherly relationships usually work, for either human or canine.

Four People and Pets

The first step in choosing a dog — or in understanding where your relationship with your pet stands — is knowing yourself. You need to take a solid, objective look at your personality and place yourself at some point within the four basic social styles. Examine your whole life, not just some portion of it, and from that overall look determine where and how you and your dog fit together.

To see how this works in practice, let's pick up the four personal stories I began in chapter 4, starting with Tim. He was, you will remember, a physical, voluble, sociable man who spent much of his time visiting with friends and competing in team sports — obviously an expressive. He needed a dog who could handle his exuberant personality and social life.

I had pointed him toward Labra-dor retrievers because of that breed's sociability, physical toughness, and imperturbability. Some Labs are more gregarious than others, and gregariousness was the quality we looked for when we visited a litter of eight-week-old pups I knew about. We had already looked into the backgrounds of the parents and grandparents of the litter, so there was good reason to believe that one of these pups would have the right blend of physical toughness and expressive personality to suit Tim.

I had no intention of telling Tim which dog to choose. I was there only to give him an objective perspective on the personality characteristics we observed together. Still, the little pup named Zack caught our attention right away. He was one of the first pups to leave the litter and walk up to us, a move that indicated a basic boldness and self-confidence in his nature. And Tim clearly liked him. Humans have an awareness — perhaps conscious, perhaps unconscious, perhaps both — of body language and facial expressions in other humans. Since dogs are much like us in the way they signal their natures through their faces and bodies, we can often sense the personality style of a given individual dog practically at first sight. Tim recognized, in some fundamental way, that Zack was a kindred spirit.

The objective of our first visit wasn't to choose a pup, but to look at the young animals, take notes on individuals, and get Tim through that first rush of puppy attraction. We went back a second time, purposely selecting a different hour of the day, so that we could be sure of observing the pups under new conditions. Zack again came up to us right away, with that same boldness and self-confidence. His tail wagged ceaselessly, up and down, back and forth, with quickness and without tension. We clapped our hands close to him, which bothered him not at all, so obviously he wasn't sensitive to loud noises. He didn't cuddle up to nap in my arms or Tim's, either. Instead he squirmed and wiggled, displaying his high level of energy. When he raced Tim across the room, there was in Zack's eyes an undeniable look of fun and play. This pup enjoyed others, too, both canine and human. He danced around Tim's feet, pressed against his leg, and jumped up on his calf, insisting on physical attention. And Zack played rough-and-tumble with his brothers and sisters, not going off on his own to explore individually, but focusing instead on social interaction. He was a gregarious dog, not a loner.

Another pup also caught Tim's attention, barking and nipping aggressively at his pants leg. Tim was drawn to this display, which showed a high energy much like his own, but he noticed almost immediately that this second animal lacked the playful and humorous eyes Zack had. This dog was more serious and more of an individual. It went off on its own to poke about the room, pre-

ferring solo venturing to socializing. The second pup matched Tim in assertiveness, but its need for responsiveness was much lower, putting it in the driver category.

Tim needed an expressive, which Zack clearly was, and he indeed chose him as his new companion. By no means was this a seat-of-the-pants selection. Tim had thought long and hard beforehand about his own needs and emotional makeup. Still, there was a distinctly intuitive way Zack and Tim recognized each other as kindred spirits. Exuberant and emotional beings that they both were, they paid attention to their gut feelings and quickly formed a relationship based on their essential similarity.

LOUISE was more difficult to work with because she was an analytical, a person given to mulling everything over intellectually before making choices and generally less in tune with her own emotions. In the course of finding her the right dog, though, we witnessed a perfect object lesson in personality mismatch.

An adult standard poodle was the breed of choice for Louise, and we looked at four of them in turn. Each dog appealed to Louise somewhat, but none was quite right. Snow was the fifth standard poodle we looked at. She was being given up, and immediately I could see why. Her owner was a powerfully emotional, outgoing woman, obviously an expressive, and there was Snow, an analytical dog, trying to fit into an environment that was simply too noisy and rambunctious for her careful nature. To protect herself, she had become even more introverted, which further frustrated her owner. Thus the wise decision had been made to find Snow a new home.

Louise and Snow recognized each other as similar practically at first glance — which was actually not a glance at all. Snow did not immediately make eye contact, but that didn't bother Louise, for she too averted her eyes on meeting new people. Likewise, Snow's initial standoffishness and uncertainty attracted Louise. She recognized that Snow was unlikely to challenge her, something she knew quiet people like her have difficulty handling. She also realized that Snow, who moved as carefully and delicately as the proverbial eggshell walker, posed no threat to her prized collection of Irish crystal.

When Louise and I went back to see Snow the second time, no doubt remained that these two were soulmates. Snow came up to Louise, met her eyes with a questioning look, and quietly stood beside her as Louise discussed Snow's daily habits with her owner. When she sat down to read the vaccination record, Snow lay her head in Louise's lap, quietly and unobtrusively. With that, the transfer was made. Snow's now-former owner said aloud that she could see how these two were connected, something she herself had never experienced.

Early on in the selection process, Louise wanted me to define precisely the rules and methodology of the selection process, a characteristic request for the analytical personality type, which prizes thoughtfulness and intellectual precision. In truth, until a great deal more research is done, we don't have a procedure. Instead, we must rely on intuitive response plus an awareness of the physical indicators of personality. Louise saw those in Snow, who clearly displayed her analytical personality. It showed in her delicate and serious movement, the controlled wag of her tail (or what little there remained of it after cropping), the quiet way she asked for affection and petting by simply standing at Louise's side. The questioning look on Snow's face indicated that, unless her hardwired instincts kicked in, she was going to ask Louise's permission for practically everything. And Louise, who knew that a poodle would at least act protective against threat, felt a subtle confidence in Snow's presence and easily assumed leadership of her pet.

Then again, Snow was an easy dog to lead — for the right person. Her quiet, sensitive, permission-asking way of life would have driven expressive, spontaneous Tim crazy. He would have considered her the dog from hell. But for Louise, Snow was a pet from paradise.

BRIAN, the young, competitive, up-and-coming businessman, had a classic driver personality. He was demanding, impatient, humorless, oriented less to process than result. He wanted to train a dog for competition in part because he wanted the social outlet of trial work, but also because he wanted to win — fiercely. However, he was looking for a companion and pet as well as a performing trial dog, and a good personality match was essential.

Brian and I had decided to look for an adult border collie who had already demonstrated some success in herding trials. An adult made good sense for Brian, who recognized that he lacked the patience to raise and train a puppy. He wanted to compete now, not two or three years into the future. He would have liked to begin with a top-performing dog, but such border collies rarely come up for sale — their owners like winning too much to part with them. But a younger dog with the right qualities and a clear proclivity for trials made sense. Brian could have the pleasure of training the dog further, and the teaching and learning process would benefit both dog and owner. So Brian and I began looking.

Wonderfully, the moment Brian saw Angus he knew he was the right dog. Angus knew it too. Both had the same eyes: serious, intense, curious. This wasn't Zack, with his intense sociability, nor Snow, with her quizzical way, but a task-oriented dog, one who wanted to be given a job and go do it. I could see this in Angus's body. He stood square and firm, his tail wagging deliberately and tightly, rarely venturing beyond the plane of his hipbones. When Angus and Brian trained together, Angus was all work, completely nononsense. He was there to do his job. And he challenged Brian only when he felt he knew more than Brian did. As soon as Brian reasserted control Angus fell back in line, accomplishing his assigned task. Work was key to their relationship. The more Brian trained Angus, the closer the two became. Angus accompanied his owner everywhere, vigilant but not intrusive, closely bonded to this human who had proved his worth as leader.

Virginia, Brian's wife, had been concerned that bringing a driver dog into their home could create an overwhelming situation for her. She was an amiable, the personality type that often mates with a driver, and her concern about being bowled over by all this directed energy in one household was real, particularly with a one-leader breed like the border collie. However, border collies are also emotionally sensitive, and with some training Virginia learned how to give basic commands to Angus and require his compliance. Angus respected Virginia and actually enjoyed her warmth and friendliness. While the two of them lacked the soul relationship that existed between Brian and Angus, their relationship was comfortable.

LIKE Virginia, Jane — the single working mother with two school-age daughters — was an amiable. Jane disliked conflict and she needed no additional hassles in a life that was endlessly hectic and pressured. She and I were looking for a golden retriever, most likely a female, to be a playmate for her girls and a friend to her. Although goldens can be good hunters, Jane was uninterested in hunting with her pet or competing in field trials, so there was no reason to look at puppies from field trial breeding lines. Rather, we looked for litters that came from show lines or were raised by breeders known for producing quiet, down-to-earth dogs. Just as I had done with Tim, she and I first investigated pedigrees, parents, and grandparents, seeking out breeding matches that looked right.

We found what seemed to be an appropriate litter close to home, and began visiting it when the puppies were between seven and eight weeks of age. First Jane was drawn to the runt of the litter, which plucked her motherly heartstrings. I advised her against this puppy, because experience has shown me that dogs who differ significantly from their littermates can be problems later. When we went back for subsequent visits, the shine came off the runt as Jane slowly came to see the pups as individuals and could pick out the personality qualities that made each different and unique. Now another pup began to appeal to her. This warm friendly little dog was neither the most exuberant nor the most intense of the litter. She came up to Jane and pressed her body against her leg in a manner that was undemanding but affectionate. When

picked up, she didn't squirm the way Zack did. Instead, she relaxed into Jane's arms and allowed herself to be cuddled. Her eyes met Jane's directly, but they lacked challenge, and they often had a soft look that requested, but did not demand, attention. Her tail wagging was exuberant, extending well beyond the body frame, but it lacked wild energy, being gentle and relaxed. She evidenced no fear of ordinary noises, and while she romped and played with her littermates as well as Jane and displayed a good sense of herself all the while, she was generally less aggressive than the others, though by no means the most shy or sensitive of her brothers and sisters.

As Jane and I visited the litter several times, again at different hours so as to catch the puppies under various conditions, it dawned on Jane that this female puppy was an amiable just like her. She chose her, and to honor the slow process of her own realization Jane named the dog Dawn. Dawn proved to be the pet she wanted: a good children's playmate and a steady friend who gets along easily in the family with little mess or fuss. And in the evening, when the girls are in bed and Jane can finally unwind, the two of them sit quietly together, Jane stroking Dawn's long golden coat, Dawn's soft muzzle and liquid eyes in Jane's lap, human and canine bonded beyond words.

On the Grid

If you are trying to put yourself on the personality grid, you may be saying that at various times you fit into each of the four types. That's right; you do. Each of us spends some time as an analytical, some as a driver, some as an amiable, and some as an expressive. That goes for dogs too. The scale, instead, types the human or dog on the basis of the personality type he or she expresses the greatest percentage of the time.

It is also important to understand how the terms *assertiveness* and *responsiveness* are used in this context. All of us are assertive in some manner or other, either actively or passively. I've watched numerous analyticals who, though they rank low on the assertiveness scale of the Wilson grid, still influence a meeting through the quiet power of their personal presence. When you score yourself, consider assertiveness only as the active, forceful effort to make something happen, rather than the quieter assertiveness that contains or influences events through presence instead of action. Think in terms of the amount of time in the day you spend asserting yourself and your ideas. You can also try to see yourself as others do: Are others likely to perceive you as someone who actively makes things happen?

You can do the same thing with the responsiveness dimension. Think about the frequency with which you initiate or invite social contact, and the relative proportion of time you spend quietly alone

rather than socially involved. Again, give thought to how others see you. Are you the party animal, the forest hermit, or something in between?

To show you how the grid formed by the two dimensions works, let's plot the positions of the four people and dogs we have been discussing. First there's Tim. He was very outgoing, talked incessantly with exaggerated gestures, laughed a great deal, and became the engaging center of attention in almost every social setting. He was also a team sports nut. He loved competition and the thrill as much as he adored applause and adulation from the sidelines.

Zack was almost Tim's canine carbon copy. Fortunately, though, he was slightly less assertive than Tim, so Tim was able to maintain leadership, and a bit less responsive, so his demand for attention didn't exceed Tim's capacity. You can see on the chart on page 92 how they pair up.

Brian was as competitive as Tim but he lacked the same high social drive. He preferred individual sports, for example, to team competition. In social settings some people perceived him as cold and indifferent, but in fact he was shy and awkward, lacking Tim's fluid social skills. When he was with close friends, Brian was fun-loving, but he was selective about his social life and wore down fast, needing quiet time to recharge his batteries. Tim, by contrast, spent virtually no time alone.

Angus was almost as assertive as Brian. He desperately wanted to work; if he had been able to drive a car, he would have traveled to trials

Each of us (and our dogs) spends some time in each of the four categories.

on his own. This self-directed quality could have caused trouble, since Angus had the emotional capacity and the intelligence to take action on his own. Fortunately, since he had already been somewhat trained when Brian acquired him, this proved to be only a minor issue. Brian could tell him, "no," and Angus followed his lead. Interestingly, though, Angus was a bit more responsive than Brian. This difference worked out because the responsiveness of Angus's personality appealed to Virginia, Brian's wife and herself an amiable. She and Angus could spend warm time together that did not detract from the relationship between Brian and Angus. In fact, Brian recognized Angus's greater need for affection and interaction and was pleased that Virginia could meet it, to the satisfaction of all.

Louise was more social than Brian, considered warm and caring by her friends. But she had relatively few of those friends, emphasizing quality over quantity in her social life and spending much of her free time reading and visiting art galleries and bookstores. In work and social settings, Louise played an involved role, but she only rarely led. She was an analytical, but compared to others of the same personality type she was relatively highly responsive.

Like Louise, Snow ranked low on assertiveness. This is very important. A human who is low to moderately low in assertiveness needs to be matched with a dog who is naturally lower in this dimension. Otherwise, the human will be forced to stretch uneasily toward greater assertiveness simply to lead the dog, a situation that can breed considerable tension. With Snow this was not an issue; she looked to her owner for leadership because she was by nature lower in assertiveness than Louise.

At first, too, Snow seemed very low in responsiveness. This was in part an emotional consequence of living with an expressive, a phenomenon to be discussed in chapter 6. Once she found herself at home in the quiet surroundings of Louise's house, Snow blossomed into a warm and lovingly responsive pet who closely matched her owner's want for affection.

Amiable Jane was nonetheless fairly assertive. She enjoyed an active social life, with friends often stopping by. Her daughters also had many friends, and Jane generally enjoyed all the comings and goings of the neighborhood children. Yet Jane did not need the organized, focused approach to life that Brian required, nor did she have to occupy center stage the way Tim did. She simply took pleasure in people and their many activities about her. Jane fell into the amiable category, with moderately low assertiveness but high responsiveness.

Dawn proved to be a little less assertive than Jane, making her comfortable with all the activity in Jane's house. A more assertive dog would have responded to all the stimulation by trying to take over, but

Dawn lay back and let life go on about her. Still, she was assertive enough to hold her own in a group setting and she genuinely liked people, both adults and children.

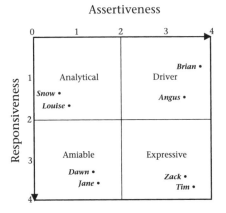

You'll notice that every human exceeds his or her dog on both dimensions, with one significant exception. Angus was more responsive than Brian, but the situation proved workable because of Virginia's natural responsiveness as an amiable. In general, it is important that human and dog match up closely in personality, with the human being slightly more assertive and slightly more responsive than the dog. This situation may be somewhat modified with a family dog, who will, of ne-

cessity, be in relationship with a number of people. Since humans tend to mate with their opposites, a dog who matches well with one partner is likely to fit poorly with the other. This could have happened between Angus and Virginia, but the difference was resolved for two reasons. First, as a border collie, Angus was emotionally sensitive and he paid attention to Virginia once she learned how to assert herself. Second, on the responsiveness scale Angus and Virginia were much closer than on the assertiveness scale. This gave them the basis for a pleasing relationship.

Complex, but Simple

As you can tell from all this discussion, the relationship between a human and a canine is complex. Still, even though the human-canine relationship is a complicated intertwining of personality, don't let yourself be daunted by it. In a manner of speaking, this is all very simple, if you will just let it be. What matters is your intuitive response to your dog and the deep way the two of you fit together. When it feels right, it is. The rest is commentary.

Chapter Six
Emotion and Action
The Revolving Wheel

O NE of the most striking, and indeed wonderful, things about the way dogs are put together is their capacity for synchrony. Dogs act much like social mirrors, reflecting the emotions and activities of their peers and leaders. Watch a group of dogs playing sometime and you'll see precisely what I mean. One dog initiates a game — say, tugging on an old knotted towel — and draws another into the play. Then the third dog, reflecting the excitement of the first two, leaps in. In mere seconds, all three dogs share much the same emotional content and pitch, as if they were in some manner not three separate creatures but one connected being.

Canine synchrony reaches far back into the evolution of the spe-

In wolves, synchrony helps the pack coalesce.

cies. In wolves, for example, synchrony helps the pack coalesce during the difficult task of pursuing and killing a moose or caribou. Synchrony ensures teamwork among the individual members of the pack.

Modern dogs carry this same capacity for synchrony with humans. By becoming aware of how it works, you can use it to manage your dog and deepen your relationship with your pet. Synchrony is also key to training and to dealing with problem behaviors. And, as we will see in the chapters on training, it is critical to motivating your dog to learn.

* * *

A GOOD image of the physical and emotional connection between you and your dog is what I call the revolving wheel. Imagine a roulette wheel or an old-fashioned spoked wagon wheel laid on its side and set spinning. If you place a cup of coffee on the rim, it will fly off and spill. But if you place the cup on the hub, in the very center of the wheel, it will turn round and round but remain stable and upright.

Two factors influence how long a cup of coffee can survive the pull of centrifugal force on the revolving wheel. One is its position on the wheel — the farther it is from the center, the greater the centrifugal force and the more likely the cup is to fly off. The other factor is the speed at which the wheel turns. Obviously a fast-turning wheel offers more centrifugal force and a greater risk of spilled coffee than does a slow-spinning one.

I find this model useful for two purposes. One is simply understanding what is going on between you and your dog. The revolving wheel is one of those working metaphors that gives you a pragmatic image of your interaction with your pet. Additionally, you can use the model to mold the dog's feelings and behavior in the way you need. I'll give a number of examples of this later on. For the moment, let's look more closely at the spinning wheel and what its various elements stand for.

The cup of coffee represents the interior mental state, emotions, and instincts of the dog, including both inherited behaviors and personality. The spinning of the wheel stands for the outside influences affecting the dog's interior characteristics — all the emotional interactions and physical activities, sights, sounds, tastes, smells, and other sensations dogs attend to. Finally, each of the wheel's spokes stands for a behavioral trait. One end of the spoke is one extreme of that trait, the other is its opposite, such as "aggressive" at one end and "defensive" on the other. Here is a list of some of the traits that belong on the wheel:

active assertive	passive assertive
dominant	submissive
energetic	lethargic
excitable	placid
enthusiastic	apathetic
intense	subdued
overconfident	apprehensive
determined	hesitant
purposeful	aimless
actively resistant	passively resistant
emotionally explosive	emotionally controlled
overly responsible	irresponsible
fearful (fight)	fearful (flight)
competitive	cooperative
dramatic	expressionless
animated	deadpan
responsive	unresponsive
constantly touching	selectively touching
independent	dependent

The speed at which the wheel spins is set by the environment. If you're listening to a Bach violin concerto at fireside after work, with your pet curled up next to you on the couch, the wheel is turning very slowly. But if you're walking along a downtown Manhattan street at rush hour, with people hurrying past, buses belching acrid exhaust, drivers in the plugged streets honking their horns in irritation, newspaper boys shouting the day's headlined atrocities, and hot dog vendors offering their good-smelling wares for sale, the wheel is spinning very fast indeed. And the faster the wheel spins, the more your dog is pushed toward the rim and the more a particular trait is expressed.

Whether this movement toward the rim poses a problem depends, first, on the personality match — or mismatch — between you and your dog and, second, on the appropri-

The Revolving Wheel

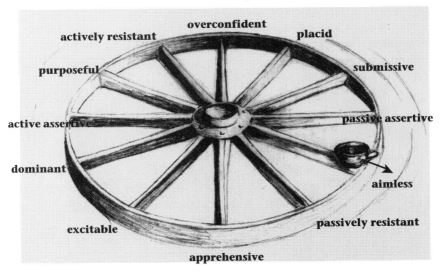

The spokes of the wheel represent different behavioral traits. The coffee cup represents the dog's outward expression of that behavioral trait based on its internal psychology. The spin of the wheel represents outside influences. A wheel with little spin represents minimal distractions or stimulants, while a quickly moving wheel represents significant distractions or a highly stimulating environment. As the wheel spins faster, the dog slides toward the edge of the wheel and that particular trait is intensified

ateness of the dog's instinctive reaction to the particular situation.

If you and your dog are closely matched in personality type, then you will both tend to be aroused in the same manner as the spinning increases in speed and to move in the same direction on the wheel. Take the example of Jane and Dawn from chapter 5. When Jane's house filled up with the neighborhood children, who ran about, played, and made themselves peanut butter sandwiches, all those sounds, smells, and sights set the wheel spinning faster and faster. Both Jane and Dawn reacted to the stimulation in the same way, being drawn into it and enjoy-

ing it as a pleasure. The wheel was spinning faster, but Dawn and Jane remained connected and in synchrony. But if Dawn had been an analytical dog, with a much lower responsiveness, she would likely have withdrawn, expressing her need for solitude even as the opportunity for that solitude decreased because of the setting. Since Jane desired social interactions, a problem could have arisen between Dawn and her.

The case of Brian and Angus shows how the wheel image applies to instinctive behaviors as well as to personality. A herding trial is a stimulating high-energy environ-

John and Hershey   Jane and Dawn

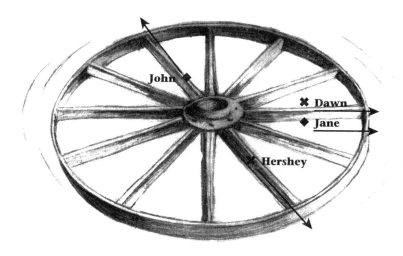

Dawn and Jane are in synchrony even when the wheel spins, while John and Hershey are out of synchrony to begin with. The distance between them increases when the wheel spins.

ment, with people milling about and the air fairly crackling with competition and pressure to win, and the wheel is spinning fast indeed. Angus's instinctive response at trials was to demonstrate heightened awareness of movement, a hardwired behavior that makes border collies adept herders and has been fostered through centuries of breeding. As a result, Angus paid intense attention to the hand signals Brian used to tell him what to do. This suited Brian's needs precisely, because he wanted to win and Angus needed to do as he was told. Angus's response fit the situation and caused no problem.

But if the dog's instinctive response is inappropriate, or if there is personality disparity between human and dog, then things can go wrong. The wheel shows why, as I can explain best by using the example of John and Hershey.

John had acquired his chocolate Labrador, Hershey, right after a painful divorce. John's personal life had been shattered, and he wanted a dog as a friend to fill in the void he felt. That was why he acquired Hershey, who was indeed a personable, companionable dog, the kind of pet John thought he wanted to come home to. But soon John found himself disappointed in Hershey.

When John returned from work in the evening, he was looking for a playful high-energy romp in the backyard. Instead, Hershey greeted John with mild enthusiasm, then curled up on the rug to watch his master. Hungry for interaction, John found himself instead with a pet apparently content to let the world go by while he took a nap. That made him angry.

John was an expressive and Hershey an analytical, by nature less responsive than John. When John arrived with his characteristic burst of expressive exuberance, the wheel began to spin at high speed. The centrifugal force pulled Hershey in the direction of the rim, arousing and activating him to be more lethargic and withdrawn. John responded with even greater exuberance, which sped the wheel further and pushed Hershey out to the edge. Then John became angry, which sent Hershey flying off the wheel into complete withdrawal, like the spilled cup of coffee.

But there is another, and better, way to handle a situation like this.

Modifying Relationships

Truth is, a relationship between human and canine of the sort I had with Gravity is unusual. Only if you are lucky enough to select just the right dog, one who is perfectly in sync with you both physically and psychologically from day one, will you avoid the common issue of having to shape the relationship with your dog. But shaping is possible,

in large measure because of the canine's exceptional ability to synchronize. The key is knowing how it works, understanding your own emotions, and working with that knowledge and emotional awareness to mold the relationship with your pet into the form you want. And this is something you have to do. The dog can't do it for you. Your task as a handler is to keep the dog where you want it on the wheel. You need to understand your own wants and to learn how to get the dog to move to the place where you want it to be.

Understand that the dog can't do this for you. Dogs, like humans, are generally versatile, capable of moving from one end of a behavioral trait — such as energetic — to the other — such as lethargic — with relative ease, depending on the setting. It is true that an individual dog or human occupies a certain natural position on a behavioral spectrum, but the same individual can move along the spectrum in response to circumstance, training, or social interaction. However, dogs cannot work up a strategy to move along the spectrum by themselves, independent of your leadership. They have no capacity to reflect on their emotions or yours, develop a cognitive understanding of what is going on, and then devise a solution. You can do that; your dog can't.

The wheel provides the model you need to move the dog in the desired direction. If your dog is in a position on one side of a given spoke and you want it to demonstrate more of that trait — that is, move

To move the dog toward the wheel's center, decrease stimuli, tone down enthusiasm, build trust, encourage gently or restrict/restrain behavior.

To move the dog more toward the rim of the wheel, increase stimuli, build excitement, enthusiasm, and heighten emotional stimuli.

closer to the rim — you need to increase the external stimuli, heighten the emotional pitch, or do whatever else will spin the wheel faster. On the other hand, if want your dog to demonstrate less of a quality, you need to decrease the external stimuli, lower the emotional pitch, or do whatever else is needed to slow the wheel's spinning. However, the technique isn't the same as simply turning the volume up or down.

I can best explain what I am getting at by returning to the story of John and Hershey. Because of his emotional history surrounding the divorce, John experienced Hershey's quiet as rejection. This distressed John and caused him to explode angrily at Hershey, who became not more socially interactive, as John wanted, but more socially withdrawn. That angered John all the more.

Pay attention to what was happening here. John and Hershey occupied opposite positions on the wheel spoke spanning the spectrum from enthusiasm to apathy. John was well past the center toward the excitable end, while Hershey found himself closer to the other, placid end of the spoke. The two were out of sync on this basic personality characteristic. John expected Hershey to figure this out on his own and take steps to express excitement, something no dog can do. When Hershey failed — as he had to — John's anger and distress grew.

But this had the exact opposite effect of what John wanted. In Hershey's emotional eyes, John's growing anger set the wheel spinning faster, which pushed Hershey farther and farther down the spoke toward greater and greater placidity. The angrier John got, the more apathetic Hershey became in response. Round and round they went, the wheel spinning faster by the moment.

Dogs can't devise an emotional solution to such a situation. They respond at the gut level in terms of fight or flight. Had John continued to spin the wheel faster and faster by growing ever angrier and more resentful, Hershey, who disliked the emotional display every evening brought, would have simply begun avoiding John's homecoming — which would, no doubt, have irritated John still more and made him angrier yet. Dog and human both would have been locked in unhappy place at opposite ends of a fast-spinning wheel.

The dynamic in this situation was very similar to what I observed between Snow and her first owner. There, too, a low-responsive analytical dog was linked to a high-responsive expressive human. The owner grew even more expressive, which pushed Snow into even lower responsiveness. Round and round the cycle went, the wheel spinning ever faster, human and dog moving in opposite directions.

Fortunately, once John figured out what was happening and where

his own distress arose, he took a different tack. He made a concerted and planned effort to move Hershey nearer his own position on the revolving wheel. First, he moved himself closer to the hub of the wheel and Hershey. Then he encouraged Hershey to cross over the hub and closer to his own position. To begin with, John toned down his emotional enthusiasm when he came home. Instead of walking in through the door acting as if he were ready for a friendly wrestling match, John came in quietly, greeting Hershey in a low-key way that created a safe and secure environment. Slowly and gently, this strategy moved Hershey closer to the wheel's center. In the process, Hershey learned to trust John's emotional self-discipline. At the same time, John invited Hershey into gradually increasing enthusiasm, trading on the synchrony instinctive in canines. He reinforced Hershey's movement with treats, petting, voiced encouragement ("Good dog!"), and lots of smiles — all the motivators we will discuss in greater detail in the training chapters.

As his trust increased, Hershey moved down the spoke in the direction of the more excited end of the spectrum. Once he passed the center of the wheel, John could raise his own excitement from the subdued level he had been maintaining. Over time and with care, the two of them came much closer together.

Soon Hershey was greeting John's homecomings eagerly. John, having understood that he himself had to catalyze the emotional reaction with Hershey and could not expect the dog to do it on his own, had gained the companionship he wanted. By nature a more placid being than John, Hershey was not about to initiate the greetings John sought. Instead, John had learned how to draw the dog toward him by consciously working with the revolving wheel of centrifugal force.

THIS story of John and Hershey brings home a couple of critical points. First of all, moving your dog along one of the wheel's spokes is a matter of both increasing and decreasing your own emotions and activities. If you are closer to the center than your dog is, you decrease any stimulus that arouses the dog and pushes it toward the rim — in this case, John's enthusiasm and anger — and increase any stimulus that pulls the dog closer to the center — John's encouragement and invitation as Hershey made his first moves toward the center. If you are closer to the rim than your dog is, you do just the opposite — increase any stimulus that pulls the dog toward the rim and decrease any stimulus that pushes the dog closer to the center.

Second, the amount of effort required to move your pet depends on how close to the rim and how far from you the dog is. Hershey was so far out he was about to spin away into empty space. It took concerted effort, both to decrease the level of threat and to encourage enthusiasm, to bring Hershey closer to John.

Brian and Angus provide an example of the situation where lesser effort is required. You will recall that Angus was more responsive than Brian and therefore more interested in attention, but the distance between them in this respect was fairly small. On the fast-spinning wheel of a herding trial, Angus asked for attention by sidling up to Brian. To move Angus back toward the center and keep him on track for the trial, Brian simply decreased his own responsiveness, refusing to touch Angus, talk to him, or give an approving facial expression. Quickly Angus went back where Brian wanted him. This required little effort because dog and human were so close together to begin with. Had Brian and Angus been farther apart, Brian would have had to say "no" or use a stronger negative reinforcement.

ANOTHER friend of mine, Jessie, faced a problem that was quite the opposite of John's. Her pet at the time was Keila, a black Labrador who later became my dog when Jessie moved away and had to give her up. In terms of the four basic personality types, Keila is an expressive, highly desirous of social interaction. Jessie, however, was a driver. Though she was moderately interested in social interaction, Jessie was less keen on touching than Keila.

Jessie and Keila

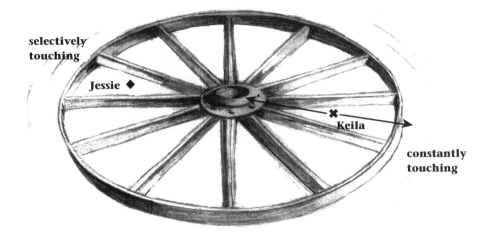

selectively
touching

Jessie ◆

✖
Keila

constantly
touching

Shaping with an emotionally controlled approach stops the wheel's spin, and allows the dog to be maneuvered closer to the person.

Increasing anger at Keila speeds the spinning and increases the intensity.

That led to difficulty between human and canine. Every morning when Jessie bent over to tie her shoelaces, Keila was in her face, literally, licking and nuzzling. It didn't stop there. As Jessie typed at her computer, Keila would suddenly nuzzle her or jump up and put her front paws in Jessie's lap. This unexpected intrusion would cause Jessie to lose her train of thought, and in her frustration she would explode angrily at Keila.

To Jessie's surprise, the anger did no good. Every day was a repetition of the day before. Keila intruded unexpectedly, and Jessie responded angrily. Clearly, Keila wasn't understanding that Jessie disliked such sudden intense interaction — which led Jessie to ask me why.

The answer is obvious from the revolving wheel concept. Consider where the two of them were positioned on the spoke representing the spectrum from great desire for touch at one end to no desire for touch at the other. Jessie was just past the center hub toward desire for touch, but Keila was much closer to the rim. Keila's constant drive toward touch frustrated Jessie, who wanted less. That frustration elicited in Keila a reaction much like Hershey's, in that the human's response increased the spinning of the wheel and pushed the dog further toward the rim, making its behavior increasingly extreme. John's anger made Hershey more placid. In Keila's case, Jessie's anger made her more eager for touch. As with John and

Hershey, Jessie and Keila were locked in a downward spiral helping neither party in the relationship.

Jessie needed to apply a different technique than John did, since her goal was to decrease Keila's seeking after touch. Every time she reacted to Keila's insistence with an emotional outburst or by pushing the dog away, she was inadvertently reinforcing Keila's need for touch. This was particularly true when Jessie gave Keila a shove, because she was providing precisely the kind of physical interaction the dog wanted.

Instead, Jessie learned not to react with negative emotion to Keila's unsolicited desire for touch, but to tell Keila, in a clear and objective tone of voice, that she was to stop. Alternatively, she ignored Keila altogether, thereby leaving the dog in a void without reward of any kind. Since Jessie wanted to move the dog from the emotional end of the spectrum toward the calmer center, her approach was purposely controlled and restrained. In the absence of stimulation related to her behavior, Keila became less insistent. This allowed Jessie to take the initiative and encourage touching with Keila at the times when she wanted it, not when Keila insisted. Jessie had to be consistent to make this work. When Keila initiated, Jessie told her to go away, always in a cool and restrained tone of voice. But when Jessie herself started touching the dog, she was enthusiastic and upbeat. Keila quickly understood the new ground rules, and the relationship brightened. Both were getting what they needed, with closer synchrony between the two of them.

Keila never completely stopped initiating touch, but she became much more selective about it. Instead of pushing all the time, Keila learned to initiate only when Jessie was in a soft-touch mood and would respond to her. Still, Keila's insistent behavior of times past did not reappear — except in circumstances when the wheel was spinning very fast, such as a party with a houseful of guests or high excitement on Jessie's part. Then Keila was likely to become pushy once again, and Jessie again had to use a verbal "no" command to move Keila closer to the center of the wheel and to herself.

Instincts, Psychotics, and Bad Dogs

When John exploded into anger at Hershey for what he perceived as his dog's rejection, he was facing a classic handler-pet situation: Hershey wasn't meeting his needs. John had alternatives in dealing with the issue. He could have done what many people do: give the dog up. This, in fact, happens to about 60 percent of all dogs adopted each year in this country — including Snow, the poodle we talked about in chapter 5. John's second option was to accept Hershey as he was and modify his own life to suit his pet's instincts and personality. This is the choice made, often unwittingly, by many families who reshape their lives to accommodate their dogs. The third option was the one John chose.

John decided to move Hershey in a direction that would make him more satisfied with his pet. John assumed leadership and moved Hershey the way he needed him to go.

All too often, people give up leadership and take the second option, shaping their lives to their dogs and in the process augmenting the disturbing behavior by pushing the dog closer and closer to the rim of the revolving wheel. This would have happened to Hershey if John had continued his angry displays. Hershey would have become more and more withdrawn and simply avoided John's evening homecoming. More times than I care to remember I have seen situations where a person of low assertiveness takes on a highly assertive dog, usually as a protector. The dog takes over, and as it assumes greater control, the human becomes less assertive while the dog becomes ever more so. Such a dog can be made into a good companion capable of protection by controlling and restraining its aggressive displays, a strategy that pulls the dog toward the wheel's center and its less assertive owner. But when such a dog is unrestrained, the wheel turns faster and faster and the dog moves out to the rim, where it becomes highly aggressive and possibly dangerous.

Another common predicament is the expressive, emotional person who takes on a sensitive dog, one who, for example, becomes anxious when visitors arrive. If the owner coos over the dog and coddles its sensitivity, he or she pushes it farther out toward the rim of the revolving wheel and makes the animal even more sensitive. In time, the dog is transformed into a quivering and overly sensitive pet who runs and hides under the bed at every knock on the door. Instead, the owner could have reacted to the dog's original displays of sensitivity by not reacting at all, using a cool and controlled response that pulled the dog toward the center and closer to its human partner.

Sadly, some people like creating emotional messes with their dogs. For example, I have seen people who got some kind of kick out of being angry with pets, in the same way that some parents fulfill misplaced emotional needs by browbeating and abusing their children. Some people also use their dogs as a compensatory mechanism that fills in where they feel wanting. This is a kind of synchrony, but instead of making dog and human alike, the dog takes over where the human is lacking. You can see easily how this dynamic arises between the shy, low-assertive person and the forward, highly assertive guard dog. The pet becomes wish fulfillment for the human's missing machismo. Such situations serve both human and canine poorly.

IN working on the communication dynamics between you and your dog, it is important to be aware of what you can and cannot do. You cannot, for example, create sanity in a psychotic dog by moving it closer to the center of the revolving wheel. Nor can you fully extinguish instinctive behaviors your pet inherited.

Psychosis refers to severe mental disorder, and dogs, like people, are subject to such emotional dysfunction. Psychosis is by no means common among canines, however, and most problem behavior in dogs arises from miscommunication between owner and pet. If you are concerned about the emotional and mental stability of your own pet, consult with your veterinarian. Because vets are familiar with the behaviors that are normal and abnormal for the particular breed, they can give you sound advice about your pet's status.

Understanding the instinctive, or inborn, behaviors likely to appear in your pet is one of the reasons why it is important to know about your pet's breed and specific ancestry. Dogs enter the world bearing a number of behaviors, reactions that are essentially hardwired into them and that will occur in response to certain stimuli. All other things being equal, Rottweilers guard, border collies herd, greyhounds pursue, spaniels flush, and terriers dig.

With the revolving wheel, you can shape these instinctive behaviors, but not eliminate them. Instincts cannot be removed entirely because they are as much a part of the dog as its bones and blood vessels. Still, because of the canine's equally inborn capacity for synchro-

nization, you can shape instinctive behavior to fit your lifestyle. The key is understanding your relationship with your dog, using the revolving wheel concept, and determining what you yourself need.

A good example was a friend named Mary, a seventy-year-old grandmother living alone. She wanted a watchdog to alert her to strangers and a lapdog for affection, and so she wisely chose a terrier cross named Peta. The relationship was good, except in one place: the garden. Mary was an avid gardener who daily spent hours tending her flowers, and Peta, true to her terrier legacy, was a digger who loved nothing more than tearing into turned earth. Mary could have devoted a great deal of time to training Peta not to dig, but she decided it wasn't worth the effort. Instead, she fenced part of her yard so that when she put Peta out in the morning to urinate, the terrier had access only to a small patch of ground well away from Mary's prized flower beds. When Mary was working in the garden, Peta came with her, but she was allowed among the flowers only when Mary herself was there and could correct Peta if she started digging. This way, Mary and Peta enjoyed each other's companionship, yet the flowers were safe.

Mary solved her problem in a way that respected Peta's instinctive propensities and also protected her own values. She recognized what she needed and devised a way of getting it. Peta wasn't a bad dog; she was a terrier. Mary created a relationship in which Peta could still be a terrier and also be Mary's watchdog and companion.

Din, the pet of another friend, was also no bad dog, but a German shepherd. Like most shepherds, Din was protective and territorial when strangers approached the house she shared with her owner, Fred. Again like most shepherds, Din was devoted to her handler, but she was also more assertive than he. As a result, she generally obeyed him, but only when it was her choice to do so, never his. In essence, she was leading the relationship, not he. Most of the time, things went along well enough, but conflict erupted when visitors came to the door. Din barked, snarled, and growled despite Fred's commands to stop. Invariably, he had to confine the dog to another room before he could let his friends in. Nobody — not Fred, not Din, not the visitors listening uncomfortably to the stream of snarls from the back of the house — was happy.

When the revolving wheel began spinning faster at the approach of visitors, Din moved out closer to the edge, becoming even more aggressive and assertive, as Fred's uncertainty about the right action to take pushed him the other direction, making him less aggressive and assertive. Under these circumstances, Fred had no control over Din and she did what she wanted, despite his verbal commands to the contrary.

So Fred faced a choice: lock Din in the back room whenever friends came over, or change her behavior. He chose the latter.

The process began with a set-up. Fred had asked a friend to come over at a specific time. Before the friend arrived, Fred slipped a choke chain and leash on Din and, while he waited for the friend to arrive, he sat and petted her, creating a synchrony between them through the mutual pleasure of touch. When the bell rang, Din broke and ran toward the door. Immediately, Fred said, "No!" quietly but with authority, his manner controlled and restrained, and he corrected her with the choke chain (using the jerk-and-release method and the objective emotional tenor I will explain in chapter 9). The correction utterly shocked Din, who had never before experienced such discipline from Fred. After an instant, she went for the door again, barking wildly as ever, and Fred corrected her again, with both "no" and the choke chain.

Din stopped, turned around, and looked at Fred, who praised her immediately but quietly for paying attention to him. Then he stood up and walked to the door, giving her the "let's go" command to come along with him. Din was confused by this sudden turn of events, but she already knew enough not to lunge at the door again. Instead, she took a few tentative steps at Fred's side. Realizing in a split second there were no repercussions for walking alongside her owner, she again bolted for the door, barking wildly.

Fred and Din

The wheel's center represents stability. No matter how fast the wheel is spinning, whatever is at the center will remain in place. You can temporarily resolve problems resulting from your dog's inborn, instinctive behavior by shaping the dog's behavior to the center of the wheel, thereby stabilizing it for the specific period of time you are directly controlling the situation.

Retaining his quiet and controlled emotional air, Fred corrected Din with the chain alone. She came back to his side, both because she knew that was a safe place and also because, as dogs do, she was moving toward synchrony with her leader.

Fred opened the door and said hello in a soft voice to his friend. Din, still confused, barked. Fred corrected her with a firm "no" and praised her the second she stopped barking. Meanwhile the friend, following the plan he and Fred had worked out beforehand, stood quietly, making no moves that might lead Din to doubt his peaceful intent. All the time, the wheel was spinning slowly. Keeping Din on the

leash, Fred invited the friend in and they talked for a while. Din minded her manners the whole time.

Fred and his friend repeated this routine several times over a period of days, with the leash on until Din got the message fully, then with a longer leash as a safeguard. They also raised the level of stimulation from quiet talk to enthusiastic conversation. After a while, Fred was able to use voice control alone and forgo the leash, even when he was talking excitedly with friends.

At that point it might have looked as if Din's aggressiveness had been completely eliminated, but this was not the case. Instead, Fred had assumed the leadership position in the relationship. Also, he had used another aspect of the revolving wheel concept — namely, moving Din's behavior temporarily to the center of the wheel and thereby stabilizing it, creating a balance against her her inborn aggressiveness. This worked, however, only when Fred was present to slow the spinning wheel and move her to the center. When the wheel spun faster — say, when Fred was gone and Din was home alone — she was just as aggressive as before, obeying her inborn instinct to protect.

Getting into Your Guts

The idea of achieving synchrony with your pet through the revolving wheel is really nothing new. You probably do it all the time with the people in your life. No doubt you realize that you can't calm a crying child by jumping up and down and yelling, nor do you bolster job security by shouting obscenities at your boss. Assuming that you want a healthy relationship, you already know inside yourself, at the gut level, how to fix problems and improve communication.

The same realities apply to you and your dog. First, you need to be aware of your own motivation in regard to your dog. Sadly, some people are committed to being a part of their own problems, enjoying the emotional charge of things going badly. Others may put the dog in a leadership position, wanting the animal to fulfill their emotional

needs, essentially playing the child to a canine parent. It doesn't work, for either dog or human.

What complicates this emotional dumping and makes it even worse is that dogs mirror their handlers emotionally. When you feel fear, your dog feels fear; when you are exuberant, your dog is exuberant. However, this emotional information is processed through the dog's fight-or-flight response, and either your pet may move to assume your emotions or it may go in the opposite direction. In a fearful situation, for example, you may choose to run while the dog stands and fights. At the same time, your dog looks to you as an emotional role model, particularly when it meets new situations, in some manner asking you how it should behave. This works to your advantage if you are willing to take emotional responsibility for your pet and provide leadership, but it leads to all sorts of unhappiness, for both canine and human, if you are not.

Emotional responsibility is key. For those people who want a mature and meaningful relationship with their dogs and who understand the canine's limitations, capabilities, and gifts, there is one right way — pay attention to your own instinctive, intuitive emotional reactions. When you look at your dog, what you are looking at is your own self unfettered by cognitive thinking. The animal is your mirror; it seeks synchrony with you. The relationship between dog and human is true, deep, honest, meaningful, and forthright. What you see is what you get, and the deepest human pitfall is to ascribe to this relationship complexities that do not belong.

The greatest wonder dogs bring to our lives is honesty of intent. This doesn't mean the dog is always right. As I have shown in the stories in this chapter, canine behavior often has to be shaped to make for a happy relationship. But shaping does not belie the fundamental truth of the dog, which is that it connects with the truth in us. Separate yourself from your cognitive mind, and you separate yourself from the capacity for deceit. Then you become like the dog, who cannot tell a lie, and the dog can become like you, which is its deep drive. At this level of awareness, you won't be ascribing to your dog all sorts of badness, evil intent, or purposeful sabotage that it is incapable of doing. Instead, you will be enjoying the wonderful gift that the dog is, shaping its behavior to your needs, and reveling in the joy of perhaps the purest relationship you will ever know.

Part Three

Educating Your Dog

I F YOU have ever stood in a rain
forest while monkeys trooped
overhead, or if you have simply
watched them in the zoo closer to
home, you know how noisily hyperac-
tive these small primates can be. Monkeys fill the air with screams and
chatterings and shake the branches of
the tree canopy wildly with their endless
movement. Everything is sound and
motion, without apparent melody or direction, as if chaos had put on flesh and
fur and climbed loudly into the trees.

Buddhists use this image to describe
an internal state of confusion as monkey mind. Mind, in this context,
doesn't carry its usual narrow meaning
of reason or intellect. It refers instead
to the whole form of being, both mental
and physical, that makes a particular
creature what it is.

I don't consider myself a Buddhist,
but I like the concept of mind applied to
educating your dog. Only by entering

the mind of another being can we ever
understand who and what that being
is. The challenge for you as a human
wanting to deepen the relationship with
your pet is that you must first enter dog
mind. You must see, feel, and experience the world — and yourself — as a
dog does. The point of this necessary exercise is not to become a dog. You can't;
your sense of smell is too rudimentary
and you have but two legs. Rather, the
objective of entering dog mind is to become familiar enough, particularly in-
tuitively, with the psychological and
physical workings of the canine that
you can relate to dogs as they are, not
as convention says they are. Then, and
only then, can you begin to teach and
train your dog in the skills you want it
to learn.

This section begins by mapping dog
mind, then it moves on to detail the
specific training approach I use, from
basic commands to advanced tasks.

Chapter Seven

Learning

The What, How, and Why of Educating in Dog Mind

*T*HERE'S a great deal more to education than training. Training refers broadly to what are called motor skills, and it covers that typical series of events in which a human teaches a dog a command like "sit" and the dog learns to sit when the command is given. Training is only part of the picture, though, both in terms of how one educates a dog and how the dog learns. Dogs are more like us than we commonly care to admit, and educating them entails more than instilling motor skills.

Learning is in fact an exciting, integrated, all-over process. Dogs learn much as children do, with great emotion, using their bodies as well as their brains, and assimilating lessons about attitudes and modes of thinking as well as motor skills. In describing learning in humans, psychologists often use words that demonstrate the complexity and integration of the process, particularly such adjectives as *psychosocial, attitudinal,* and *perceptual motor.* These terms are rarely applied to canines, however, as if learning in dogs were only rote training. In fact, such words hold for dogs just as validly as humans. We will all do much better with our pets when we admit that complex and integrated learning is common to both species.

But, truth be told, we don't really know a great deal about learning. There are many books on the subject, but these represent largely the opinions, observations, and analyses of individual scientists. Education is more art than science, a skill that requires sensitivity in addition to knowledge, whether your subjects are children or dogs. Many of the same insights hold true.

Brain Basics

As we have already discussed, humans and dogs share many similarities at the level of brain function. The differences are important, too. Dogs lack a word-based language, so a great deal of educating your pet involves efforts to show the animal what you want without benefit of verbal explanation. You can't simply tell the dog what you're after in language, the way you can with even a small child, and expect it to understand. And even after a dog does understand, there is a greater likelihood that it will behave contrary to its training than a child will. The reason is simple: Dogs have less cognitive capability than humans. All other things being equal, humans rely much more on cognition than on hardwired instincts, while dogs are just the opposite. They fall back on instinct, often in mere thousandths of a second, with the right stimuli.

In dogs a large portion of the behavioral repertoire is under the control of the autonomic nervous system, which responds automatically and outside control of the conscious brain. Instinct functions in the autonomic realm, as do emotions and feelings. We humans share feelings and emotions with dogs, but we process them differently. In canines, feelings happen and behavior changes, just like that, without any processing in the conscious mind. In humans, emotions are at least partly processed into consciousness before behavior occurs. I am convinced, though, that like dogs we humans have rich emotional lives in our guts, below consciousness. The difference is that we often ignore or turn away from these feelings, using the conscious mind as a kind of emotional police force.

I call this range of feeling, both conscious and unconscious, the affective domain. As I have said before and will say again and again, connecting with your own affective domain is key to working with your dog effectively.

Dogs and humans begin life at a

similar starting point, with most behavior originating in the autonomic nervous system. As the brain develops in babies, functions first controlled by the midbrain and considered reflexive move into the cognitive domain. In dogs, though, a significant amount of reflexive behavior remains in the midbrain and outside conscious cognitive control even in adulthood. In dogs, much more than in humans, a substantial proportion of behavior derives directly from the inheritance of the species and the breed rather than individual learning. If a squirrel dashes out in front of a viszla or weimaraner or German shorthair pointer, it will give chase — not because the individual dog has learned to, but because hunting breeds have been shaped over the centuries to pursue when something small runs away.

Babies and puppies entering the world carry such unlearned behaviors with them. For example, newborn babies know how to suck milk from a nipple, just as puppies do, and both know how to swallow at birth. At this early stage, the limits of learning are set by the baby's and puppy's physical capabilities. Babies have no bladder control, nor do puppies, but puppies can be guided to urinate in only one part of the yard. Likewise, as the pup gains skills, education can begin with simple commands like "sit."

Readiness is all important, in humans just as in dogs. You cannot toilet-train a child before he or she has control of the sphincter muscles.

Trying to toilet-train too soon is nothing but an exercise in frustration for both child and teacher. The same applies to dogs, whether the issue is housebreaking or learning a difficult and demanding command. Education can occur only when the dog is ready and able to learn. The command curriculum I develop in the subsequent chapters follows an order based in part on the development of the dog brain as it matures.

Dogs, like humans, learn how to learn. Babies are sponges; their minds absorb all sorts of stimuli with astounding speed. Puppies do the same thing, picking up information about the world around them quickly and enthusiastically. The more opportunity a baby or puppy has to learn, the better it is equipped to learn. Experimental work has shown that the brain actually grows when it is stimulated, forming new nerve connections, or synapses, in response to incoming information. In the same way that presenting a baby with new toys enhances the child's development, it also helps to introduce new sights, sounds, smells, and situations to puppies, better preparing them to learn as juveniles and adults.

A great many studies show that stress is central to learning; in fact, unstressed dogs — or humans — learn little. Stress in this meaning can be very simple and is by no means negative. Inducing a puppy to walk on a sloped surface, for example, stresses the puppy and helps develop its learning capacity.

Arousal makes dogs ready to learn. You might call it situational readiness. I use arousal all the time in my approach to training. When I put the leash on a dog to begin a training session, I pump up the dog emotionally. "Come on, Flora, it's time to train," I might say, my voice upbeat and enthusiastic. "Remember the good time we had yesterday." Of course, Flora has no idea what I'm saying from the words alone, but she can tell from the tone and modulation of my voice that the air between us is crackling with emotion. Her tail wags; she is aroused. Emotion has been introduced into the learning environment, and Flora will learn better than if her emotions were not engaged.

Mature dogs learn much as puppies do, but they have a longer attention span, deeper concentration, and a much greater ability to discriminate — that is, to determine the significance of a particular situation. Instead of learning across a wide spectrum the way puppies do, adolescent and adult dogs become selective. On the one hand, these developments make training easier, but they also spawn new and sometimes difficult problems. For example, training a puppy to a self-disciplined command like "wait" is demanding at best, owing to the young dog's general naïveté, enthusiasm, and short attention span. Training "wait" in an adult dog is much easier, because the older animal has a longer attention span and

because it has probably already achieved some self-discipline. But the adult dog also has the ability to look at a situation, determine what is important in that setting, and choose what it will respond to. This ability is called discrimination, and it is one reason why training can seem to proceed easily for a while and then suddenly go off on a mistaken sidetrack. Say you have trained your dog to the "wait" command and it has learned easily and well. Then, one day, you tell your dog to wait by the open front door, and not two seconds later a squirrel runs out of the hedge and across the porch, only a few feet from the dog's nose. In an instant the dog sizes up the situation and decides whether it is more important to obey the command or chase the squirrel — and it may well go after the squirrel. The dog, whether consciously or unconsciously, is applying significance to the setting, deciding that all things are not equal and that some things are more important than others, and it is selecting among options. Puppies, who are more into absorbing than deciding, can't make the discriminations and selections adult dogs can because they have yet to develop the required mental capacity and capability.

Why do dogs learn? Because they are set up, in terms of their evolutionary biology, to do so. Success in the long-ago wild made the canine a creature that learns quickly and well. Contemporary dogs display that same ability to survive within the human world. Many canine drives promote learning. Dogs are naturally curious, for example. They try to figure out situations, solving problems and taking advantage of opportunities. They synchronize, with you and with other dogs. They have strong desires for play, food, love, and approval, all of which can be used as rewards in educating them and are key in creating a good educational environment.

Teaching's Many Ways

I have been asked again and again whether I think operant conditioning is the most effective method for educating a dog. Certainly, operant conditioning — also known as behavioral modification, instrumental learning, and reinforcement theory, among other similar names — is one of the tools to use in teaching a dog. But relying on operant conditioning alone belies the richness of the dog's learning ability and the many ways we humans can make use of those abilities to teach our dogs what we want them to learn.

Dogs learn at different levels and in a variety of ways. To train your dog effectively, you need to have at least some understanding of the complicated richness of canine learning.

I divide learning into three basic areas. The first is *psychomotor* learning, which includes overt physical responses, such as manipulating an object or moving the body or parts of the body in a predictable pattern.

Teaching a dog to fetch a dumbbell or to lie down exemplifies psychomotor learning. This kind of learning is often called *conditioning*, which refers to physical responses to external stimuli. You say, "Sit," and your dog sits. The word *sit* is the stimulus, and the sitting posture is the conditioned psychomotor response.

The second area of canine learning is *affective*, or *attitudinal*. Dogs learn feelings in given situations or environments. You can, for example, turn your dog on to learning by being upbeat, enthusiastic, and playful in the way you approach each training session — "Come on, baby, it's time to train. Let's get the leash and head for the park and have a good time!" Or you can drag the dog down, by being depressed, dull, and deadening — "Oh, what do you know, five P.M. once again, time for another training session with my stupid dog. Come on, Fido, let's go. At least this beats root canal." You can well imagine the attitudes Fido is learning.

The third and final area is *cognitive* learning, which includes the application of strategies, tactics, and general information. In its most basic form, you can see cognitive learning in the dog's ability to discriminate: it can tell one situation from another. If you have trained your dog to sit in a quiet room free of distractions, that does not mean the dog will obey in a different setting, like a big family reunion with the aromas of fried chicken and potato salad wafting through your grandmother's crowded house. Cognitively the dog learns the difference between the two settings and obeys selectively. At a more complex level of cognitive learning, you can train your dog to solve problems. For example, when I am teaching service dogs, I train them how to get out of tangles with their own leashes. The dogs have to determine what is wrong and take the right steps to unravel the tangle, and they can indeed learn how to do this. Likewise, a dog can be taught a concept, such as picking up a dropped object no matter where it is dropped, a lesson that requires the dog to understand the idea *everywhere*.

All methods of educating dogs across these three levels of learning are built around understanding how dogs learn. Dogs learn in a number of ways, much as humans do, and the best teaching uses all of them, depending on the task at hand.

The first way canines learn is through their own inborn, *instinctual*, hardwired behavior. Pups come into the world carrying a variety of behaviors that appear and change as their brains and bodies develop. Interactions with the world modify these behaviors at least to some extent. For example, what is known as classical, or Pavlovian, conditioning comes into play here. This phenomenon was first described by the Russian scientist Ivan Petrovich Pavlov, who rang a bell when he fed his dogs, then noted later that the dogs

salivated at the ringing of the bell even if no food was present. The dog's salivation in response to food is an inborn physiological behavior, which is itself unlearned. What the dogs learned, though, was the association between the food and the bell, and thus they responded physically to the ringing of the bell as if a meal were about to be served.

Synchronization, which we discussed in chapter 6 as the basis for the revolving wheel of centrifugal force, plays an important role in canine education. Synchronization is the instinctive drive in dogs to balance with significant others. In the wild, all canids in the pack do the same thing at the same time; they sleep together, they hunt together, they play together. You won't see one of them playing or hunting while the others are stretched out on a warm rock taking a nap. Synchronization is an important adaptive instinct; it helps ensure, for example, that all the animals are rested and ready to engage in the physically demanding task of hunting as a single unified pack. Through synchronization you can calm your dog by slowing yourself down, or speed your dog up by boosting your own activity level. Or you can assert your leadership and order a changed response in your dog. Your pet's desire to synchronize will cause it to defer to your leadership and assume the position you want. As you read the two following chapters on specific commands, you'll see that synchronization comes into play repeatedly, both for teaching specific commands and also for setting the general tone for training sessions.

Dogs also learn at least somewhat by *observation*, or mimicry, although this kind of imitative learning is by no means as important in canines as it is in mockingbirds, dolphins, or monkeys (thus the proverb, "Monkey see, monkey do"). In the case of dogs, it is sometimes difficult to tell whether a dog is truly learning by watching another dog or whether it is responding to the same stimuli. Various writers on dogs have dismissed observation and say dogs don't learn by watching, but I beg to disagree. They do indeed learn this way. Let me give you an example, one that happened just yesterday. Hoja, my Anatolian shepherd, loves to carry things around in her mouth. Usually she goes for something like an old baby blanket, but yesterday, while I was stretched out on the couch reading quietly, she picked one of my shoes, which lay on the floor where I had kicked it off almost an hour earlier. This was new and, since I was trying to teach Hoja the retrieve, I called her to bring me the shoe, praising her lavishly when she did so. Keila, my brilliant Labrador, was watching all this in her usual observant way. When she saw Hoja get praised for bringing the shoe, she trotted over to the second shoe, picked it up, and brought it to me. The shoe wasn't moving around, attracting Keila's attention and asking to be picked up; it had been lying stock-still on the floor for nearly an hour. Instead, Keila observed what had happened and saw a way for her to gain praise.

As an educational method for canines, though, observation has only limited usefulness. Learning by observation requires the dog to pay close intention to what is being taught and have a strong desire to perform that activity on its own. Rarely are these conditions met when you are trying to teach a dog motor skills. Neither the skill nor the reward is enticing enough to make the dog pay the necessary close attention. I do, however, make regular use of observation to set the stage for learning. When I am training two or more dogs to the same command, I work the first dog in an area where the others can watch. Almost always the observers learn the command more quickly than usual. In this case, observation doesn't substitute for other forms of teaching, but it sets the stage and speeds subsequent learning.

Trial and error is another common way dogs learn. Like children, dogs experiment with the world and learn from the results. Watch a puppy give a rosebush its first sniffing. The little dog explores the plant with more and more vigor and abandon until, suddenly, it draws back with a quizzical, pained look when its nose encounters a thorn. Immediately, the pup learns. The next time it approaches a rose, it will do so with care, having learned by trial and error that rosebushes sniffed too vigorously bite back.

Dogs have considerable ability to get what they want through trial and error, attempting different approaches toward achieving an objective until they find one that works. Say a favorite ball has rolled under the fence. At first the dog may try to lunge through the pickets to get the ball, but the fence is too strong. Then it tries to leap over, but the fence is too high. Finally, it lies down, extends one paw under the fence, and bops the ball back in its own direction, close enough to grab in its jaws. That is trial and error, and it works.

Different dogs have different drives, intentions, and levels of tenacity, so they approach trial-and-error situations differently. Faced with a problem, some dogs never give up; others surrender after only a try or two.

I make use of trial and error to teach a number of skills, typically by setting up situations where the dog can learn through its own mistakes. For example, I train dogs to walk on-leash close by the side of my leg, a position that helps avoid entanglement in parking meters, furniture, shrubbery, and the like. Most dogs, however, tend to walk as far from your body as the leash allows. To teach the dog to stay close, you can walk down a sidewalk lined with parking meters, purposely passing so close to the first one that you and your dog can make it by only if the dog is close to your leg. Chances are the dog will walk far out and catch the leash on the pole. You keep

walking forward and the leash tightens, tugging unpleasantly on your dog's choke chain. You wait while your dog figures out how to back up and come around the pole to return to your side. Next time, your dog realizes it has to stay close to your side to avoid the problem. Some dogs may require a third or even fourth setup, but they will come to see the error of their ways and learn to steer clear of further accidents by staying close. Such interactions are a way of telling your dog, with trial and error and without words, what works and what doesn't. In the final analysis this is what all dog education comes down to.

Then there is *insight* learning. Like humans, dogs follow a learning curve, which measures their speed in picking up a new skill, concept, or attitude. Sometimes you can see insight learning occur, when the learning curve suddenly shoots upward. The dog gets it all at once, as if a switch in the canine brain just snapped on. You were training in the same way as before, but the dog figured out — on its own and all of a sudden — exactly what you wanted. That's insight, and it happens a great deal with dogs.

A variety of teaching methods pertain primarily to psychomotor learning, one of which is operant conditioning. Operant conditioning refers to teaching a behavior by means of reinforcement. In its simplest form, the trainer gives the dog the command "sit," the dog sits, and the trainer rewards the dog with a treat or a scratch on the chest. Operant conditioning is a simple and effective approach, and it has been trumpeted as both panacea for all sorts of canine behavior problems and the one perfect way to train a dog, any dog. It's not. In fact, there is no one panacea nor perfect way. Operant conditioning has its uses, but it also has its limitations.

Operant methods are excellent for conditioning motor skills, and you'll find I use them in teaching commands in the following two chapters. Still, the simple chain of stimulus-response-reinforcement is only part of canine learning. For one thing, dogs are smarter than operant conditioning might lead you to believe. Canines can discriminate and assign significance to experience, intellectual activities more complex than operant conditioning allows for. Also, operant conditioning ignores the importance of social setting to canine learning. Dogs respond to leadership and to attitude. If two trainers use the same sequence of verbal command and reinforcement, but one of them is confident and upbeat while the other is depressed and distant, the dog will learn much more effectively from the enthusiastic trainer than the depressed one. The reason for the difference isn't training methodology. It is the social interaction with the trainer and the attitudinal learning that comes from it. Training isn't the rote process operant conditioning implies it is, but a two-being interaction between human and dog.

A training method I use a great deal is *targeting*, which takes advantage of the dog's instinctive tendency to respond to, follow, and move toward sound and movement. Targeting can involve the trainer's body, voice, and particularly arms, hands, and fingers. Any sound or movement used to get the dog to position its body, in whole or part, is targeting. It can be a simple clucking sound to get the dog's attention or an elaborate signal to focus it in a specific direction. Starting with obvious movements at first, you can over time refine your dog's response to smaller and more subtle movements later. Targeting is commonly used to train a dog to heel — that is, to walk alongside the handler's leg — by patting that leg with the open hand (Fig. 1, next page). The dog is drawn to both the movement of the hand and to the sound of hand on leg (Fig. 2). The patting isn't a command; it is instead an enticement, a way of getting the dog's attention and focusing it. When it moves with you as you say the spoken command, you praise your pet, supplying the reinforcement that forms the learning association in dog mind.

Targeting can be used to teach "down" by patting the ground in front of the dog until it lies down on its own (see page 188). "Shake hands" is often taught by holding your hand out in front of the sitting dog's chest and moving it slightly or snapping your fingers, to induce the dog to raise its own paw. Synchronization can be combined with targeting to

Fig.1 Targeting

Fig. 2 Targeting

teach "sit" or "down." Leaning over your dog and getting your own body closer to the ground both entices the animal — which is targeting — and invites the same action — which is synchronization.

Modeling is more specific, in that you actually manipulate or move the dog's body to show it what you want. "Sit" can be taught to some dogs by simply pushing their rumps to the ground when the command is given. "Shake hands" may require more than targeting, such as actu-

ally picking the dog's paw up. That's modeling. So is teaching "down" by scooping a sitting dog's paws out from under it to get it into the down position (see page 125). "Stand" can be modeled by holding the standing dog up with the hand under the belly, which prevents it from sitting down. Dogs vary in their individual ability to learn from modeling, with some picking it up better than others. With certain dogs and certain commands, modeling is very effective.

In *reflex learning*, the trainer uses the dog's own natural physical reflexes — like the human knee jerk — to show what is wanted. When a dog bumps its nose, for example, it reflexively stops forward movement. One way to teach the "wait" command is to bump the dog's nose when it walks forward past the boundary you have drawn. The dog stops in reflexive response to the bump, and you praise it for stopping, building the association. Reflex learning is used in one method of teaching the "sit" command. When the handler says, "Sit," he or she pops the dog's rump with the open hand. Moving away from the hand, the dog reflexively puts its rump down — which earns it a reward of praise. With repetition, the resulting posture is associated with the verbal "sit," and the dog learns the command. Pinching the ear makes the dog open its mouth, one way to teach the initial stages of the retrieve. Reflex learning can be combined with targeting to teach "sit" by holding a delicious treat just over your dog's head. The dog sits

Fig. 3 Targeting

Fig. 4 Targeting

Fig. 5 Targeting

(reflex) in order to look up at the treat over its head (targeting).

Association is used in various teaching approaches, but *association training* is the name given to a specific method, one that rewards a natural tendency in the dog and encourages it to associate that tendency with a command. Essentially, you catch the dog in the act, enthusiastically interject the command connected with the very thing the dog is doing at the moment, and reward it for success.

Say you want to teach "down," and you have just been playing with your dog, who is tired and ready to rest. As you notice it beginning to lie down on its own, you say, "Down," once or twice in an encouraging, upbeat voice. Then, the moment your pet actually puts its whole body down on the floor, you praise with "Good dog," or "Thank you." Repeat this procedure every time you see your pet preparing to lie down by itself, and soon it will associate the action, the command, and the praise.

What if your pet lies down so quickly you don't have time to give the command? And what if verbalizing the command distracts the dog, which promptly stops lying down and looks at you quizzically? In either case, omit giving the command and wait until the dog downs itself, then reward or praise enthusiastically. In time your pet will down on its own to win praise, having associated that action with a reward. Now you can start adding "down" and furthering the association.

Association training is time-consuming, but valuable. The positive reinforcement encourages your pet to figure out what it is doing to earn your praise, and in time it will discover that connection and make the association. Every new association speeds the learning of the next and quickens the overall training process.

DOGS learn in not one of these ways, but all of them. As a teacher I have learned to use an eclectic approach that relies sometimes on synchronization, sometimes on targeting, sometimes on modeling, sometimes on association training, and sometimes on reflex learning. There is no one right way or perfect methodology, only a bag of tricks to choose from in order to meet the requirements of the situation. The choice of approach depends on what you are trying to teach — that is, which part of the dog's autonomic or conscious system you need to affect. Obviously, teaching problem solving, which involves the cognitive brain centers, is of a different order than housebreaking, which is autonomic and reflexive. Each requires different educational tools.

Paying attention to what works for you and your dog is critically important. The most essential factor in achieving successful management of your dog is cultivating an immediate awareness of your own intuitive and instinctive emotional processes. If it works for you and your dog, then do it, no matter what the methodology.

Putting Things Together

Humans and dogs are born knowing how to associate variables in the environment. In my example of the puppy and the rosebush, the pup immediately associates the plant with the prick on the nose. *Association* lies at the core of all the ways dogs learn, from trial and error to insight.

Teaching your pet to sit is a good and simple example of how association works in training. First, you get the dog's attention, perhaps by calling its name and having it walk over to you. Now you give the "sit" command and at the same time push the dog's rump down to the ground so that the dog ends up in the sitting posture. You repeat this process two or three times, saying, "Sit," and simultaneously pushing the dog's bottom earthward. Each time, you praise the dog for sitting, scratching its chest or ears and cooing happily over it. Depending on your approach, the dog's capability and temperament, distractions in the environment, and so forth, your dog will begin to sit when you give the verbal command alone. At this point the dog has associated the sound of the word *sit* with the physical posture, and the command has been taught. As you can see, association forms the basis of successful training.

Sometimes the dog's ability to form associations works against you. For example, many people mistakenly think that when their pets do something objectionable, such as getting into the garbage, the thing to do is call the dog to you and correct it. The first time you call, your dog will come, but when you correct, the dog will learn to associate the command "come" with the correction it receives. The next time you call your pet, it will refuse to come, based on the association of "come" with the correction. That refusal — which I have heard people cite as proof of their pet's stupidity — is just the opposite. The dog is in fact displaying its intelligence and ability to discriminate.

Dogs form associations well beyond the area of motor skill learning. Canines, for example, have an internal clock, and they quickly associate times of the day with activities. If your schedule is regular and predictable, your dog quickly and accurately puts particular hours together with significant events like your departure to and return from work, its dinner of kibble, and your long walk together in the park.

Dogs also associate objects with their uses. I had a friend whose Labrador loved to backpack with him. Whenever he pulled his pack out of the closet, his dog became hugely excited and tried to climb into the car. She knew the pack meant a trip was imminent, and she wanted to make sure he didn't take off for the mountains without her.

Generalization is an aspect of association. When you are training your dog to sit, you can't say in words that you expect your pet to follow the command each and every time you give it, wherever the two of you

Fig. 1 Modeling

Fig. 2 Modeling

happen to be. When the dog first learns the command, it associates the time and place of the training as well as the word *sit* with the physical posture. You have to go beyond this, by educating your dog to the idea that "sit" applies always and everywhere. In educating a dog to generalize, you are also helping it to be versatile — that is, to handle a variety of situations and circumstances — and to learn how to solve problems on its own.

To generalize a command like "sit," you need to train your pet on

Fig. 2 Generalizing

Fig. 3 Generalizing

Fig. 1 Generalizing

different surfaces, in different situations, at different times of the day, with different tones of voice. Dogs are intensely specific creatures adept at equally specific associations. Suppose you always train the "sit" command under the same circumstances — in the kitchen, on the linoleum floor, after you get home from work, leaf through the mail, throw out the junk ads and put the bills on your desk, take your dinner out of the freezer, and pop it into the microwave. You are indeed training your pet to sit, but only in the kitchen, on the linoleum floor, after you get home from work, leaf through the mail, throw out the junk ads and put the bills on your desk, take your dinner out of the freezer, and pop it into the microwave. So when you go out for a walk on Saturday morning after breakfast and try to put your dog on a sit while you chitchat with the neighbor down the street, and your dog just stands there with its "What was that?" look in its eyes, it isn't disobeying. It simply has not generalized the "sit" command. Because the dog has been trained under only one specific set of circumstances, it hasn't had the opportunity to learn that "sit" includes Saturday morning walks and neighborly chats as well as in the kitchen, on the linoleum floor, after you get home from work, leaf through the mail, throw out the junk ads and put the bills on your desk, take your dinner out of the freezer, and pop it into the microwave.

Since dogs are good at generalizing, you don't have to introduce them to every possible circumstance. Instead, you need to present the dog with enough variety to give it the message that training comes in various forms and is not regulated by the clock, the weather, or the geography. "Sit" means "sit," whenever, wherever, whyever.

When behaviors are consistently associated with other behaviors, they form *patterns*. Patterns are central to the ways both dogs and humans learn. Typically, patterns arise for some good and important reason in the moment, but soon they become self-sustaining even if the original reason no longer applies. For example, you probably get up pretty much the same way every morning. Once upon a time there may have been a meaningful explanation for why you always brush your teeth before you take a shower, rather than the other way around. But now that's just the way you do things, which has its own logic and lasting power.

When a pattern forms, a trained or synchronized behavior becomes habitual without direct input. If you get up with an alarm clock at the same early hour all week long but sleep in on weekends, your dog is likely to grow restless at the usual alarm time. That's a pattern. Likewise, if you repeatedly tell your dog to go to a particular spot in the house and stay while you eat dinner, soon it will go there on its own without command.

Reinforcement

Learning in dogs is largely self-motivated. Dogs want to learn, and their very nature drives them to investigate their world and learn from it. Learning requires feedback; the student has to know whether he or she has achieved the desired result. Since you yourself cannot tell the dog what you want it to learn, you must guide its learning by means of your interactions. This is what reinforcement is all about. Since dogs can't talk, you have to show them, largely through your actions, what you want — and don't want. Reinforcement lets you do that. It gives you a way of "talking" to your dog and molding its behavior into desired patterns. Positive reinforcement tells your dog which behaviors you want, and motivates it to do them again. Negative reinforcement tells your dog which behaviors you don't want, and motivates it to cease them.

Once your dog has been trained for a time, you can put some of the responsibility for right behavior on its shoulders. But in the beginning stages particularly, it is your task as the handler to motivate and reinforce your pet.

The word *reinforcement* is borrowed from the language of operant conditioning. Also called praise and reward, positive reinforcement includes any method that encourages your dog to do what you ask and lets it know it has succeeded. Positive reinforcement makes your dog want to repeat the activity. In the techni-

Appreciation is an important motivator.

you want. You give the command "sit," the dog sits, and you give it a treat. Positive reinforcement says, "That's right," in various ways, including words. An association is forming.

Suppose the dog doesn't sit and you say, "No," firmly and meaningfully. The "no" is a negative experience, one the dog wants to put an end to. This is a negative reinforcer, one that tells the dog you don't want it doing what it is doing at this very moment — in this case, ignoring your order to sit. So it sits, at which point you give it the positive reinforcement of a chest-scratch or a treat, telling your pet it has done the right thing.

Praise Repays

The actual act of giving a command should be objective and emotion-free. You want your dog to hear it and do it. You are the leader of the pack, your dog is the follower, and its job is to obey your command. Your dog will do its assigned task because it expects that a reward will follow success. You are the one responsible for defining the task the dog is to do, for letting it know that it did what you wanted, and for showing appreciation of its success. This is the essence of training.

You yourself are really no different. When you take on some project at school or work because it was assigned to you by a leader, just completing it is insufficient reward. You want to know from the leader that

cal language of learning theory, motivation refers to encouragement to perform, while praise, reinforcement, and reward describe the feedback. However, a good feedback system also serves as a motivator for the next round of training, and so I combine the terms.

Positive reinforcers are rewards, like a vigorous chest-scratching or a treat, and they tell your pet what your work is valuable and appreciated. Point to someone you admire as a group leader — whether a corporate CEO, a symphony conductor, or a football coach — and you'll be pointing to someone expert at communicating appreciation for success to his or her followers.

For dogs, too, appreciation is an important motivator. You can communicate it in a variety of ways — by light touching, vigorous petting and rubbing, enthusiasm and heartiness in the voice, softness and gentleness in the voice, a bright smile with an encouraging voice, food treats, games (chasing a tennis ball or Frisbee, running together, tugging on a knotted rope), roughhousing, or combining any two motivators, like gentle touch with soft voice.

Food treats do make good positive reinforcers, but they need to be used sparingly and carefully. Choose only a food your dog really likes and one you can serve in such small pieces that your pet can take it down in one gulp. Cheese cut into small cubes is an example. Remember: This is a reward, not an extra meal. Also, time and energy your dog spends chewing is time and energy taken away from attention to training.

All reinforcers are ways of giving praise, of telling the dog how much you appreciate what it has done. The particular kind of praise you apply has a lot to do with your dog's makeup. Reinforcers have to be stimulating and titillating to the particular dog. If your pet is prima-

rily auditory, spoken motivators are the most effective. If it loves touch, then petting and rubbing are called for. As you work with your dog, watch for the kind of motivator that best gets its attention.

The dog's style makes a difference, too. Some animals are so soft and sensitive that enthusiastic rubbing combined with a strong voice would make them shrink in fear. Others are so strong-willed and physically insensitive that only vigorous touching, a loud voice, and hard-played games qualify as turn-ons. Anything less such dogs won't even notice.

The revolving wheel of centrifugal force comes very much into play in choosing and measuring praise. Any time you motivate and positively reinforce your dog, you are intensifying its feelings and moving it closer to the rim. As a result, you need to pay attention to your intuition and select a form of reinforcement that works in the current situation. For example, if you are reinforcing an already excited dog, you probably don't want to set the wheel spinning so fast that it catapults your pet off into space. Instead, put out a quiet but sincere message about how pleased you are, perhaps with a quiet voice and soft stroking of the ears. Your dog will know it has done well, but the praise won't send it flying out of the emotional ballpark.

What's going on in the moment matters, too. Say you have a dog who is usually motivated by nothing more than a soft voice and a gentle pat on the head. In a high-energy environment, like the sidelines during your child's championship soccer game, with excited parents and kids jumping and screaming, softness won't get through. You'll have to raise the praise level just to connect with your pet. Mood matters as well. At the end of a long day, a very tired dog will likely need more motivation than the quiet praise that worked earlier, when its energy level was high. An excited voice and an enthusiastic stroke or two under the chin might be required.

Here are a few basic guidelines to keep in mind:

- If your dog is fawning, use voice, not touch, to praise.
- If your dog is showing fear or has just been frightened, speak loudly and confidently and touch vigorously.
- If your dog is highly energized, keep your voice quiet and your touch light. The animal is already motivated enough on its own.
- If your dog tends to be resentful or is showing resentment right now, use an excited and vibrant voice. Do not acknowledge or reward your pet's resentment by playing to it.

For positive reinforcers to work, they must be given at every successful completion of the command in the initial stages of training. For example, when you are teaching "sit,"

a good chest-scratching after every success in the first few training sessions is called for. But once the teaching has sunk in and the association forms, reinforcement should be scaled back to verbal praise at each success with chest-scratching every now and again. You want to keep things interesting and just a little unpredictable. If you reward your pet with chest-scratching each time at every training session, constant reinforcement becomes the norm and its motivating power is lost. Intermittent reinforcement arouses the dog's desire by keeping it in a state of expectation and anticipation. The situation is something like playing a slot machine. The first time you get lucky, bells ring and the money falls out. So you keep sitting there, feeding in more quarters, pulling that one arm again and again, hoping for the next reward —which, you will notice, never arrives when you expect. In the same way, reinforcement focuses your dog's attention on learning, and intermittent reinforcement after learning retains the reinforcer's power to motivate.

Another thing about positive reinforcement: shake things up. If you usually use chest-scratching, try a food treat every now and then or throw in a game of Frisbee for a complete change of pace. Just because a particular form of praise worked two minutes ago doesn't mean it will work again, right now. Dogs love the new and abhor the boring, so the same old thing only works for so long. Variety is the spice that makes praise work over time.

These basic guidelines about using praise with your dog will help:

- Praise should encourage your dog to repeat what it just did.
- Connect the type and level of praise to the dog's temperament, its mood of the moment, and the emotional environment. The whole point is to make the dog feel happy and good about itself in the here-and-now.
- Keep it varied. Don't let your manner of praising become the same old boring thing.
- When you are teaching something new or the dog is tired, praise your pet for getting close to what you want. If your dog has high energy or if the command is already familiar, require more precision before praising.
- Be sincere. If you fake praise, your dog will see through the deception and mirror your own insincerity the next time you give that command.
- Praise is given only after a command is completed. Should you praise before the action is finished, your dog may stop midway through its performance. Use praise as you would the phrase "thank you" with a human — that is, only after the task is finished. In fact, I often use "thank you" to give praise

as a way of ensuring that I await the completion of the command.

- Sometimes motivators are needed to encourage your dog to follow the command as you request. You can also use motivators to get and hold your dog's attention as you give a command.

Correction's Rightful Role

Spend some time watching a group of dogs and chances are you will see one of them tell another what not to do by growling, body bumping, display fighting, or, if the point fails to get across, by outright conflict. In all my tens of thousands of hours of dog watching, I can't remember a single example of one dog telling another what to do. They cajole, entice, and encourage through body language, barking, and facial expression, but they never tell each other what to do. Actually, they don't have to. Because of their pack psychology, capacity to synchronize, and observational learning, canines generally do what the pack needs. If one of them exceeds the boundaries of the allowable, the pack leader tells the offending animal about it in no uncertain terms. It's a clear message about what not to do.

It seems probable that the original human-canine relationship worked the same way. When the hunter-gatherers of fifteen thousand years ago who first domesticated dogs hung meat out to dry, they told their pets not to help themselves. Dogs who disobeyed likely didn't live long. This selection process favored individual animals who paid attention as closely to humans as to the canine pack leaders, and it probably opened the way to the training of dogs to do everything from hunting quail to pulling wheelchairs. That has been a positive development. The downside, though, is we humans sometimes assume we can correct a dog into doing what we want. This is a mistaken idea. Correction, also known as negative reinforcement, is best left to its original purpose, which is telling a dog what not to do.

Correction is an effective way of delivering information to dog mind. Correction is never punishment. I have read that dogsledders in the Klondike days considered it standard practice to beat their teams, thinking this maltreatment instilled character in the animals. That was and is nonsense. Beating is abuse, pure and simple, and it instills only fear and anxiety. Under no circumstance do I recommend that you punish, abuse, or physically maltreat any dog.

Punishment occurs some time after an incident and is therefore not associated with it in dog mind. By definition, punishment doesn't stop when the behavior stops. Negative reinforcement does. Essentially, punishment is a way for a human to vent his or her destructive feelings on a canine, not to solve a problem. Negative reinforcement entails no dumping of emotion, and it does indeed aim to solve a problem by conveying clear information about what not to do.

You can often distinguish punishment from correction by the attitude of the person administering it. Punishment often entails anger ("I'll teach you, you little —") or self-righteous retribution ("You deserve it, and I'm only doing this for your own good anyway"). Anger has nothing to do with correction; in fact, for reasons we will discuss in chapter 8, it confuses the dog. Correction is introduced to the dog as a learning tool that is administered coolly and objectively, with neither rage nor retribution, and it learns that the appropriate response to correction is to change its current behavior. You are not trying to say to the dog, "You are bad!" Anger sends exactly that message; it mires the dog in bad feelings and distracts it from looking at its own behavior to discover and fix what is wrong.

Correction in the proper form is information. It tells the dog that whatever it is doing now — such as standing after the "sit" command is given — is unacceptable. Correction can involve pain or the threat of pain. In dog mind, though, pain is not limited to physical discomfort. It also includes emotional distress, such as the feeling that the master is unhappy with the dog's behavior. Since the drive toward synchronization is so strong in canines, the mere feeling that they are out of sync causes pain and constitutes a sort of correction.

Let me give you an example of the appropriate use of correction. Your dog has been trained to sit on command and it has shown it knows what to do. You start a training session, with your pet apparently fully alert and listening to directions, yet when you say, "Sit," the dog just stands there without response. Immediately you say, "No!" with authority. That tells your dog it is doing something wrong — that is, not paying attention to you. The instant it does pay attention, by turning its eyes to you, you praise it, for doing the right thing. The likelihood is that, because of the correction and the praise, your pet will become more attuned to you and responsive to commands.

Correction delivered in an unemotional manner that's quick and to the point sends the dog information, like the authoritative "no" for the pet who is not paying attention. As soon as the dog becomes attentive, you praise it, charging the interaction with the very emotion missing from the correction. The correction told the dog clearly what you didn't want, and the praise encourages the behavior you do want.

When a correction is delivered in the right way, the dog looks to you for direction. Its mood becomes intense, interested, and questioning. Dogs like leadership and direction, and appropriate correction strengthens the relationship between human and canine.

There are a number of different kinds of correction to choose from. The right one depends on who you are, who your dog is, and what the problem happens to be. The following are the basic types of correction, both nonphysical and physical:

Nonphysical corrections:

- *"No!"* The more authoritative your tone of voice, the stronger the correction. "No!" affects a dog emotionally very much the same way that a firm talking-to affects a child.
- *Use other words or spoken sounds.* If your dog walks into you or steps on your foot because it isn't paying attention, say, "Ouch!" Employ a noise or word appropriate to the situation. A guttural "ah!" or "aw!" is a good choice.
- *Loud noises.* Clap your hands hard, or slap the flat of your palm against a table or counter. The idea is to use the dog's sensitivity to sound to shock its hearing and bring its attention to you.
- *Time-out.* Ignore your dog completely or remove it from the current setting. Since dogs learn in mere tenths of seconds, a time-out must be administered immediately for the canine to make the association and for the correction to be effective.

Physical corrections:

- *Body bumps.* Use your knee or elbow against the dog's body. Be forceful enough to get your dog's attention.

- *Shake the dog down.* Face the dog and grasp its neck ruff firmly. To the dog this feels like having someone shake your shoulders, and it approximates what a pack leader does to a disobedient follower in the wild.
- *Bump the dog under the chin.* Make a fist and give the dog a firm bump, either under the lower jaw or into the soft part of the nose.
- *Jerk and release the choke chain.* To a dog, a choke chain correction feels like someone pulling you up short by your suspenders and then letting go. We will discuss correct choke chain technique in greater detail in chapter 9.

Obviously, this list is like a ladder of escalation. Saying "No!" is less correction than a hard jerk-and-release on the choke chain. But don't use this list by starting at the bottom and working up, until you find a correction that works. The key to correcting effectively is giving just the right correction the first time.

Correction should match the dog's infraction. The hand bump under the chin, because it closes the jaws together, is an excellent correction for mouth offenses, like barking at visitors or eating from the garbage can. A loud "ouch!" corrects for canine clumsiness that gets you stepped on — no small matter if you're training a Saint Bernard or an Irish wolfhound. I reserve choke chain corrections and shake-downs

for clear-cut dominance issues only — never, never for confusion, uncertainty, or ignorance in the dog — and I make sure the dog cannot misunderstand my meaning. "I am the leader here," I am saying in response to canine rebellion, "and you *will* pay attention to me." Likewise, a choke chain correction is a good way to stop an unwanted display of aggression against another dog, because it reminds your pet who the leader is — you, and you alone.

The second aspect of selecting the correct correction is to be aware of the individual dog's temperament and emotional makeup. Remember Zack, Tim's hard-nosed, physically tough, highly expressive Labrador from chapters 4 and 5. Zack was such a rough-and-tumble dog he didn't even notice a light-voiced "no." He required strong verbal or physical correction — a loud noise or a harsh "no!," occasionally a quick jerk-and-release of the choke chain. Snow, Louise's softer-temperament poodle, however, was more sensitive and rarely required a choke chain correction. Usually Louise had only to say, "No," clearly and quietly, and Snow got back into line.

If you correct too severely for your dog's temperament, the behavior you want to stop may or may not change, but the overcorrection will lead to new problems. For example, your pet may cower or appear confused. Likewise, if you correct too lightly, the dog will remain stuck in the problem behavior without changing. Amiable dogs abhor correction and will work very hard to avoid it. As long as you have the dog's attention, a sharp "no" is a strong correction to an amiable. Analyticals stand up better to correction, amending their ways immediately, but an unjust negative reinforcement sends them into orbit. Because they are so much more assertive and tend to test boundaries, drivers and expressives typically require more correction than analyticals or amiables.

Understand that there is no such thing as a partial correction. Either you correct or you don't, and if you correct, you need to use the correction necessary to achieve the behavior change you want. Correcting too lightly turns into nagging, which feeds resistance and even more problem behavior. Correcting too severely turns into punishment.

Where nagging ends and correction begins, and where correction ends and punishment begins, depends in part on your dog. And it also depends on your personality.

Because they want to be liked and are generally not highly assertive, people classified as amiables find correction uncomfortable. They tend to deliver too little negative reinforcement, and descend into nagging rather than correction. Since they too are not highly assertive, analyticals are often uncomfortable with correction. But since they are thoughtful people, they might mull the issue over and decide to correct — possibly too late. Similar mistiming may happen with the praise that must follow correction, and the praise may also be lower key than necessary. Since drivers are impatient, their timing is excellent, but they may overdo correction and forget how important it is to follow up with praise. Expressives are both impatient and enthusiastic, so they are perhaps the best equipped to correct well. Sometimes expressives are too harsh and too quick to correct, but their powerful personalities are so attractive to canines that resentment or fear is usually forgotten.

Mix, Match, and Timing

Study after study, including research done by myself and my associates, shows that the most effective training mixes positive and negative reinforcement. Positive reinforcement alone does inform the dog of what you want, but it leads the animal to anticipate performance rather than wait for the command. For example, the dog sits before you tell it to. As a result, positive reinforcement alone fails to establish your leadership. Your dog is doing what it wants to get the reward it craves, and it is not following your lead. Also, with positive reinforcement alone, the dog performs only for the reward and displays little or no interest in the performance itself. As for negative reinforcement used by itself, it is something like going to jail, an unpleasant experience that creates fear, resistance, and apprehension in the dog. Mixing positive and negative reinforcement together creates the most effective emotional learning environment for your dog and the strongest relationship between you and your pet. Negative reinforcement demands that your dog pay attention to the task at hand and follow your leadership, and positive reinforcement develops your pet's desire to do the task.

Shaping, which uses both positive and negative reinforcement, can be used effectively as part of any teaching approach and for managing your dog in general. Studies of the educational process in children show that learning through discovery is important. The same, I am sure, applies to dogs, and shaping is a method of guiding the canine's discovery through a process of trial and error in which you provide feedback in the form of positive and negative reinforcement. In a way, mixing negative and positive reinforcement serves as a learning game. Like a red light, correction means "stop," and praise is a green light or "go." You alternate reds and greens based on the appropriateness of your dog's actions and shape its behavior as surely as traffic lights control the flow of cars, trucks, and things that go.

Teaching "sit" serves again as a ood example. You say, "Sit," and your dog — who perhaps has learned the command only tentatively and needs reinforcement, or who knows it yet has chosen to ignore you — fails to respond. Imme-diately you intercede with the negative reinforcer "no" said over and over in different tones and tempos, and you give the "sit" command now and again. The negative reinforcer tells the dog you are unhappy with its performance, and "sit" provides direction. Upset by the negatives coming at it, your dog will seek a solution, perhaps running through a repertoire of behaviors to find the right one, perhaps sitting right away. In either case, the moment the dog begins to sit, you stop saying, "No," and instead pronounce an enthusiastic "That's it!" to tell your pet it's on track. Should your dog falter, go back to the "no"'s until it starts to respond correctly again, then switch to "That's it!" When the dog completes the whole command, respond even more enthusiastically, adding physical praise if the dog has had a particularly hard time.

In this type of shaping, you create a negative environment when the command is not being carried out. The dog will find this emotional setting not to its liking, and it will try to change the feeling by seeking out the correct action. When it discovers the right response, relief from the negative reinforcement and the pleasure of the positive reinforcement instills knowledge of the correct response plus the desire to do it right — and even faster — at the next opportunity.

I strongly suggest you use "no" rather than other forms of correction to create a negative environment in such situations. Admittedly, your pet will not respond immediately because it still must understand this new approach, and you too must learn how to make it work. If one or two "no"'s aren't enough, keep at it. You may need to say, "No," over and over, alternating it with the original command, while your dog tries to figure out what you're after. Be patient; this will work. Once your pet discovers how the negative environment evaporates in favor of a positive one as soon as it demonstrates the right response — in this case, sitting on command — it will be eager to comply. You will be pleasantly surprised at the new-found willingness and speed in your pet's response, and you will be delighted to find the need for harsh physical correction eliminated.

Whether reinforcement is positive or negative or a combination of both, timing in delivery is critical. You need to ensure that the dog grasps the association between the reinforcement, either negative or positive, and the behavior. Since dog mind works so fast — remember, there is little time-consuming cognitive processing going on — reinforcement must follow completion of the task practically instantaneously. When you're teaching "sit," you cannot wait till the end of the training session to reward your dog for getting it. Don't reward before the command is completely executed, though, for the dog will learn to do only the portion of the

command leading up to the reward. If you praise the dog at the first wiggle of its rump in the direction of the floor, it will stop right there and learn no more. Likewise, negative reinforcement well after the fact doesn't work. In dog mind, it looks like random punishment completely unassociated with anything the animal was or was not doing.

There are two other timing aspects of learning in dog mind you should know about. One is that dogs need to rest between training sessions because time-off consolidates learning. Often I have worked with a dog who experienced difficulty, let the animal sleep on it, then gone back to training the same command in the morning, and discovered that the canine had figured it out and was now doing what I wanted. Apparently, dog mind creates associations among experiences during time-off, in essence learning during rest or sleep. I find this terrifically exciting because it shows how dog mind works on its own, quite outside human control or intention.

The other issue is that dogs do not learn at a constant rate over a number of training sessions. You may find your dog coming along nicely, only to stall or even slip backward and seemingly forget what it has learned. These plateaus in the learning curve are normal, and actually indicate progress. Theories about these plateaus vary, but I think two things are going on. First, the dog is likely losing interest. It has figured out what it needs to do, so now the whole process feels boring. Second, the dog may recognize, at least subconsciously, that it is surrendering control to you and it is making a last-minute effort to hold back before giving in. When you and your dog hit a plateau, keep going. Restrain your own frustration or impatience, but keep training your pet to its level of knowledge. In time, depending on the dog's personality, it will move on to the next learning phase.

Learning in Dog Mind

Now let's put this together. I want to show you how all the aspects of learning we have been discussing apply in training your dog to a simple command. "Sit" is a good place to begin, because it is an easy command to teach and one of the first most dogs learn.

The first requirement is to associate the physical sitting action with the word *sit*. Say, "Sit," then show your dog how by pushing its rump down to the ground. This is modeling. As you model the action and push down the rump, repeat the word "sit," thereby building the association. Also, you are leaning over the dog as you push its rump down, and the arch of your body is a form of targeting.

Praise your dog for getting its rump down as if it sat down all by itself. Positive reinforcement develops motivation and encourages the dog to learn.

Now repeat these steps of association, modeling, targeting, and reinforcement, watching the dog carefully to see if it begins to sit on its own, without your physical intervention. If it does start to sit, avoid touching the dog further until its movement fails. Only then should you take over, moving as smoothly as possible to avoid any obvious break between the dog's actions and yours in finishing the sit. On the next go-round, your dog will do even more itself. As the dog gets closer and closer to full compliance, continue to reinforce each step in its progress even if you have to help it complete the command. This maintains the motivation and tells your pet it is doing okay.

Once your pet demonstrates the ability to do the full command in response to the word alone — be patient; this will happen — reinforce its success enthusiastically. You want your dog to know you are truly pleased, and enthusiasm communicates that it has gotten the whole thing.

Now you can start to eliminate targeting. Lean over less and less at each successive exercise until you are standing fully upright when you say, "Sit." This eliminates the body posture cue and teaches your pet to associate sitting with only the verbal command "sit." That's important, so you can tell your dog to sit even when you can't lean over it. It also demands more of your dog, since in dog mind it is much more difficult to respond to the word alone than to targeting's physical cues.

Here comes the inevitable plateau in the learning curve. Usually, once the dog has demonstrated its ability to respond, it refuses to obey. The dog is in essence saying that this is a game, not a command, and can't we please go do something different now? You need to tell the dog in no uncertain terms that "sit" is a command and refusal is unacceptable. Time has come for a correction, ranging from a series of "no!"'s to a choke chain jerk. Be ready for this and give the correction immediately, then reinforce the dog positively the very instant it complies.

With the full command learned, you can help your dog generalize by having it respond in a variety of settings. This teaches the dog that "sit" means "sit" always and everywhere.

Tighten up performance standards as progress continues, using both targeting and shaping techniques. Early on, sloppy is okay. As your dog gets it, you can expect more and more precision. Shaping through positive and negative reinforcements communicates your expectations.

When the command is fully learned and performance is up to snuff, reduce positive reinforcement. Limit praise to those times when the dog's performance is outstanding or when it was truly difficult for the dog to comply — for example, when it sits perfectly in the presence of three good-friend dogs who want to play. At this stage in learning, constant reinforcement loses its significance and becomes merely ordinary and expected. To make praise significant, you need to keep it unexpected and unique. Your dog shouldn't know what is coming, when, or how much.

Be sure to end every training session on a positive note. If it has been a rough session, go back to something the dog knows well and reinforce its success. This supplies motivation for the next training session.

As training progresses, you will discover that other aspects of your relationship with your dog change. It may look to you for leadership at times when it used to go off on its own. And you may find your pet synchronizing more closely with you, anticipating your actions and flowing along with them. This deeper bonding is one of training's many benefits and joys.

Chapter 8

Setting

How Relationship and Emotion Affect Canine Learning

*B*EFORE you can begin to train your dog, you must instill a sense of security in your pet about its continued survival. Simply, a dog has to know where its next meal is coming from and where it will sleep tonight before it is centered enough to make training possible.

Survival needs greatly influence canine behavior. Like humans, dogs require food, water, shelter, and safety. If any one of these needs is not met, the dog will direct its activity toward satisfying that need. Wild canids spend much of their day seeking or preparing to seek food and water. In human society dogs can't launch out on their own to hunt wild game or dig dens for the night. We humans must meet their needs for the basics.

Supplying a dog with food and

water is obvious enough and easy. Satisfying its need for safety and security is more complex — but equally necessary.

Setting and consistently enforcing rules for your dog tells it the world is safe, because you are the leader in charge and will therefore provide for its needs. Love and praise also add to security. If, instead, you take your anger out on your dog, or if you are inconsistent in what you ask of it and how you react, you are sowing mistrust and insecurity in your pet.

Say you leave for work in a heated rush one morning and forget to fill your dog's water dish. Or maybe you come home late after a tough day and fall into bed without feeding your pet. In either case, the trust your dog places in you erodes; you are failing to meet the animal's needs. Continue this pattern of neglect, and soon your dog will do whatever it must to survive. If your dog's sense of frustration grows because you do nothing to win its trust back, it may well take to chewing, digging, or running away to express its insecurity.

Caring for your dog's basic needs does not require you to live your life according to its schedule. But your dog must come to trust that, no matter how hectic your day, you will devote some of your time — even if it's just a little bit — to care for, love, praise, and play with your pet.

Provide for your dog first. Then you can ask your dog to provide for you.

Fears and Phobias

What upsets dogs, robs them of their sense of security, and leaves them anxious and fearful? The answer is simple. The same kinds of things that bother you at work, in school, or in a relationship also upset your dog in its relationship with you.

If your boss, teacher, or spouse launches into you with an undeserved tongue-lashing, your first response will be confusion, followed by fear, anxiety, and insecurity. The same thing holds for your pet. If you come home after a tough day and yell at your pet for no particular reason other than your own pent-up feelings, it will be confused. The dog knows it is being yelled at, but it can't figure out why it merits such ill treatment. Besides confusion, your pet feels as if it has failed at its job of being your dog. Keep up the yelling and your pet's continuing sense of failure will lead to insecurity. An emotionally insecure dog is as difficult to train as one whose physical needs are not met. Fearing that it will continue to fail, your pet will be hard put to follow your commands.

Dogs reflect their owners' insecurities and anxieties, as well as their strengths. Emotionally, your dog knows what gets to you; deception on your part is impossible. You can try to put on a happy face when you've got the blues, but your dog won't buy the act. It knows how you feel inside, despite your attempted concealment. That lack of candor can also lead to insecurity in the

New and unusual sounds attract a dog's attention.

dog, who loses trust in you as the leader of the pack emotionally.

As a result, one of the most important aspects of working with your dog is paying particular attention to the things that upset you. Stay aware of your feelings, particularly ones of insecurity and fear. And don't bluff; your dog always knows what cards you're holding.

Distractions and Attention-Getters

The dog has been taken from the wild, but the wild has yet to be taken from the dog. Like the wild animals from whom they are descended, dogs rely on powerful instinctive reactions to their surroundings in order to find prey, sense danger, and tend social relationships in the pack. Because they are such instinctive creatures, dogs are much more attuned to external stimuli than we humans are. We tend to think through our days; your dog sees, hears, feels, and smells its life. And although these sensory responses can be shaped somewhat by training, they are an inborn and given part of dog mind.

Dogs see in black and white

rather than color, so you'll never come across a group of canines in the Louvre admiring the *Mona Lisa*. But let a loose cat race through the museum and all the dogs will chase after it. Visually, dogs respond to color and composition much less than to movement and motion, which draws them into the chase. Hunters that they are, dogs respond to anything running as if it is a possible meal. If it moves, it will attract your dog's attention. And if it keeps moving, your dog will be drawn to pursue.

Hearing is highly acute in dogs, who can detect frequencies well above the normal human range. Dogs are constantly listening to what is going on around them, attentive to clues about basic needs like food and prey. Novelty is all. New and unusual sounds attract a dog's attention much more than old and familiar ones.

Canines are also tactile, responding strongly to touch. Dogs groom themselves and each other with great relish, and touching is a central way wild canids cultivate relationships in the pack. The same goes for humans and dogs. Touch can and should be a central aspect of your relationship with your dog. And, as we will see further on in this chapter, massaging your dog is an excellent foundation for training.

It is in the sensory arena of smell that dogs come into their greatest glory. Dogs enjoy an acuity and discrimination of smell humans can only begin to imagine. There is a

A dog will constantly sniff air and ground for clues about its surroundings.

depth of experience here we can recognize but not share. Wherever you take your dog on excursions and outings, it will constantly sniff air and ground for clues about its surroundings. As with hearing, new and unusual odors will draw canine attention more than the usual and everyday.

It is important that you come to understand which stimuli in the environment can attract your dog's attention — that is, you need to enter dog mind with your senses. There are two pragmatic purposes to this task. The first is to become aware of distractions that can intrude on training and sidetrack the process. The second is to understand how to get and hold your dog's attention, which is an essential part of training.

A distraction is any stimulus that draws your dog's attention away from what you want it to be doing.

If you're letting your dog romp in the backyard and it is running all over, sniffing every square inch of ground, smell is no distraction because you're allowing the animal to follow its nose as part of playtime. But if you want your dog to walk by your side on leash down a busy sidewalk and it turns aside to sniff a half-eaten pastrami sandwich discarded in the gutter, then smell indeed becomes a distraction.

The best way to deal with distractions is to be aware of them *before* they pull your dog's attention away from the task at hand. Ideally, you should become so attuned to dog mind that you spot the pastrami sandwich before your dog does and prepare yourself in advance to counter the tug on the leash as it lunges out to sniff.

Distractions depend greatly on setting. In the familiarity of your home, your dog is used to the usual odors, sounds, and movements of dinner cooking, the cat meowing next door, the garbage truck making its slow noisy way up the street, and the neighborhood children playing. But in a new setting — say, a friend's house where you are spending the weekend — your dog will be in a state of heightened awareness, wanting to explore every novel sight, sound, and smell that comes along. This is the dog's way of checking out its environment, discovering what new surroundings have to offer and where possible dangers and opportunities may lurk.

You can use this canine interest in novelty to focus your dog's atten-

tion on the training process. Part of training is letting the dog know you are a powerful individual deserving respect, someone fully capable of leading it. But you will have little opportunity to convince your dog of this fact if you can't get its attention. No dog, no matter how well trained, will obey a command unless it hears the command and has its focus on you. Any other focus is distraction.

Say your dog is engaged in that excited sniffing excursion of the backyard and you want to get its attention. In this situation, it's your job to be the initiator, to make the dog respond. Motion is one way. Moving your hand or arm or taking a step away from the dog will draw its attention. Touch is another way. A sudden touch rather than a slow gradual stroking surprises the dog, bringing its attention to the source of the stimulation, which is you. Sound also works. You can call the dog's name in a new way, cluck your tongue against the roof of your mouth, or suck your lips together in a wet kissing noise, as if you were calling a horse.

But as soon — and I mean *as soon* — as you have the dog's attention, you must give the command you want. You can't wait around. There is only a moment in which the dog's attention is focused on you and only you. If nothing comes from you to hold its attention longer, your pet will move right on to the next interesting sight, sound, or smell in the environment.

Communicating Clearly

It is remarkably easy to distract a dog without even realizing you're doing it. When you get your dog's attention and give it a command, you are communicating with it. But if you communicate something other (or more) than what you want to, you're putting out a distraction as well as a command. That will end up confusing both you and your dog.

Dogs and humans are complex communicators. Dogs do it without words, which are the mainstay of human communication, but they still communicate in sophisticated, effective, and efficient ways. Among themselves dogs use smell, sounds (whines, barks, yips, growls, snarls), sight (facial expressions, tail and body postures), and touch (striking, rubbing, face-licking) to signal their feelings and also to relay cognitive information, such as the approach of a strange dog or dinner in a bowl. We humans don't have an acute enough sense of smell to pick up olfactory messages from dogs, so our communication with them is limited to visual (facial expression, gestures, and body movement), auditory (clucking your tongue, the word sounds of a command), and tactile cues (rubbing, touching, chest-scratching).

To make training with your dog work, you have to communicate clearly what you want. That entails more than saying what you want. Cognitive as we humans are, we tend to pay attention to words and their meanings alone. Dogs do at-

No dog will obey unless it hears the command and has its focus on you.

tend to words, though not to their meanings in the way we do, but they also respond to a wide range of other signals. As long as your whole body and being communicate "sit" in the same way the word does, the dog will perceive one message and is more likely to obey. But if there are other messages coming through along with the command, your dog may react to them more than to the command. In this case your dog may follow those other signals instead of the command and fail to obey.

Frankly, this happens all the time, and it causes considerable grief for dog owners and their pets. Miscommunication can arise from a number of sources.

One is tone of voice. Since dogs are pack animals biologically evolved to live in a hierarchical social order, they respond to lower vocal ranges as more authoritative. This response is instinctual, hardwired into puppies at birth. Unfortunately, it puts us women at something of a disadvantage since our voices are generally higher pitched than men's. Fortunately, dogs do learn to respond to higher tones over time, but it's important to remember that when push comes to shove — say, when you need your dog to lie down and stay in a demanding emergency situation, or if your pet is challenging — it pays to drop your voice and make it as forceful and authoritative as you can. Never raise your voice to a high pitch, the way many adults do in talking to babies and children. To a dog, baby talk betokens fear and anxiety or play. If you try to give a command in such a voice, the dog may well pay more attention to the meaning of the vocal tone — "I'm afraid and not in authority" or "Let's play" — than it does to the command itself — "down." Thus the tone of voice becomes a distraction from the command and invites failure to obey.

Another common distraction is throwing extraneous words into the command. For example, assume you've trained your dog to down on the "down" command. Then one day you say, "I want you to go down." Your pet may pick up the word "down" and obey, but it also may not. This isn't stupidity or disobedience. Your dog is trained to "down," and that is the command it expects, not a string of additional words tacked on fore or aft that serves simply as distraction.

Visually, dogs respond to body posture and language, and it is important that your body says the same thing your words do. In large measure, body posture tells your dog how you feel about your sense of power. Watch dogs interact among themselves, and you'll see the powerful role posture plays in sorting out relationships of leader and follower. A leader dog looks like a leader: head and tail erect, body raised to full height, face aware and focused. Likewise, canines respond to humans who communicate power in their bodies. You don't have to look like Arnold Schwarzenegger pumping iron, but you should take a stance that is well balanced on the balls of your feet, upright through the spine and head, square across the shoulders, and energized throughout. This posture tells the dog that you are in charge and that when you give a command, you must be obeyed. On the other hand, if you give a command when you're sitting on the couch half asleep, slumped, and tired, you're sending a message of weakness. For training purposes, standing or sitting upright communicates to your dog that commands require compliance. Sitting in a slump, or even standing with your shoulders down and your face dejected, distracts from the command and invites noncompliance.

Movement is another unwitting distraction. For example, you give the "sit" command while simultaneously reaching out your hand in order to pet your dog as soon as it obeys. The dog, who was beginning to sit, sees the hand coming and stops to receive the petting. Thus the intended reward becomes a distraction. Much the same thing happens if you give your dog a command, then decide to adjust your sleeve, unbutton your collar, or tie your shoe while waiting for the dog to obey. The movement distracts your pet away from the command.

Touch is a powerful communication medium and reinforcer for dogs, and it can easily become a distraction. This one happens all the time: you are petting your dog and, in mid-stroke, you tell it to sit. Like as not, your dog will fail to obey. Perhaps the canine realizes that its back will no longer be at a good petting angle if it sits, and so it refuses. Or perhaps the petting is so enjoyable that the dog simply fails to notice the command. Either way, the dog is distracted from the command.

Similarly, moving or prodding

your dog to get it to obey can be a distraction. In the training chapters, you'll see that I commonly advise modeling your pet into the desired posture to show it what you want. Once your dog gets it, though, the modeling is gradually withdrawn. If you keep it up, even after the dog has learned the command, the prodding is more distraction than learning aid. Depending on the dog and your manner, the dog will move toward or away from your touch, and its concentration on the spoken command is lost.

To communicate clearly in training, you need to be very careful to identify your own patterns — which can be much more difficult than it might seem and quite central to how successful your training is. It is remarkably easy to create an unwitting pattern that undercuts the purpose of training.

Often people will follow one command with another and, unconsciously, always give them in the same order. A typical case is "sit" followed by "down." The dog learns that "down" always follows "sit," and the two commands are never separated. After a while, if you give the "sit" command, the dog will sit and then, unbidden, it will lie down. Again, it is not resisting or challenging, only following the pattern you have unwittingly instilled in its learning. Whenever training is done in the same order, it is the order itself that is learned, not the individual commands.

I've also watched people training

the "sit" command who, when the dog fails to sit down promptly, say, "Sit," once more, often with greater emphasis. Do this two or three times, and the dog will sit only when you say, "Sit," twice, the second time more emphatic than the first, because that is the pattern you have trained.

Patterning is often the reason why training goes awry and why small canine behavioral problems become big canine behavioral problems. Training can seem to jump the tracks when you have changed the command by changing your pattern. Many breeds instinctively pay more attention to movement than to sound, which means they are attending more closely to your motions and gestures than your spoken commands. If you add a motion to the command, your dog is attending both to your body and to the word. This is fine, as long as you know you are doing it. A distracting pattern arises if you add a motion unconsciously and then stop doing it. For example, many people lean over their pets as they train the "down" command. The dog picks up two cues: the word *down*, and the handler's leaning body. Then, as often happens once the dog begins responding well, the handler stops leaning over altogether — and the dog stops obeying. The noncompliance arises because the dog expects both cues, and when it gets only one, it fails to obey. In the training chapters to follow, you will discover that when I incorporate targeting

into training, the body movement is withdrawn incrementally, so that the dog gets the clear message that the verbal command alone is sufficient.

Patterning is one source of behavior problems, even in well-trained dogs. For example, let's say your dog makes a small mistake: distracted, it fails to come when called. Say you are distracted too, and you fail to correct the dog and insist on follow-through. Then it happens again, the same mistake by your dog and the same failure by you to correct. See the pattern. If it occurs a third time, the dog has learned something new and problematical: When it is called, it need not come.

In a case like this, the dog isn't bad. It isn't good, either. It has simply learned, in the subtle and attentive ways dogs learn, that this new pattern is acceptable.

One Step Ahead

Your dog is mentally quicker than you are by a long shot. The canine's elaborate sensory consciousness keeps it attuned intimately and immediately with its environment, giving it the capacity to react practically instantaneously. And dogs do react. They don't stop and think. They do what the stimulus prompts them to do, and they do it right now, in this very instant, in the quickest blink of an eye. There is no thought about consequences, about right and wrong, in dogs. There is simply reaction.

We humans, with our thinking ways, are usually one step behind our pets. We get many of the same messages from the environment as the dog, but we take time to process them cognitively. And the process does take time, so much time in fact that your dog has already reacted and gone on to something else before perception of the stimulus enters your consciousness.

One of the key aspects of training is learning how to react in dog time, within that critical one or two seconds of the canine attention span. With good timing, you can educate your dog to a point you want to make in only a moment. With bad timing, it may take a month.

How can you train your dog if you're always a step behind? You can't. If you trail your dog physically or psychologically, then the dog is leading you, not vice versa. Much of training is learning how to get ahead of your dog. For one thing, you need to work at anticipating distractions and new points of canine interest before they intrude upon you and your pet. For another thing, you need to learn how to train from your own instantaneous emotional reactivity, not from the slow thinking mind. That change may appear difficult. But this is the only real and true way to work with your dog, because this is the real and true way dogs work.

When I was involved full-time in training service dogs and teaching people how to handle them, I found I often had to shock humans out of

their thinking minds. They looked at working with the dog as an intellectual puzzle, something to be doped out by dint of analysis, like a crossword puzzle or a word-processing program. Of course, the dog was far ahead, leading the way, while the human hung back, trying to think his or her way out of a dilemma. That had to stop. I found myself flustering the humans, pushing and pressuring, making demands, refusing to accept explanations for failure, until they dropped the pretense of thought and took command emotionally.

It's something like learning to play a sport. You can't shoot a basket or hit a curveball or swim the 1650 freestyle in your head. The sport can happen only in the wholeness of your body. Don't think. Focus on the basket or the baseball or the pool and make it happen, in all of your being. It's exactly the same with training your dog.

Trying on Dog Mind

An exercise I use in teaching dog trainers can help you understand how the world looks in dog mind. All you need is a friend and a sense of play.

The exercise is simple. Get down on all fours and act like a dog while your friend tries to teach you a command. Typically I use the retrieve commands explained in chapter 10, but you can use any command you care to. Mimic your own dog as closely as you can while your friend puts you through your paces.

Many of my students who try this exercise tell me afterward that their handler's slowness amazed them. They were ready and able to pick up the item to be retrieved, while the handler stumbled through the command sequence and unwittingly delayed the performance of the "dog," who felt frustrated. This is a strong lesson in the shortened time frame of dog mind. You'll see precisely the same frustration, usually manifested as distraction, arise in your own pet when you take too long.

My students also tell me that getting down on all fours gives them a new understanding of the canine view of the world. They become more sensitive to vocal intonation, their friend's leadership skills or lack thereof, the surroundings at canine eye level, and the potential for distraction if the handler is slow or fails to display enthusiasm.

Another way to increase your awareness of dog mind is to speed up the pace at which you work with your pet. The faster you respond, the more likely you are to move from thinking to just doing it — which is the essence of dog mind. You will likely make mistakes, but don't worry about them. It's more important to let go of thought processes and let yourself experience what dog mind feels like.

For example, as you teach your pet the commands in chapters 9 and 10, try speed drills. Give your dog the "heel," for example, then walk quickly across the floor much faster than usual. Make one or two sud-

den, sharp turns and demand that your pet stay right next to your side, as the command requires. Follow this with an urgent "sit," then an immediate "down." Then let the dog up with "release," "heel" over to a chair, sit down, and give your pet the "my lap" command. Say, "Off" and "Let's go," then "heel" to an open door and give the "wait" command, while you zip into the next room and back out.

There's no right order to all this, of course. The point is to be ingenious, clever, and, above all, fast. Require your pet to go as fast as you do. If it falls behind, give instant firm corrections followed immediately by praise.

The point of this exercise is to force yourself out of thinking into the quicker, more agile pace of dog mind. If the process feels as if it is flowing, you are on the right track, but if it becomes herky-jerky and chaotic, you are probably still trying to think and therefore moving awkwardly, full of hesitation and reflection. Try it again. The more you work at this, the easier you'll find it to enter dog mind.

Emotion Junkies

Dogs crave emotional interactions with humans the way some of us lust after sweets. Since canines live primarily at a reactive and noncognitive level, emotions are all-important to them. Emotion drives the interior life of the dog; its whole being revolves around a core of feeling. Dogs are drawn to human emotion, both positive and negative, and the more emotional input a dog gets, the more it wants. Watch any dog with its master, and you'll quickly see how adept the canine is at eliciting emotion from the human.

Of all the many tools that can be used to shape a dog's behavior — from interesting sounds to food treats — human emotions are by far the most powerful. This power can be used either constructively or destructively, as you yourself choose. The effect humans have on canine emotionality is so powerful that you use it to turn your dog into either a quivering, fearful, devastated creature who urinates submissively at your approach or a fun-loving, happy, secure pet who lives to please you. The responsibility and the choice are yours.

The key to understanding the effect of human emotions on dogs lies in the dog's sense of dependency and its fear of rejection — feelings dogs share with humans. Remember what the world was like when you were small. Every child figures out early on that it depends wholly on its parents for food, shelter, and love. In a family where love is assured and the physical environment secure, a child can be confident and happy. But if the child comes to fear that its parents will reject it or fail to feed it, then the child becomes desperate, frightened, and fearful. The same process continues for adults, though more subtly. Whenever an important relationship is threatened, anxiety arises. If you have ex-

perienced or observed a divorce, job loss, or death in the immediate family, you know what I mean.

One day the child grows up and leaves home. At some point, it will achieve independence and resolve its fear of dependency by becoming independent. But a dog never leaves home. It depends on its master throughout its whole life. The dog knows how dependent it is; instinctively dogs understand their need for attachment. The sense that the relationship is threatened, the fear that the human will reject the animal, raises enormous and devastating anxiety in the dog.

Handle it well, and your dog is a happy and fulfilled animal. Handle it inconsistently and abusively, and the animal collapses into a heap of fear, aggression, or catatonia. Which direction your dog goes is largely up to you — yes, you.

Why Anger Doesn't Work

You give your dog a command — say, "sit" — and it fails to obey. Now what do you do? You may be tempted to vent your frustration by becoming angry at your pet. But if you do so, you will be going in the wrong direction, for complex reasons arising in the nature of dog mind.

The dog can have two basic reactions to your anger. The first is to feel that it is a bad dog, and that you are pushing it away and rejecting it. The canine fear of rejection is so strong that it will get in the way of teaching. Your dog won't learn about the correct way to sit. Instead, it will feel confused, insecure, and anxious.

The other possible reaction provides fascinating insight into how dog mind works. Dogs love emotion, any emotion, and who says all emotion has to be positive? In the absence of other emotions, dogs are as attracted to anger or frustration as they would be to exuberance and happiness. Emotion, any emotion, reinforces what the dog was doing. That goes for anger and frustration as much as happiness and exuberance. So if you react angrily or with frustration to your dog's failure to follow a command, you are in effect rewarding it for failing to follow through. The next time you give that command, the dog will again fail to obey — because it has been rewarded for this failure by your negative emotion.

Then, too, because your dog synchronizes with you, it mirrors your emotions. When you get angry, the dog gets angry, either actively or passively, depending on its position on the revolving wheel. So you get angrier in response and the dog gets angrier yet, which pushes you into a really big anger, which in turn drives the dog to an equally negative response — and so it escalates, round and round and round, getting you and your dog exactly nowhere except stuck.

To avoid the temptation of climbing onto this frustrating merry-go-round, you need to base your training on what motivates a dog positively — that is, what draws it to do what you want. And you need to correct your dog for failure to obey in the cool objective manner that avoids confusing it about the issue and rewarding it for its failure.

How Dogs Fight Back

You are standing in line to buy movie tickets when somebody, seemingly accidentally, pushes against you and steps on your toes. Probably you will just give way, taking the incident for nothing more than a misstep. But then it happens again; somebody else steps on your foot. This time your anger flares. And the third time a nameless somebody pushes against you, you don't give way. Instead, you plant your body and push back, maintaining your position and your boundary. Should there be yet another push, you may lash out verbally to tell the intruder in no uncertain terms to stay out of your space and off your toes.

Dogs do much the same. I call it *resistance* because that's what it is — a direct resistance to your command, a refusal to obey. You want the dog to complete a certain action and it decides not to, typically by resisting you and your command. It is the animal's way of defending personal rights, holding physical and psychological space, and wielding power.

Puppies sometimes resist being handled. Unable to scramble away or protect itself, the puppy may scream in protest or simply tense its body. Some puppies roll over and urinate submissively, as a way of saying, "Please don't." Others ground — that is, the pup acts as if its four feet are glued to the earth.

Adult dogs employ a number of different methods of resistance, both active and passive. Active resistance, or challenge, is easy to recognize: growling, biting, pulling away from you or tugging at the leash, and jumping around. There's nothing subtle about it. Passive resistance is harder to recognize for what it is, since the dog is taking an indirect route. Adults dogs, like puppies, may ground. The dog is saying, in its exquisite body language, "I shall not be moved." Sometimes the eyes roll and look heavy. The tail may wag only at the end, or it may be tucked under the belly. Dogs, again like puppies, may resist by rolling over and exposing the belly. This apparent submission means, "I give up," but the dog avoids completing the command — which is precisely what it is trying to accomplish. Some dogs resist by developing selective hearing. Suddenly, they hear only what they want to hear. Or, instead of obeying, the dog takes off on a happy romp, starting some game it likes to play and inviting you to drop this training nonsense and join in.

Whatever form it takes, resistance means one thing: The job you asked the dog to do didn't get done because the animal refused. What are you going to do about it?

And, yes, you must do something about it. The dog is a pack animal who needs leadership and continu-

For both you and the dog to achieve security and satisfaction in the relationship, you must respond appropriately to resistance.

ally tests its leaders as way of ensuring its own safety and security. Failure to respond to resistance says that you no longer have the right stuff to lead. For both you and the dog to achieve security and satisfaction in the relationship, you must respond appropriately to resistance.

Resistance arises from the dog's feeling of violation. It is entering territory with you where it feels uncertain, perhaps incapable of fully trusting you. Chances are something you did alienated your pet or took away its motivation. Perhaps you were inconsistent or you displayed anger. In countering resistance, you show your dog that you are trustworthy, that following you works, that it remains secure under your leadership. And you can send that message only by acting as the dog's leader, not by submitting to its rebellion.

The first thing to do is to recognize resistance as resistance. You said do X, and the dog by resisting is saying it will not do X. Don't turn this into a contest of wills, however. If you meet resistance head-on with angry insistence, the dog's resistance will grow, not diminish. Instead of ending the resistance you will reinforce it — and that's the last thing you want to happen.

To counter resistance, you need to change the dog's immediate emotional focus. You need to shake things up, shift the dog's balance, and change the game. Here's where knowing your dog's motivators comes into play. Use them to provide the dog with a new direction that changes the current situation and induces the dog once more to follow you.

Let's say your dog grounds. It is tense and locked up. Simply telling it to come with you and moving forward two or three steps may break the tension as the dog complies and comes to your side. Or you could start acting silly, drawing the dog into a romp that sheds the physical lock-up through movement. If the resistance is expressed by playing a cutesy game, try a sharp, forceful voice that startles and shocks your pet out of its romp. If the dog rolls over, try just walking away and paying attention to something other than the dog. Quickly the animal will realize the resistance isn't working because you are no longer reacting to it.

The model of the revolving wheel of centrifugal force works well in showing how to meet resistance effectively. Think of the resistance as your dog's position on the wheel, which is somehow stuck and unmoving. You want that position to change immediately, right now, to get the wheel moving again, to jerk it forward and alter your dog's position. That's why a sudden change of focus works, because it gets the wheel spinning and knocks the stuck dog loose.

Once you disrupt your dog's resistance, go back to the command that started the resistance, but move three to five feet away from the original point to avoid building a pattern of resistance around a physical space. It is important that your dog obey you in the original task. If it resists again, continue knocking it off balance until you are able to bring the dog to perform the original command.

To sum up, here are the essentials to keep in mind when you are dealing with canine resistance:

- Take away the dog's motivation to resist. Ensure that you don't resist the resistance, especially with anger, and thereby create more resistance.
- Knock the dog off its stuck spot on the revolving wheel by offering a different activity or interest; change is the name of this game.
- Finally, go back and deal with the original issue.

Let Your Fingers Do the Talking

Resistance is about tension. You very likely know from your own experience how touch can help resolve tension. Sometimes just having a loved one lay his or her hands on you can help dissolve stress, lower blood pressure, dissolve headache, and instill an overall sense of well-being.

Dogs respond to touch as eagerly as people. This tactile hunger in dogs offers an excellent way for you to build responsiveness between you and your animal. Massage helps both you and your pet feel good together, which clearly promotes the intuitive connection critical to a healthy relationship. Also, massage can help dissipate resistance, calming the dog and making it more open to paying attention to you and your commands. In fact, I recommend that every training session begins with massage. You will enjoy it as much as your dog does. The technique is simple:

- Position one hand just behind your dog's ears, with the thumb on one side of the neck and the fingers on the other. Pinching the thumb and fingers together vigorously, work down into the muscles. Slide down the neck slowly, and don't be afraid to apply considerable pressure. The dog will like the deep sensation.
- When you reach the top of the shoulder blades, bring the other hand into play. Put the thumbs together on the midline at the base of the neck, and work your fingers into the muscles on top of the shoulder blades, massaging them deeply.
- Over the rest of the body, grasp the coat in large folds and roll your hands backward. Use this technique to massage the remainder of the back, the sides, and the legs.
- As you work, note how the dog relaxes. It may actually seem to melt. You may, too. A warm, pleasurable feeling flows to and from your hands. The dog may become so relaxed that it lies down.
- When you finish the massage, you will discover that the dog is now more interested in you than in the environment. This connected responsiveness sets the emotional stage for a productive training session.

Besides using massage to begin training, you can use it to bring the

The dog will like the deep sensation behind his ears.

Use both hands to massage the shoulder blades.

Grasp the coat in large folds and roll your hands backward.

As you work, note how the dog relaxes

dog's focus back to you in the event of distraction. It is also an excellent way of working through resistance. Massage reconnects you with the dog, and it fills the animal with well-being and trust — precisely the feelings a resisting dog is looking for.

Meeting Challenges with Pack Savvy

As I have said again and again, dogs require leadership. They evolved as pack animals who attend to their daily survival needs by means of complex teamwork coordinated by a leader. *Leader* in this context does not mean *dictator*. The top dog in a pack isn't a four-legged Hitler or Stalin, who rules an enslaved populace with brute force. He or she is instead the animal who exhibits the greatest strength, together with courage and personal power. In trusting the leader to lead, the other dogs are creating a secure social system that assures their own survival.

Challenging is a dog's way of ensuring that its leader is strong. It is the method canines use to assess their own security. If the leader is strong and competent, the dog feels safe. But if the leader does not meet the challenge, then it's time to raise up a new leader who has the competence to do what needs doing.

When a dog challenges you, it is simply doing what its nature tells it to do. Challenging is as basic to the dog's inborn survival ability as its capacity to smell, chase, and defend against attack. Dogs challenge the humans who make up their domestic social group as readily and as frequently as they would challenge other dogs in a wild pack.

Some people shrink from challenges, but they are in fact opportunities to reaffirm your role as the dog's leader. Answering the challenge with a strong clear message that you are still doing the caretaking and giving the commands tells your dog that it has every reason to feel safe and secure. And the clearer this message, the longer it will be before the dog challenges again.

Without challenges, a dog has no way of knowing whether it will survive in the hands of its leader. Securing your leadership is no one-time event. Your performance will come up for review any time the dog has reason to doubt your ability to command.

You may find yourself surprised at how clever, inventive, and strong your dog can be in mounting challenges. In a wild pack, only a quick, tough, smart dog can challenge the current leader and win. The strong will and inventiveness you see in your challenging dog is part of its survival mechanism. The personality traits that come into play in a challenge — much as they may get your goat at the time — are part and parcel of the attributes that makes dogs such fascinating companions.

Accepting Inequality

Whatever else it may be, the human-dog relationship is no democracy based on the absolute equality of both members. It is instead a cooperative team, with a human leader and a canine follower.

Two elements are required to make the relationship work. One is leadership of the pack by a responsible leader, and the other is cooperation among pack members following the leader. Dogs are followers, good followers, but they keep a constant critical eye on their leader at all times. It isn't that they want to lead. In fact, dogs would much rather follow. Remember: Dogs want to be sure their leader still has the capacity for leadership.

When the leader falters, a dog who has been a follower will challenge. If the challenger wins, it takes over and sets the rules. Should your dog feel stronger than you in your house and family, it may revert to behaviors, like barking at visitors, that are unacceptable to you but acceptable to the dog. To prevent this, you need to meet every challenge and provide the dog with a continuous sense of security.

Recognizing Challenge

Anytime you're working with your dog and you feel your neck stiffen or your stomach clench, pay attention. That's an animal reaction to animal behavior. Your dog is challenging and you are reacting, one creature to another.

We've already discussed one form of challenge: resistance. Resistance is largely passive. The dog isn't taking you head-on, in a canine *mano à mano,* but challenging by diversion. Still, you must meet that challenge and remain in control.

The same thing goes for overt challenges, which can be tellingly dramatic. Dogs understand the things you value — say, the signed first edition of Jack London's *Martin Eden,* your favorite softball glove, or the heirloom rug from your grandmother's house — and they may go right for them when they are in a challenging mood. It isn't that the dog is vengeful or mean; it's that it wants to make sure it has your attention. That's why it will chew the Jack London instead of some utterly

forgettable pulp novel you picked up at the airport last week. The pulp you would hardly notice, but the Jack London definitely gets your blood up.

If you react emotionally to the destruction of a favored possession, you are playing right into the dog's paws, confirming its underlying suspicion that you are guided more by unchecked emotion than by leadership ability. Remember, too, that an emotional reaction rewards the dog's craving for emotion, reinforcing its challenge rather than meeting it.

Anytime you feel insecure or fearful, your dog will challenge. What you must do is recognize your fears as such, not deny or mask them, and lead your pet in a way that honors your fear but without communicating weakness. For example, when I was training service dogs, I often heard about the situation where a person with a newly acquired service dog was overwhelmed with attention the first day back at school or on the job. A crowd would gather around and want a demonstration of this wonder canine who could turn lights on and off and run an elevator. Of course, being on the spot like that is scary and the new service dog handler would find himself or herself doubting the dog's ability to perform such a complex task — not because the dog couldn't do it, but because the human was afraid of public failure. Recognizing the fear, the human would instead command the dog to do something simple, like lying down or shaking hands. The human was retaining control and leadership, making the best of a situation where the dog might question its master's ability to lead.

For that is the whole point of meeting a challenge — retaining your control and communicating clearly to the dog that you still provide the leadership it needs to feel safe and secure.

In Fairness

Part of preparing to meet a dog's inevitable challenges is preventing them before they happen. Anything and everything you do to instill a sense of security in your dog will help. For example, a dog whose daily job it is to fetch the evening paper and protect the house while the master is away at work enjoys a well-defined role within the pack. Feeling secure, valued, and well led, it is more likely to overlook its master's occasional minor slips and errors of leadership than to rise to each as an opportunity to challenge.

An important aspect of preventing challenges is eliminating ambiguity. There is a critical difference between confusion and challenge. Even a dog who very much wants to fit in and follow won't know what to do if the rules are inconsistent or changing. You can't give a dog permission to urinate in the house one night and forbid it the next; the dog simply can't figure out what the standard is. Your job as the leader is to determine the rules and insist on them, consistently and unambiguously.

It's also your job to recognize who's capable of what when. It's not a good idea to embark on training a difficult command when you're feeling tired and exasperated after a long day. The same holds for your dog. Be kinder and gentler when the animal is hot or fatigued. Should you command your dog to do something altogether too difficult for its current physical state, it may balk. You can regain control by recognizing the situation and making the dog's life easier. Instead of demanding something difficult, give the dog an easy job to do — and reward it lavishly for success. Your leadership will be reinforced and the dog will experience strong satisfaction.

Another pitfall to avoid is boredom, which is a common cause of challenges. If you ask your dog to do the same command again and again — say, "heel-sit," "heel-sit," "heel-sit" — it may well challenge you the seventh or eighth time you give the same command. Your job is to keep things interesting and to provide sufficient stimulation to the dog that it finds training fun.

Walking Your Talk

One of the ways you can lessen your dog's need to challenge you is to assume leadership of every interaction between you both. You don't have to do anything special. Instead, it's a matter of communicating leadership — clearly, and without distraction — in the very way you speak and move toward and with the dog.

Personal power is in some ways the crux of educating your dog. To this day, I can still hear the anguished cry of the woman who came to an obedience class I was teaching. She had this ninety-pound German shepherd on a leash and every time she said, "Sit," in her soft questioning voice, the dog simply ignored her. "But he listens to my husband," she explained, as if a canine who obeys one person will automatically obey every other. It doesn't work that way. The dog is a pack animal hardwired to live in a leadership hierarchy. The German shepherd in question knew the commands, but he was an assertive canine, much more of a driver than the woman, and he recognized that he could lead her. Thus he refused to obey, having assumed the position of leader toward her. For the woman to change the relationship, she had to project an assertiveness that put the dog into a follower position and required it to obey. Physical correction can help in such a situation, but on a day-to-day basis it is much more important to project power personally, in one's being, than to rely on a choke chain. Fortunately, once the role reversal occurs — in this case, after the young woman knew what it felt like to assume power and project it — the authority can be assumed and projected at will, when the occasion arises.

Projecting personal power is easier than you think — if you let yourself do it. Think of a military drill sergeant, the kind who stands tall, shoulders squared, body flexible and ready for action, face determined, open, and confident. The voice is like that too — deep, certain, less loud than authoritative. This is an extreme, of course. Most of the time you spend with your dog, you need not act as if you were aiming for a career in the Marine Corps. But when you feel that your leadership is challenged, when you realize that your own confusion or fear or frustration is undermining your leadership position with your dog and giving it emotional cause to doubt your ability, call that image up and put yourself into it through body language and voice.

The most important aspect of giving commands is tone of voice, not volume. The louder you have to speak to your dog to get its attention, the more it will associate the greater volume with the command and the less responsive it will become to lesser volumes. Simply, once you start shouting at your dog to make it pay attention, you'll have to keep shouting.

Focus instead on the quality and emotional tenor of your voice. Turn the volume down; the idea is to get your dog to listen to all your spoken commands, not just the loud ones. Imagine yourself in command and control, full of power and light, and speak to your dog from this self-image.

This is particularly important in meeting a challenge. You want to respond firmly, not angrily, from your status as leader, not from the emotional insecurity of confrontation. Your voice should be objective and firm. It must communicate a clear message: "I'm in control here."

The same thing goes for body language. If you meet a challenge by kicking the ground, sagging your shoulders, and staring the dog directly in the eye, it's going to go badly for you and your pet. You're saying very clearly that the dog has gotten to you and that its challenge is working — precisely what the dog doesn't want to find out. And you will increase its challenge by staring, which in the body language of dog mind invites further confrontation. Instead, you want to regain control and communicate your leadership.

You can use body language in all interactions with your dog to reinforce the nature of the relationship. Here are some basic and useful guidelines.

- *Hold your head up.* Leaders stand tall; they don't slump.
- *Make your dog watch you.* Become the center of attention for your dog. Keep its eyes on you rather than keeping your eyes in it. For example, when you are walking with your dog, vary speeds so that it has to pay attention to you. It's a subtle but effective lesson in leadership.
- *Avoid staring contests with your dog.* It just advances the challenge. Instead, change the game. Move in order to interest your dog in following you with its eyes, then give it a simple

command so you regain control.
- *Refuse to feel beaten.* Keep at it, trying new approaches, until you establish leadership again. It may take a while, but it's worth the effort to conclude the interaction with both your leadership and the dog's security unquestioned.

Training and Personality

Personality affects everything in the human-canine relationship, training included. Because each of us is put together somewhat differently, there is no — nor can there ever be — one right way to train your dog. Equally successful professionals use markedly different methods. The key to their success is less the method itself than the trainer's belief in his or her approach and the right fit between that approach and the trainer's personality. You too must train with methods that fit your personality.

The same goes for your dog's personality; the training method has to fit properly with your pet's emotional makeup. There is simply no substitute for getting to know your dog as an individual. You need an intuitive connection with your pet. Without such a connection, I can prattle on and on about training methods and none of them will really work for you, because that essential link between you and your dog has not been forged. If you try to follow a method you don't believe in or one that runs against your grain, you will only confound yourself and your pet.

What follows are general guidelines and ideas on how to fit a training approach to the personality types detailed in chapter 5. Start with what feels best for you and alter it with experience. We'll begin with canine personality, then discuss human.

Analytical dogs are relatively low in both responsiveness and assertiveness, expecting leadership and focusing on the task at hand. In working with such a dog, it is important to show the canine exactly what you want. Precision helps. Be sure that information about right and wrong is clear-cut. Don't overwhelm the dog emotionally. Remain calm and controlled, and don't push hard or threaten. Patience is required; don't rush the learning process. Give the dog time to check out the situation and achieve accuracy, but also be persistent. If you need to increase the responsiveness of an analytical dog to training, interact in a friendly and social way and encourage risk taking by creating a secure but upbeat environment.

Snow, Louise's standard poodle from chapters 4 and 5, was the classic analytical dog, and training her required that Louise be precise, controlled, and gentle. However, when Louise asked Snow to stretch, it didn't work to feed into her passive outlook. Instead, Louise found she needed to create a dynamic setting while retaining a sense of trust and security. Using synchronization,

Louise encouraged Snow with smiles and enthusiasm and made sure she herself felt grounded and secure in what she was asking.

With a driver dog like Brian's border collie, Angus — highly assertive, but relatively low in responsiveness — brief training sessions that move quickly and have a clear point work best. When it's time to train, don't mess around. Stick to business and be prepared; don't come to the training session disorganized and awkward. Performance, not personal relationship, is the focus. Motivate and persuade the dog by encouraging positive results. Expect resistance and challenges. Respond to them clearly and unequivocally, letting the dog know that training is a necessary and serious business. To make your dog more responsive to your training, you need to demonstrate your own strength of leadership and encourage — that is, reward — patience and empathy in your pet.

Brian discovered in training Angus that his pet focused so much on performance that he had trouble relaxing enough to enjoy even an ordinary social interaction. Such a dog can burn out, and it also pays more attention to the task than to its leader. To lighten up the situation and keep Angus's focus on him, Brian invited his pet into spontaneous play, drawing the dog to him through synchronization. Brian would purposely assume a social, relaxed, patient mood. Angus relaxed, developed his capacity to play, and learned better how to attend to his handler, as well as to the job at hand.

In the case of an amiable dog, who is highly responsive but relatively unassertive, the first requirement is to build the relationship. Be soft in your approach, avoiding harshness, coldness, and indifference. Don't threaten your dog or act domineering. Instead, be patient and train slowly and gently, with a sense of casual informality. Offer personal reassurance frequently ("Yes, it's okay"). Keep an eye out for any sign of dissatisfaction in your pet, and reduce risk by presenting everything in small increments. Ask not for great leaps forward but for small steps in the right direction. To increase responsiveness to training, instill confidence and security in your dog and encourage its initiative and sense of urgency.

Dawn, Jane's amiable golden retriever, was by and large a joy to train. She was so relaxed and socially involved that she went right along with the program. Amiables, though, are laid back and their pace is casual. This is just wonderful until you confront a situation requiring initiative and urgency, such as retrieving a dropped object within a tight space, like behind the couch. Jane found she could increase Dawn's initiative by acting enthusiastic and upbeat and imparting a sense of urgency. Jane's own excitement drew Dawn toward her, in the way of the revolving wheel, and increased her pet's ability to take the initiative in a timely manner.

Expressive dogs, who are both highly assertive and highly responsive, learn best when they think it's fun — within limits. Ideally, you want to communicate that learning is a good time, but not a laugh riot. Vary the work; expressives abhor boredom and repetition. Keep the dog stimulated and motivated, and move fast. Don't be rigid; stay loose and flowing. And be sure to include time for relating and socializing in the training session. Since expressives are high-energy dogs, increasing responsiveness to training means restraining their enthusiasm, encouraging them to focus on the task, and rewarding them for practicing emotional control and self-discipline.

Zack, Tim's expressive Labrador, had the short attention span typical of his personality style, and he also tended to execute commands imprecisely. To encourage him to focus and to perform each command all the way through, Tim adopted a training attitude that was controlled and restrained. Synchronizing with his handler, Zack slowed down and became better able to concentrate. Tim rewarded him enthusiastically for self-control and precise execution, and that taught Zack to pay increasingly close attention to what was expected of him.

When it comes to human personality styles, analyticals are the least exuberant in giving praise and may, to an outside observer, appear too cool to provide the quality feedback the canine needs. However, if you yourself are analytical, it is likely that your pet already knows your personality and its limits and will greet your subdued praise with the significance it deserves. This fact underscores a basic reality about canines: Dogs are so versatile, and so adept at synchrony, that they will work hard to fit with you.

Analytical and amiable people both experience difficulty with effective timing, that is, in giving praise or correction promptly. Analyticals are slow, methodical, and thoughtful, and often fail to respond before their dogs have moved on to something else. Amiables pay less attention to detail and may miss opportunities to reward or correct. Also, neither amiables nor analyticals are particularly enthusiastic about giving corrections. Since both personalities rank relatively low in assertiveness, giving a correction can be a personality stretch. Also, amiables are loath to do anything that may cause pain or hurt.

Because they are more assertive, drivers and expressives generally find it easy to give a correction, but for different reasons. Drivers like results and they see correction as an efficient way to get what they want. Expressives are impatient, and they simply don't want to wait around for the slower association-training methods of behavior change favored by analyticals and amiables.

Expressives give praise easily, but they can be so exuberant that they overpower a dog who is markedly less assertive. Amiables likewise find praise easy, but they tend to give it in a manner that asks the dog to approve them, typically by giving commands and tendering praise in a questioning tone of voice that seems to say, "Are you okay with this command? Did you like doing it?" This undercuts the handler's authority and lessens the positive emotional effect of praise.

Once again: There is no one best method of training, and no right or wrong personality type. If you are a high-energy driver who believes absolutely in operant conditioning and who demands that his or her dog produce results, your confidence and leadership will succeed. Likewise, if you are a thoughtful analytical whose style is subdued and patient, and you have faith in your own quiet way of working with your dog, that approach will also succeed. The key is to find an emotional approach that fits for you and your pet, pay close attention to what happens between you two, and be willing to be as versatile with your dog as your dog is with you.

The Responsible Dog

When you are training a dog, you are leading it through a series of steps that instill a new pattern in its behavior. In this progression, you yourself are the motivator, the source of all reinforcement, positive and negative. You are drawing the dog's attention to you and making your praise the reward for completing the task correctly. But you are also making the dog responsible for follow-through, as it learns the command and you require it to do the task correctly, each and every time.

The dog's assumption of responsibility for doing the job right is itself a new and important pattern. The dog is learning to learn; it becomes more adept at responding, at figuring out what you want and doing it. As it learns, the interaction between you and the dog changes.

When you start training your dog, it doesn't know what you want. But since canines are social and quickly discover that doing the job earns them praise, they learn quickly. Your dog has achieved some competence at this point, but its skill is limited, so praise remains essential to building the association. As your dog learns the job, it will perform because of the success it experiences and the praise it receives.

But dogs can go beyond this level in certain areas, completing some tasks not only because of the reward from you but also because of the animal's own internal satisfaction at completing the task. In the human world such self-motivated action is the provenance of the architect who designs a building because he or she loves it, not because of the fee, or the poet who labors for years over an epic out of passion for the story and the language, not fame or fortune. In the canine universe, self-motivation is largely reserved for those dogs who must work with great independence and autonomy and who are follow-

ing pursuits natural to them, often inborn. Herding and guardian dogs are examples, as are hearing dogs, whose job it is to alert their deaf masters to significant sounds in the world around them. Praise isn't the point for them. It is the task itself, and the sheer joy of doing it.

When it comes to tasks that are not natural to the particular dog — such as going into the "down" position and staying there until you say it's okay to move — you yourself must be your dog's motivator. Since the task isn't inborn, the motivation must come from the outside — namely, you.

Self-motivation explains why it can be so difficult to deal with problem canine behaviors. Practically all of them are inborn in the particular breed: the German shepherd who rushes the front door and snarls at arriving guests, the terrier who uproots the newly planted roses, the coonhound who assiduously trees every small furry four-legged critter, both wild and domestic, in the neighborhood. Negative reinforcement doesn't extinguish or eliminate such self-motivated behavior. Correction only gives you control of it under certain circumstances, as we saw in the example of Fred and Din in chapter 6.

A sometimes-successful approach to problem behavior is to train your dog to the opposite activity. For example, some dogs lack any instinctive ability to hold an object in their mouths and will drop it at the first opportunity. Negative reinforcement won't make the dog hold on, but training it to let go with a "drop it" command may. In other words, broadening your dog's perspective to include an alternative can sometimes counteract the problem. Likewise, a dog who lunges forward on a leash can be trained to "back" up to you on command.

The Twelve C's

Over my years of training dogs and people who work with dogs, I developed a number of catchphrases that summarize important elements of my approach. I call them the Twelve C's, because they lay out a basic code of behavior. Keep them in mind as the basis for all our training work as we go on to study specific commands.

1. Communicate Clearly

It goes both ways, but primarily it is your responsibility. For training to work and the relationship to flourish, you and your dog must communicate clearly. Dogs, unlike cows, horses, and most other domestic animals, strain to understand what humans tell them. In their eagerness to comprehend and their wide sensitivity to us, they may misinterpret or misperceive the signals we send through voice or body. It is your task to prevent this by communicating with your dog in a way the animal understands. Likewise, you need to pay careful attention to what your dog is saying to you in its behavior, its facial expression, and its body language.

2. Concentrate on Reacting, Not Thinking

People think and dogs react. Human cognitive process is an ace for scientific discovery and rocket-building, but it is far too slow to be the only tool you use in training your dog. Instinct and intuitive reaction are extremely important, because it is in your guts, not your cerebral cortex, where you connect most effectively with your pet.

Thought processes are thorough but slow. In the time it takes you to size up a situation, analyze the possibilities, and make a choice among options, your dog has already reacted and has moved on. The more you can come to rely on intuition and instinct, the more your emotional timetable will match up with your dog's, and the more effectively you and your animal will communicate.

3. Command and Show, Then Command and Order

It's one thing to teach your dog to do something and quite another to teach it to do the same something on command. In teaching "sit," as an example, first you are teaching the dog how to assume the correct posture. That's basic psychomotor training. Then comes the issue of getting the dog to sit on your command, a second level of teaching that draws from both the dog's learning of the posture and its deference to your leadership. If your pet feels that you are not leading properly, or if it is distracted, it may refuse to sit even though it knows full well what the expected behavior is.

You face two tasks in training. One is instructing the dog in a particular psychomotor skill. The other is teaching it that, everywhere and always, it is to obey you. Training isn't about tricks to impress the neighbors; it's about your leadership in building and maintaining the relationship with your dog.

When you are teaching your pet a command, first give the command and then demonstrate physically what the dog is to do. Whenever the dog shows that it is trying to do what you want, offer encouragement and let the dog do as much of the task as it can without your help. Once you know the dog understands what you want, give the command and insist that the animal complete the task. If the dog refuses, make it clear that you weren't asking, but ordering. A correction is called for.

4. Connect Action with Commands

Dogs learn largely by association, so it's important to help your dog connect its physical movements with the commands you give. Dog training is literally hands-on. When you give a command and prepare to show your dog what you're after, physically maneuver the dog into the position you want. That's the whole point of the downward push on the rump for the "sit" command. You are putting the dog into the physical position you want it to take in "sit." Usually in two or three run-throughs, the dog will associate "sit" with the sitting position.

5. Chart Training to Your Dog's Personality

Dogs are not automatons, and no two dogs can be trained in exactly the same way. Their personalities vary greatly. A task that may be easy for one dog is difficult for the next. Some dogs require a great deal of praise; some, very little. Some dogs retrieve automatically, and others must be encouraged enthusiastically before they even get the idea. Learning to read your dog is part of the benefit of training, because you will come away from the process with a deeper understanding of the animal as an individual being.

Dogs are as susceptible to mood swings as humans are. Their emotional state is affected by diet, weather, distractions, fatigue, exercise, illness, success or failure in training, and, very important, your mood. Whenever your dog seems to have jumped the track during a training session, chances are one or more factors is affecting its emotional being. If you understand what is going on and why, you may be able to do something about it. Above all, remember not to display anger or frustration toward the dog and be sure to end every training session with a success, even a small one.

Set your expectations according to what is going on for the dog in the present moment. If, for example, your dog is tired, it will perform slower than usual. This is fine, as long as the dog does indeed follow the command you have given. But slow performance isn't fine if your dog is brimming with energy. Then it's important to insist that the dog obey quickly and well. Throughout, adapt your technique and expectation to your dog's current state of mind and body.

6. Control Emotions

When a dog seems slow to catch on to a new command or fails to obey an old one, you can easily become frustrated and angry. Trouble is, once you lose control of your emotions, you also lose your ability to instruct the dog — which is the whole point of training in the first place. Strong emotions interfere with the command you give the dog, putting the animal in a state of confusion, frustration, and resistance. The result is an emotional stalemate.

Complicating the matter is the fact that to a dog any human emotion is better than no human emotion. Anger can actually reinforce a dog's incorrect behavior and lead it to repeat the incorrect action again and again.

There's a wise rule of thumb: *Never pick up your dog's leash when you're angry.* It need not even be the dog who is the source of the anger. If you've just had a bad day at work, completely destroyed a two-day-long experiment in chemistry lab, fought with your spouse, or gotten a traffic ticket, don't turn to dog training as therapy. It won't work. Instead, give your dog a good massage. You'll both have

the good and relaxing time you need.

Initiate training only when you are ready to train. Don't train when you are fatigued, angry, or distracted. You will work from your own internal emotional state, not from what is going on between you and your pet. And that — what is happening between you and your pet — is the whole point and basis of training.

7. Consistency Is Critical

With dogs as with humans, double, triple, and quadruple standards don't work. It is essential that you use the same word or words each and every time you give a command. Varying the command confuses the dog and prevents it from learning the association between your command and its behavior.

Consistency in training also means not letting the dog off the hook or making exceptions. Simply, don't let your dog get away with something for which it has previously been corrected. With dogs, the exception soon becomes the rule. Once you've set the standard, stick to it.

Look at it from the dog's point of view. Say you're learning to drive a car and your instructor tells you over and over again to stop at red lights, letting you know in no uncertain terms anytime you don't come to a full stop. Then one day, just as you approach a red light, the instructor tells you to run it. Next time you're in the car, you go right through a red light the same way you did the day before — only to have the instructor jump down your throat. Probably feeling a little confused there, aren't you?

This kind of emotional anarchy is precisely what befalls a dog subjected to double standards. Consider the canine equivalent of red lights and driver's education. During toilet training, your puppy has trouble rousing you from a deep sleep and it urinates inside. You don't react, making an excuse for the pup because you feel guilty about sleeping so soundly. The pup doesn't know from guilt; instead, as it sees the situation, urinating inside is now allowed. The next night, when the puppy dumps its full bladder without even trying to get you up, you scold the little animal. Now you have a confused puppy. One night it can urinate in the house; the next night it can't. If it could talk, it would look at you and say, "But yesterday you let me do it. Why can't I do it now?" And it would have a point.

For a dog, consistency creates security and safety. Inconsistency upsets the dog's emotional state, and makes your job of training and the animal's job of learning that much harder. If you don't want your dog to urinate in the house, be sure it knows that this is the rule — all the time. And "all the time" applies to every house rule you set up. Anything less is unfair to your pet.

8. Correct, Don't Punish or Nag

It has been my experience that correction is the most difficult and least understood aspect of training, working, and living with a dog. No doubt, most humans generalize from their own bad education in correction, and see it as torture (inflicting great pain with glee and pleasure on the part of the torturer) or nagging (harping continually and ineffectually). In humans, torture does deep damage to both victim and torturer and nagging doesn't really do any good, except to create unpleasantness in a relationship and generally reinforce the behavior that is the object of the nagging.

Correcting a dog is quite different. The whole point is to use pain or discomfort — often in a small dose, and always for only an instant — to induce the dog to change its behavior. A correction is given quickly, and then it is over. And a correction is given objectively — that is, when you correct your dog, you must do so without anger or any other emotional baggage.

There's good reason for this show-no-emotion requirement. Remember that any human emotion reinforces canine behavior. If you correct your dog for some infraction accompanied by a display of pluperfect anger, you are in fact rewarding the dog for doing what it just did — which is precisely opposite to the message you want to send. Instead, you should remain emotionally cool and objective as you give the correction. A cool unemotional correction sends the dog a clear message in canine terms: "Don't do that."

Typically, you need to use correction when your dog is distracted and won't give you its attention, despite your attempts to motivate it. Correction also works as a countermeasure to challenge. But, you ask, how much correction of what sort is called for? That's a good question. And here's the answer: It depends — on you, on the dog, and on the behavior being corrected. As with everything that has to do with you and your dog, the point isn't technique. It's what the relationship requires.

Many people worry about overcorrecting to the point of abuse, yet the same potential holds as well for undercorrection. If you correct too little, the problem behavior doesn't change and the dog must be corrected again, only harder, because its resistance has risen. Should you undercorrect yet again, the resistance only increases the more. I call such repeated ineffective corrections nagging, and nagging is definitely unpleasant for the dog.

9. Complete Corrections with Praise

Immediately — and I mean *immediately* — after you give a correction, praise and encourage your dog. Let's look at what is happening in canine terms. Your correction tells the dog to change its behavior. As soon as its behavior changes, you then praise it — which takes the dog's mind off the correction and encourages it instead to continue the changed behavior, making the point of the correction even more emphatically. Always keep it in mind that correction is about communication, not punishment.

With correction as with all other aspects of canine behavior, praise fittingly. A small correction calls for small praise. A big correction calls for big praise.

Praise following a correction reminds the dog that it is safe and secure, that it still has a place in the pack. Praise erases doubt in the dog's mind, freeing it to focus on learning and providing the motivation it seeks to work well with you.

10. Create Desire

It's no fun to go to school or work every day and feel as if you have accomplished nothing despite all your labor. In fact, if you continue to feel that you are accomplishing nothing, soon you won't try at all. The same holds true for dogs, who come into this world wanting nothing more than to please their leaders. Leaders — that includes you — have the responsibility of seeing to it that this basic canine need is met.

Dogs have limited attention and stamina; long training sessions wear them out and are ineffective. Keep your work to no more than twenty minutes at a stretch, and no more than three times a day. If you can only train once or twice a day, that's fine. The training process will still work. It's better to be focused and brief than scattered and lengthy. Also dogs, like humans, learn better when they can sleep on it — literally. Rest periods give the animal the opportunity to consolidate learning.

Make training fun. Start by massaging your pet, which will bring it to focus on you as the source of good feelings and good care. Use a bright voice with upbeat energy as you teach. Dogs like to learn; behave as if you enjoy training too.

For a dog to continue to want to learn, training sessions must end on a positive note, each and every time. The dog needs to feel it has succeeded, particularly on days when training has been tough. Always finish your training session with a command you know the dog can do easily and well and follow with praise. A good ending sets the right tone for the next beginning.

11. Change When and Where Training Occurs

If you train a dog in only one setting — say, your front room, or out back on the patio — the dog will learn to obey only in that setting. When you take the dog for a walk to the park and tell it to sit, it won't — simply because it has learned to sit in only one particular setting, which the dog takes to be part of the command.

To help the dog generalize, you need to vary the training setting. Dogs are quick to learn patterns. If you teach it to sit in the front room, out back on the patio, in the park, on an asphalt parking lot, and on the side porch at your mother-in-law's, the dog will figure out that the point is to sit, anywhere and everywhere the command is given.

Training in different settings is also a good way to accustom your dog to different sorts of distractions and to teach it to follow your lead no matter what is going on in the surroundings. This appears to be particularly important to puppies, whose brains, it appears, mature faster and become larger than normal in response to new stimuli.

Whenever you're introducing your dog to new things and settings, be positive and enthusiastic toward both yourself and your pet. Encouragement teaches a dog to be confident and comfortable in any and all settings. But don't force the dog to accept new stimuli — the emotional equivalent of teaching someone to swim by throwing him or her into the ocean. Remain aware of the dog's reactions, and if it reacts with fight, fear, or aversion, employ motivation to allay the dog's anxiety and teach it to accept the new stimulus.

12. Challenges Result from Democratic Treatment

You and your dog are a team, but you are the leader. Remember that always. Whenever your dog senses that your leadership is slipping, it will challenge you. In other words, anytime you treat your dog as an equal rather than a follower, a challenge will result. Your dog has no choice in the matter. Its nature pushes it to seek leadership and to demand reassurance that leadership is strong, that the dog itself will be secure. Just as it is the dog's responsibility to challenge whenever it doubts the strength of your leadership, it is your responsibility to respond to the challenge, reminding the dog that it remains safe in your hands.

Chapter Nine

Basic Commands

The Twenty-four Must-Have's

THERE is good reason to begin at the beginning. Even if you have a particularly intelligent and tractable puppy or dog, avoid the temptation of jumping ahead to teach the optional commands of chapter 10. Wait until your pet has mastered the basic commands covered here. For one thing, you'll avoid confusion; as an example, "shake hands" in chapter 10 is taught after "sit" in this chapter because it is taught most easily from the sitting position. For another thing, these commands instill the basic skills your dog needs to be a well-behaved member of the household. Also the commands in this curriculum build in difficulty from simple to complex, helping your pet learn how to learn.

These commands can be taught

effectively to puppies between eight and twenty-four weeks of age as well as to adult dogs. With puppies, of course, expectations should be much lower than with adults, whose longer attention spans, full brain development, and greater fund of experience allow them to learn more quickly and precisely.

The twenty-four must-have commands are arranged by days — so many the first day of training, so many the second, and so forth — so you can teach the whole batch of them in just two weeks to adult dogs. Pups should be trained over a longer period set by the individual animal's ability to assimilate. It works best if most of these early commands are taught more or less simultaneously, whether to a puppy or an adult. They are central to promoting good behavior right from the beginning and avoiding the long stretch of frustration that prompts so many people to give up their pets.

Walk the Wider World

As you gain more and more control of your pup or dog, and as the relationship and trust between you and your pet grow, you can begin exposing it to more and more of what I call the five S's: sights, sounds, smells, surfaces, and situations. Start taking your pet on walks around the neighborhood, introducing it to all the things and beings in the world outside your home.

Turn these walks into training adventures. Approach them with en-thusiasm and excitement. Encourage your dog to keep pace with you — that's an important part of its training — but also give it plenty of opportunity to explore whatever is new. It is important that your pet feel safe and confident during these excursions. Keep your own enthusiasm high, and the dog will mirror your feelings, which will build its self-confidence.

These walks serve an important purpose in the overall training regimen. In working with your dog, the command and the required action remain the same at each and every training. But changing the setting gives your pet the opportunity to generalize. Train your pup or dog in as many different situations as you can — out back, in the kitchen, over near the rabbit pen, at the park, on your father-in-law's front porch, in the kids' bedroom, on the sidewalk next to the corner gas station, and so on. You want your dog to obey you whenever and wherever you give a command. That can happen only if you give the dog adequate opportunity to generalize.

On your walks, seek new kinds of terrain for training sessions. Work on grass, cement, asphalt, gravel, and sand. Expose your dog to loud outdoor sounds: car backfires, chain saws and lawn mowers, rock music, diesel trucks, and buses. Be on guard for noises that frighten your pet, but remember to remain calm and collected, rather than falsely solicitous over any fear it shows.

Pay careful attention to anything

and everything that draws your puppy's or dog's attention. Watch for attractive odors, sounds, and motions that can turn into distractions. In your training, you may need to counteract them.

Also, vary reinforcers. Use treats, praise, petting, ear-rubbing, a good game of Frisbee or chase-the-tennis-ball. Avoid the predictable, the humdrum, the same old. Keep reinforcement motivating to keep your pet interested.

Longer Reach

Distance, like body posture, affects how your dog responds to you. In dog mind, the closer you are to your pet, the more control you exert. Since most owners want to have their pets obey commands both close by and at some distance, you need to incorporate distance training as part of your canine educational regimen.

Typically I begin training a new command with the dog on a three- to four-foot leash at my side. Then, as the dog gets the command, I gradually increase the distance, working the dog about two or three feet from my body. Only after the dog consistently follows the command at this distance do I put on a longer leash and let it out five or six feet from me. And I do mean *consistently;* that is, the dog obeys whether I am on its right, left, in front, or behind, each and every time. The next step is a retractable leash or lunge line ten feet long. When consistency

is achieved at that distance, push the distance to twenty feet. Once the dog is precise and consistent there, you can start working with it off-leash, first close by your body, then gradually at greater and greater distances as your pet learns to obey completely and consistently.

As you add each increment of distance, be certain that distractions in the environment are under control, particularly in the initial training. The first time you try a new distance, do it in a safe, enclosed space with little else going on. Don't, for example, give your pet its first twenty-foot off-leash training session in a crowded shopping mall on Saturday afternoon. Save that kind of setting for much later, when your pet has already demonstrated its ability.

The Choke Chain

All too often, people use the choke chain, as well as other forms of correction, to break their pets. It pains me terribly to see a misinformed person walking down the street dragging a recalcitrant dog behind, every muscle in its body tensed, its eyes bulging from slow strangulation. Such ignorant folks have gotten it wrong. They are causing unneeded physical and emotional pain and undermining the human-canine relationship.

Used well and properly, a choke chain is one method of giving correction and an excellent training tool. It gives you a high degree of control, and it allows you to communicate to your dog, quickly and unambiguously, what is acceptable and what is not.

A choke chain is used to correct, and only correct. It is a method of neither punishment nor torture. Likewise, a choke chain should never be used to restrain a dog, and it should be removed following a training session. Do not, under any circumstances, allow a dog to run free and unsupervised while wearing a choke chain because of the risk of accidental strangulation.

A choke chain shouldn't be used until your dog reaches six months of age. Before that, use a regular flat collar for training and forgo collar corrections.

Correct fit is a must. Don't use one of those thin-linked, jewelry-like choke chains, which can cut into the neck painfully. Instead, choose a half-inch-wide chain that slips easily through the metal ring. Be sure the links lie flat, so they slide smoothly without catching on the ring. As to length, the chain should have about three or four inches of slack when it is snugged around the dog's neck. A shorter chain will fit too tightly and a longer one will make it difficult to deliver the quick snap required of an effective choke chain correction.

When you are using a choke chain, remove the dog's regular collar. The flat collar may act like a pad and dissipate the choke chain's snap.

Some people consider the choke chain inhumane and prefer to use a flat collar only. This is a mistaken view. The choke chain distributes pressure over the entire neck, but a flat collar concentrates the force on the side of the neck opposite the leash. If a flat collar is jerked from above, it focuses pressure on the windpipe and causes a strangling sensation in the dog. With a choke chain, the same jerk would be felt around the whole neck. Clearly, the choke chain is the better alternative.

How the choke chain goes on the dog depends on whether you are training from the right or left side. Conventionally, right-handed people train with the dog on the left, and lefties train on the right. However, I am a firm believer that a dog should be trained to obey from both sides. But always remember that if you change sides during training, you may want to change the choke chain too — at least until you master the jerk-release motion.

To put on the chain, hold it out horizontally and drop a loop through one of the end rings. You will notice that the chain forms the letter P (see photo on page 176). Now, with your dog on your left side, place the chain over its head so that the long part of the chain — the straight leg of the P — lies across the top of the neck. To train with your dog on the right side, reverse the chain.

After you have trained your pet for some time and mastered the choke chain jerk-and-release, you'll find that you can correct effectively from any angle and any position

The choke chain, ready to be put on the dog.

It takes practice to get the quick snap-and-release action of the choke chain. I recommend that you practice on yourself first and then work with your dog. Don't put the chain around your neck; instead, use your forearm. With your free hand, take the chain by the end-ring and snap it tight. Pay attention to the feeling; the pressure on your arm is sharp and quick. Now, pull the chain tight and hold on. As the muscles tense against the pressure, your arm will pull away from the irritation. Your dog will pull away — that is, resist — in just the same manner if you keep pressure on the chain. Now, try snapping the chain tight and releasing immediately. Notice how the pressure catches you by surprise and that it is gone even before the arm muscles have time to tense. That is the perfect correction.

A further issue concerns the right amount of force to use. There is no such thing as a partial correction; either you correct, or you don't, with no in-between. And if you jerk, and the attempted correction fails — that is, the dog keeps on doing what it was doing — then the force was too little and it wasn't really a correction. Simply put, correct as hard as you need to get the point across. You can tell whether the dog has gotten it. When it stops what it was doing and looks to you for direction, the correction has worked. Until you get that look, the attempt to correct has fallen short.

Always praise your pet the moment it stops the unacceptable be-

without switching the chain around. In the initial stages, positioning the chain to fit the side you are training from helps ensure the most effective correction.

But putting the chain on is simple compared with learning how to use it in a manner that delivers a clear, unequivocal correction to dog mind. People tend to apply pressure to the chain and then hold it. Actually you want to do just the opposite — apply the pressure quickly, and release immediately. And I do mean *immediately*. If you hold on even briefly, the dog's neck muscles will begin to tighten, and the animal will pull away from the pressure rather than surrender to it. In other words, instead of correcting the dog you will be spawning resistance.

havior and looks to you. This tells your dog it has done what you wanted: ceasing the unacceptable behavior and accepting your leadership. That's communication, and it is the whole point of correction.

Besides correction, the choke chain is also used in training to encourage a dog to move in a specific direction. I use this method minimally, however, since I find other methods of targeting, such as patting the legs with the open hand, more effective.

Taking Command of Problems

Your personal attitude in training should encourage your dog to cooperate and respond, and you should use as positive reinforcers what your dog finds most desirable — food treats, praise, play, petting, and so forth. Correction is used only to tell your pet what you don't want and what it should change immediately.

But correction isn't the only answer to problem behavior. For example, let's assume that your pet has this annoying habit of jumping up on you. Reinforcement keeps this behavior going; it feeds the problem. So if you follow the logic of the revolving wheel and simply ignore your dog when it jumps up, you end the reinforcement and stop feeding the behavior. In many cases, such treatment will end the problem.

Another approach to problem behavior is to teach your dog to do it only on command. Take jumping up as the example again. Training your

pet to "up" on you only when you say so brings this behavior under your control.

Yet another solution is to train your dog to a command opposite to the problem. If your pet pulls against the leash when you two are out for a walk, try "back," a command that tells the dog to walk backward. "Back" eliminates the need for correction and it gives your dog an alternative behavior, something it can do positively and productively. It also helps educate your pet to the big picture: If it goes too far forward, you will require it to back up. For a dog with a powerful forward urge, that alone is a form of correction, and it will learn to change its behavior.

Make It Work for You

Years ago — so many I have forgotten exactly when or where or who wrote it — I read an article that posed an important question. Freud argued that toilet training is critical to child development, yet many people who endured unenlightened toilet training grow into healthy adults. The issue, the article concluded, isn't the specific toilet-training process used by the parent. It is whether the child understands that it is loved unconditionally by its mother. Unconditional love triumphs over poor technique and gives the child the emotional grounding it needs to grow into health and wholeness.

The same holds true for dogs. The

point of my training program is to help you build your relationship with your pet. Your dog, by its canine nature, wants to learn and fit into the role you define for it. Training your dog isn't a matter of following the right recipe step by rigid step, but of communicating clearly to the animal that you love it and are its source of safety and security. When that gets through, the dog is yours.

Likewise, understand that there is no one right recipe. The training curriculum developed here is drawn from my twenty years of work with dogs, and it has succeeded for me and the dozens upon dozens of professional trainers I have taught over the years. I combine synchronization, targeting, modeling, association training, and reflex training, and the following pages offer a variety of ways to teach the commands suited to different people and different dogs. Don't be afraid to experiment and find what works best for you and your dog. There is an artistry in this that comes from understanding the interactions between yourself and your dog and learning from them.

Whenever your dog fails to respond or behaves inappropriately, stop and think before you blame your dog. Because canines follow and synchronize with humans, it's always good to consider the possibility that you yourself are misdirecting your pet. Throughout training, pay attention as much to yourself as to your dog. Your feelings and emotions, conscious and unconscious,

affect training as powerfully as do your chosen words and intended body language.

Day One

This elementary curriculum covers twelve calendar days, or two five-day work weeks with Saturday and Sunday off. Introduce the commands on the specified days, but practice them regularly throughout the training period.

Unless you have no fenced yard or enclosed area for training, leave your puppy or dog off-leash this first day. Entice and encourage your pet's responses, giving it the freedom to respond without restraint.

Command 1. Your Dog's Name

Most people confuse calling a dog by name with telling it to come. This leads to a problem when you try to get your dog's attention by calling its name, then deliver a command, like "down" or "wait," that does not entail coming to you. Instead, you want to teach your pet to attend to you when its name is called and await the next command, whatever it is.

Simple association-training methods will teach your dog to associate its name with paying attention to you. Call out your dog's name — say, Freckles the Dalmatian — and praise it with "Hi, sweet dog" the moment Freckles looks at you. If Freckles is paying close attention to something else, like the cat in the neighbor's yard, call out "Freckles!"

with authority, then praise it as soon as your pet turns its eyes your way. Likewise, associate the name with various commands as you go through this series, such as "Freckles, come here" and "Freckles, sit," so that Freckles learns over time that the name is connected not with one command but many. In later training, stop using your pet's name when it is already looking at you. Call out the name only when your pet's attention is directed elsewhere.

Command 2. "No!"

This is the only command that doubles as a correction. It is the mildest correction in the repertoire and the first one to use with your pet.

Teaching the "no!" command is straightforward. Whenever your dog does something inappropriate, say, "No!" in a quick, startling way. By reflex your pet will likely stop what it's doing, at which point praise it. In all likelihood, though, your pet will go right back to that inappropriate something. Say, "No!" again, with force and authority. Again, praise as soon as the behavior stops, then entice your pet into some different activity, like a game. If the pup continues or resumes its unsuitable behavior, repeat "no!" and add a firm bump under the chin. If that still doesn't work, you can combine "no!" with yet firmer corrections, like a shake-down or body bump. Refrain from showing anger as you make the correction, lest you damage self-confidence. You want your pet to learn that it has behaved badly, not that it is a bad dog.

As soon as your pet corrects its action in response to "no!," praise it. You can also draw the pup into a favorite game to divert its attention away from the correction.

Never leave a "no!" situation assuming the lesson is learned for life. Strong drives, be it digging in the garden or going after the neighbor's cat, are not easily overcome with correction alone. Either remove the problem (for example, fence the garden) or maintain careful watch. And make sure your dog never is allowed to enjoy the fruits of unwanted behavior. Getting away with it, even occasionally, reinforces the behavior and makes it that much more difficult to control or extinguish.

"No!" is an important part of shaping, one of my favorite training techniques, which is described in chapter 7.

Command 3. "Come Here"

This is one of the most important commands your dog will learn. It brings the dog close to you physically, a great aid in keeping it under control in all sorts of situations.

Practically every puppy or dog will come when it is called unless it learns that it is likely to receive a correction. Your job is simple: You must teach your pet that every time it comes, it will experience something positive — food treats, praise, chest-scratching, whatever turns your dog on.

The targeting approach uses voice and body language. Give the "come here" command when you have

Fig. 1 "Come here"

Fig. 2 "Come here"

you bend over only slightly. Later, stand fully upright.

Initially, teach this command with your pet off-leash but close, and entice it by stooping and patting your legs or moving quickly and enthusiastically away from your pet (remember, dogs respond to and follow motion). Later in the week, after the leash has been introduced, use it to ensure promptness or correct your pet if necessary. If it should run from you when you give the "come here," do not chase it! That would teach your pet to run away from you and let it know, subtly, that it has assumed leadership over you.

"Come here" can also be taught with association training. When your pet is coming to you on its own, give the command, then reward it for coming as if it had obeyed entirely on its own. Continue this routine, and your pet will come to associate the command with coming to you.

In the course of teaching "come here," you can also educate your pet to "that's it," which communicates that it is on the right track even if it hasn't quite arrived. Use just enough enthusiasm to encourage your pet through the process without signaling that the endpoint has been reached. In dog mind "that's it" — said with an upward inflection on the "it," much like a question — means something like, "Keep going, kid, you're almost there." "That's it" works particularly well with analytical and amiable dogs, who need encouragement to respond, and with

your pet's attention, then step back, drawing the dog or puppy to you. With pups and less assertive dogs, it often helps to get down in a crouch before you say, "Come here" (Figs. 1 and 2). Down close to canine eye level, you appear less threatening and your pet feels more confident about approaching. Once your pet is obeying "come here" consistently, begin issuing the command when expressives, who revel in the spotlight. Driver dogs often need less encouragement along the way. Watch how your own pet responds and use "that's it" in the most effective way for you and your pet.

Command 4. "Better Go Now"

Yes, you can teach your puppy or dog to relieve itself when you tell it to — a convenient command if there ever was one. The approach uses both reflex and association training.

With both puppies and adult dogs, the smell of prior toileting will reflexively prompt urination or defecation. Select a spot where your dog has defecated recently (pick up old feces, which canines find objectionable; the residual smell is enough). Take your dog to the chosen spot and let it wander about on its own unless it leaves the designated area. Keep saying, "Better go now," while your pet sniffs about. Be patient. If it begins to void, continue the "better go now" and perhaps add "that's it" as encouragement along the way. Once the voiding is complete, praise enthusiastically. Keep working on this association and in time your dog will respond to the toileting command by voiding when you say so.

This command should be taught both on- and off-leash. In your own yard you won't need a leash, but if you're traveling, the leash makes it easier to stop at a highway rest stop to let your pet urinate. You should also learn your dog's signals and respond to them, using the command when you take your pet outside. Your responsiveness encourages your pet to let you know when it needs to relieve itself, and helps make life a good deal easier for both of you.

With puppies, "better go now" can easily be incorporated into the housebreaking routine I explain further in chapter 11.

Command 5. "Settle"

This command comes into play when you want a bouncy pup or dog to cool it, but there's no reason to put the animal on a "sit-stay" or a "wait" command. "Settle" can be very helpful, for example, if you have more than one pup or dog and their roughhousing on the living-room floor is getting to be a bit much. It is also one way to move an energized dog closer to the center of the revolving wheel and more under your control.

Teaching this command involves both synchronization and association training. You are using your own toned-down emotions to lower the dog's; that's synchronization. You do not acknowledge or reinforce the rambunctiousness. Instead, when your pet changes its behavior in a suitable direction, you reinforce the change, but quietly enough to slow the revolving wheel and move the dog toward the center. Enthusiasm would speed up the wheel and send an already-excited dog flying.

Teach this command when your

dog is in a high-energy stage. First, calm yourself by breathing in and out slowly and mindfully. Since your dog mimics your moods, it is important that you be calm, not angry or demanding, when you give the command. Then in a firm but quiet voice, say, "Settle." If the pup ignores you and continues its display, walk up to your animal and face it with one hand on each shoulder, then give it a firm shake. In dog mind, this is the action of the pack leader disapproving the behavior of one of its followers. The shaking will surprise and startle your pet, much as if someone took you by the shoulders and said, "Cool it." As soon as its demeanor quiets and calms, praise it — but again, peacefully and with reserve, lest your enthusiasm pump the animal back up.

Use "settle" as often as necessary, and mean it when you say it. Quickly your dog will learn that it must change its emotional act whenever it hears the command.

Day Two

It's time to introduce the collar and leash. Use a plain flat collar for puppies under six months of age, a choke chain on older dogs. Be sure you're familiar with the choke chain guidelines on pages 174–177. It is very likely that your pet will at first pull and fight against the collar and leash. Give it time to settle in, merely holding on to the leash firmly but not pulling or jerking it. I prefer a three-foot leash to the standard six-foot length so there's no slack to deal with when I'm working the dog close.

Use the "come here" command to bring your dog close for petting and relaxing. Your pet will learn quickly that responding and moving closer eliminates the neck pressure created by pulling away. Don't hesitate to give treats, praise, or a massage. If your pet gets out of hand, use "no!"

Command 6. "Get Dressed"

This command teaches a puppy to put its head through a collar and a dog to put its head through a choke chain. It can become a part of your regular training routine, so that "getting dressed" tells your pet training is about to begin. It also invites your dog to be responsible for what comes next, be it training or a walk around the neighborhood.

The command is taught with targeting and association-training techniques. If you are working with a puppy whose neck is too small for a regular collar, make a loop in the end of the leash. With an adult dog, use the choke chain. Say, "Get dressed," hold the loop, collar, or chain in front of the dog's face, then slip it down over its neck. As soon as the loop, collar, or chain settles, praise the dog.

Repeat this action several times, until your pet begins to associate the movement of the loop, collar, or chain over its head with praise and with pleasing you. When it begins to anticipate by sticking its nose through the loop, collar, or chain on its own, use "that's it" to tell your pet it's on the right track. Once it achieves skill at slipping its head through, repeat the same training but limit your part to sliding the loop, collar, or chain over the head just enough to finish the task.

Since you must take the loop, collar, or chain off your dog for this stage of teaching the command, be sure you are working in a safe enclosed area. That way your pet is protected in case it tries to escape.

Command 7. "Let's Go"

Unlike most commands, which demand precision, "let's go" allows your pet to walk to the front of you, out to the side, or even behind, as long as the leash doesn't pull taut. "Heel," which is included in chapter 10, is more regimented and precise. Both "heel" and "let's go" are useful in their own ways, but "let's go" is the place to begin, because it's easier to teach and learn.

Targeting is key to teaching "let's go." With your pet on-leash, pat your leg at about the dog or pup's eye level, and say, "Let's go," as you start walking. Adjust the enthusiasm of your patting to your dog: the more enthusiastic your pet, the quieter your patting. Lagging behind or lunging ahead are common. If your pet falls behind or lunges ahead and the leash tightens, do not drag it along or pull it back. Instead, change directions, and pat your leg to encourage your pet to follow or come back beside you (Figs. 1–4, page 184). Repeat the command as well, and

praise the pup or dog as soon as the leash slackens. Follow this procedure of changing directions, patting your leg, giving the command, and praising for compliance every time your lagging or lunging pet responds. Your pet won't like being surprised by the changes of direction, and to avoid them it will learn to pay attention to you. Also, enthusiasm will draw a lagging dog to synchronize with you and catch up. A firm, calm, and decisive approach will deflate some of the enthusiasm of a lunging pet and draw it into synchrony with your self-controlled emotional state.

An older pup or adult dog who lags or lunges may need correction. A firm "no!" or quick choke chain jerk-and-release may be required to put an end to it. Be measured; use just enough correction to get your dog in line, and no more.

Once your pet has learned to walk with you at a steady pace, help it to generalize by varying your speed, sometimes faster, sometimes slower. Avoid patterns. Be sure to keep slack in the lead as you walk. If you keep the leash tight all the time, you are telling your pet you don't trust it to hold position on its own.

Command 8. "Back"

Used primarily with dogs who lunge ahead, "back" is a useful tool for positioning your dog at will. It stops lunging by requiring the animal to do the exact opposite.

My approach entails both targeting and reflex training. Holding your leash short, position yourself

Fig. 1 "Let's go"

Fig. 2 "Let's go"

Fig. 3 "Let's go"

Fig. 4 "Let's go"

directly in front, facing your pet, and walk into it saying, "Back." Because of the short leash, your pet has no place to go but back. Praise it exuberantly when it does. Repeat this until your pet starts to get it, then do a "let's go" with your pet on-leash at your left side. Now, with the leash held firmly, give the "back" command while patting your leg and backing up yourself. Encour-

age your dog to stay close to your side as you back up; at first, allow the dog to walk sideways as you back up. Intermittently repeat the walk-into exercise with the "back" command to freshen the association between the verbal cue and backing up.

As the concept sinks in and more precision can be taught, put your pet between your body and a wall, leaving the animal too little room to move sideways. Repeat the "let's go" and "back" commands. When your pet gets this down, train the "back" command while you are standing still and not moving backward yourself.

Command 9. "Sit"

Perhaps the most commonly given command in the canine lexicon, "sit" is an excellent way to gain immediate physical control over your dog. And since it demands stillness rather than movement, it helps an excited dog collect itself and synchronize with you on the revolving wheel.

Fig. 1 "Sit"

Modeling is the best way to teach "sit," but reflex learning combined with targeting, modeling, and association training also work. While holding your pet's head up, either by gently lifting the collar or raising the head with your hand, push down on the dog's rump with the other hand and repeat the word "sit" (Figs. 1 and 2). As soon as the dog's bottom touches the ground, I suggest you scratch its chest with your hand. Most dogs love this, and it reinforces the notion that they must sit upright to make the chest readily available to your hand.

Fig. 2 "Sit"

Repeat this routine several times. Then give the command to sit, but hesitate for a moment before using your hands to move the dog into the sitting posture. Watch to see whether your puppy or dog makes the move to sit without help. If it does, even partly, say, "That's it,"

help it complete the movement if need be, and scratch its chest to show how pleased you are. If it doesn't make a move toward sitting, calmly move the dog physically into the sitting position. Repeat this until it gets the idea.

Quieter amiables and analyticals will usually accept the sitting posture readily and hold it, but the more assertive drivers and expressives will be ready to move on to the next item on the agenda almost immediately. Until you start teaching the "stay," play it by ear and let the dog sit for the length of time that suits its nature. Remember that all you want to teach here is getting the rump to the ground, not holding the position for some predetermined period. That comes later.

Some dogs are so hard-headed or short of attention span that reflex training is the best approach to teaching "sit." Pop the rump abruptly with your open hand as you say, "Sit," and the dog will sit down reflexively. Some canines can be taught "sit" simply by holding a food treat over their heads as you say, "Sit." To better arch the neck and look up, the pup or dog may sit (see Figs. 3–5 on page 123). When bottom touches earth, your pet gets the treat.

Day Three

Start off with a review of the first two days' work, encouraging your pup or dog to focus and get it right. Practicing the initial commands will help take the edge off your pet's energy level and allow it time to settle down. Success will feed your enthusiasm too, and that will set the wheel spinning in a way that benefits training for both of you. Once again and from here on out, begin with your pet on-leash.

Command 10. "Stay"

This command is used primarily to control your pet's movement,

Fig. 1 "Stay"

particularly with dogs who are exuberant and ever-moving. Also, "stay" begins to teach the dog about self-discipline and accountability for its own actions, relieving you of the unsettling feeling that your pet has no mechanisms for self-control. You can also use it to hold the dog in place when you answer the door, keep it on the examining table at the vet's office, or calm it when it is agitated.

"Stay" is taught with both modeling and targeting. First, put your dog in the "sit" position, then stand directly in front of it and give the "stay" command in a firm voice. If your dog is exuberant, you will probably doubt unconsciously that your pet will obey, and you are likely to give the command in a questioning voice. This is ample reason for your pet to refuse to go along. Synchronizing with you, it hears the question in your voice and assumes you don't really mean this.

Therefore, you must sound confident, secure, deliberate, and unwavering when you give the "stay." Your firmness alone may take your dog enough by surprise that it will indeed sit quietly and wonder what's going on. Reinforce its quiet with another "stay" command.

In this initial training, remain right in front of your dog and keep it on-leash. Praise quietly lest your enthusiasm encourage your pet to come to you. Standing in front also prevents your pet from breaking the "stay."

If, however, your dog breaks the stay and moves out of the "sit," put it back exactly — and I do mean *exactly* — where it was sitting in the first place. If you put the dog or pup back down even a foot or two from its original position, it will learn that you are less than definite and some cheating is allowed.

To model the "stay," hold your pet in the sit for a moment while you repeat the command. At some point, though, you will need to let go, because the essence of this command is self-discipline. When you let go, hold an open hand in front of your dog's face at nose level (Fig. 1). This targeting suggests to the dog that it will run into a barrier if it moves forward, and helps hold it in place.

As your pet develops awareness of the command, take a small step away, holding your hand up and saying, "Stay," as you move. Keep hold of the leash, lest your pet bolt and learn it can get away with it. Gradually increase the distance you

move away. Shake things up. Sometimes come back to your dog and praise; other times, call your pet with its name and "come here" and then give praise.

Once your pet shows a fair understanding of the "stay," be ready to correct with "no!" or the choke chain. Following correction, put your pet back in the exact spot where it was when you gave the command. If you place the dog closer to you, you will unwittingly give it incentive to break the command again in order to creep toward you.

You can also train your pet to respond to "stay" even when it is receiving other cues. For example, with your pet on-leash and sitting, pull gently but firmly on its collar or choke chain as you give the "stay." The first time you do this, your pet will acquiesce to the pressure and come to you. Correct it, put it back exactly where it was, and praise, then repeat the leash pull with the "stay" command. Soon your pet will learn that "stay" takes primacy over any other stimulus or cue.

Command 11. "Down"

Like "sit," "down" gives you both physical and psychological control of your dog. The goal is to have your dog or pup go down the very instant it hears "down."

"Down" is taught primarily by modeling, though targeting or association training works with some dogs. Begin with your dog in the sitting position and you on its left side.

Fig. 1 "Down"

Fig. 2 "Down"

Fig. 3 "Down"

Put your right hand on the animal's shoulders. As you say, "Down," push down on the shoulders and use your left arm and hand to scoop the dog's front legs forward (see Figs. 1 and 2, page 125). Be gentle. Remember your goal is to induce your pet to lie down, not to knock it flat. As it slides to the ground, repeat the "down" command. As soon as it is lying on the ground, praise.

Another approach is to face the same way as your sitting dog, again on its left side, and reach the right hand over its shoulders to take hold of the outside elbow. With the left hand, grasp the inside elbow. Now ease the legs forward, dropping your dog into the "down," applying pressure to the shoulders with your right arm if needed.

Yet another way is to crouch in front of your sitting dog and tap the floor or ground while saying, "Down." Some dogs will mimic your body position and follow the tapping to the floor (Figs. 1–3). With others, it helps to conceal a food treat in your closed hand, encouraging the dog to lie down and try to nuzzle your hand open.

Finally, in a classic example of association training, you can wait until your pet lies down on its own, then say, "Down," as it drops. Repeat this a number of times, and the dog will begin to associate the physical position with the word.

Whichever method you choose, remember to praise your pet exuberantly when it downs.

Once the pup or dog achieves initial understanding of the "down," combine it with "stay" to give another essential lesson in self-discipline. As always, teach in small increments, moving a short distance away, then a longer distance away, and calling your dog to you to reward it. Slowly increase the distance, and try walking around the dog, even stepping over its body, while it is on the "down-stay."

Some trainers teach the "down" with the choke chain, jerking forward and down quickly to cause the dog to move reflexively downward. I don't recommend this method, unless all else has failed. As far as I am concerned, learning should be as pain free as possible and the choke chain is to be reserved only for correcting your pet's inattention or refusal to acknowledge your authority. Using the chain to teach "down" by reflex qualifies on neither ground.

Command 12. "Release"

Up till now, performing a command ends when you call your dog to you and praise it. "Release" is the formal way to tell your dog a command no longer holds. "Release" doesn't mean the dog is supposed to come to you, although it may choose to do just that. It means instead that your pet is free to do what it wants — something like recess.

"Release" is most easily taught via synchronization. Put your pet on a "down-stay," then say, "Release," in an excited, upbeat, fun-loving voice. You may also have to target by patting your legs, which will induce your pet to end the stay and move around. Give praise when it does so.

Use "release" also with "sit-stay" and later with other restraining commands, like "wait."

Day Four

Once again, begin by practicing the previous three days' lessons, and this time pay special attention to your targeting and modeling. I'll bet that by now your pet is sitting on the word alone, but you're still bending over, maybe even touching its hindquarters for extra encouragement. Begin to minimize and eventually end these hints and prompts. Unless you gradually eliminate them and cut back to the command alone, your dog will come to expect both physical and verbal cues before it complies. That will make life difficult when you try to give a command with your arms full of groceries, wet laundry, or a crying baby.

Command 13. "Out"

This command tells your dog to walk from one place to another, namely through doorways, from indoors to outdoors, between rooms, or from one section of a fenced yard to another. It's much easier to use this command than to pull or push a dog through a doorway. You can also use it to send the dog out into the yard, then stand in the doorway and say, "Better go now" — a comfortable way of handling toileting on cold winter nights.

This command is taught primarily with targeting, though some modeling may be needed. A good place to begin is a door leading out-

Fig. 1 "Out"

hesitate, walk forward with greater momentum, gently propelling your pet through the door. Yet another approach is to teach "out" with another person, who stands on the other side of the threshold and calls the dog as you say, "Out."

When the command sinks in and the dog figures out what you want, gradually stop walking through the door or pointing. Rely on the voice command alone.

After you can stand at the doorway and send the pup "out" without pointing or stepping outside yourself, take a few steps farther inside and give the command from that position. Then reverse the direction. Stand outside and send the dog inside with the "out" command. As the dog learns to generalize, practice sending the dog between various rooms of the house with the "out" command. Be sure to praise for every success, and don't let your pet become bored by repeating the command too many times in the same place.

Remember that the "out" command doesn't require your dog to stay in place right on the other side of the threshold. Once it gets across, it is free to wander where it wants.

Command 14. "Wait"

Readily taught along with "out," "wait" tells the dog to remain on the other side of a threshold or boundary. The animal may do what it wants there — sit, lie down, play with a ball, nuzzle the cat, wander around — but it may not cross the boundary. "Wait" is very useful around the

side. With your pet on-leash, open the door. Stand on the inside threshold and say, "Out," as you make a sweeping motion from the dog toward the door and end up pointing out (Fig. 1). Canines are quite capable of learning to follow a point, a form of targeting that initially pulls them along with the motion itself but later generalizes into the understanding that they are to move in the direction of the point. If the pup hesitates, repeat the command and take a step outside, encouraging your dog to follow and modeling the desired action. Praise your pup as it moves outside. Should the dog still house, for purposes like keeping your pet out of a room where you don't want it, and it can also be used in exiting a car, as we shall see.

Reflex training is easiest, although targeting works with some dogs. Put the pup or dog in a room and back out across the threshold. Your pet will try to follow you. When it approaches the threshold, say, "Wait," firmly, while you draw an imaginary line across the doorway with your hand. Stand aside so your body doesn't form the barrier, and be sure the line is drawn at the pup's or dog's eye level (Fig. 1).

The dog will likely try to cross the line. Bump the end of its nose with the flat of your hand right at the boundary line while again saying, "Wait." Praise your pet as if it had remained there by itself. Repeat this routine until it gets the idea.

As the dog understands the command, test it by walking back and forth across the line in and out of the room, telling your pet to wait even though you have crossed the threshold. Play with the dog on its side of the line, so that it comes to realize it can move about freely there. But this interaction may cause the animal to forget the command. If your pet tries to follow you across the threshold, again bump it on the nose and say, "Wait." This correction reinforces the notion that it must stay behind the line even if you do not. Praise every time you correct as well as each time your pet stops on its own.

Once the pup or dog is staying on its side of the line consistently, test

Fig. 1 "Wait"

it further. Rush energetically through the doorway and out again or bounce a tennis ball on your side of the line. Use any distraction you can think of to induce your pet to cross the line, except calling it by name or using the "come here" command. If the distraction succeeds in pulling it across the line, correct and then praise as before.

When you first start teaching the command, leave your pet behind the line for only a few minutes at a time. As it becomes more accustomed to staying in the room alone, gradually add to the time you leave it on the "wait" command. Also, as your pet comes to understand the command, you will be able to give the command verbally, without drawing the line.

To release the dog from the "wait," call it to you from your side of the line with the "come here" or give the "release" command.

Day Five

Feeling your enthusiasm drain away there, are you? Remember the revolving wheel and your dog's ever-uncanny ability to see right through you. Pump yourself up and approach this twenty-minute training session with genuine enthusiasm, or your pet will begin to build negative associations with the commands. Praise, praise, praise, and practice, practice, practice.

Command 15. "Move"

This is a command no dog owner should be without, because it gets the dog out of your way whenever that's necessary. If your pup is lying on the floor next to the kitchen table, you can tell it to "move" so you can pull out a chair. If it is sleeping in front of the fireplace and you want to put another log on, "move" is an easy way to get your pet out of range of flying sparks. "Move" works whether the dog is lying, sitting, or standing.

Reflex training is the best approach to teaching "move." When your pet is sitting or standing near you, say, "Move," and walk briskly right at it. If it fails to move, keep walking. Bump it in the chest with your knee if it still hasn't moved by the time you reach it. As soon as it moves, even partially, whether before or after the knee bump, praise it. "Move" doesn't tell your pet which way to go, but once the dog gets it, it will start figuring out the best place to go on its own.

Repeat these steps until your pet understands that on the command "move" it must shift away from wherever it is. When that lesson has sunk in, increase the distance from which you give the command.

Command 16. "Closer"

This is another of those so-useful-around-the-house commands. "Closer" tells your pup or dog to move next to you, whether for a "let's go" or a warm snuggle at TV time.

Targeting is the training method of choice. As you say, "Closer," pat your leg if you're standing, your chair if you're sitting, or the floor next to you if you're lying down. When the dog moves toward you, praise effusively. Repeat this routine, gradually eliminating the targeting once your dog gets it. You may want to return to using the targeting, however, whenever you need to tell your dog where you want it to be. Say you're sitting on the couch and you want your pet close to your feet. Then target the floor by tapping your foot against it. But if you want it up against your body, pat the couch itself.

Days Six and Seven

Ah, the weekend, the blessed weekend. Relax. No training, no practice. Do use the commands your dog has learned whenever you need them, but only as a part of your day-to-day routine. Let formal training go until day eight. This gives you and your pet a chance to rest and restore your energy and enthusiasm. Time off also helps prior training sink in.

Day Eight

Back to work. Start off practicing the sixteen commands, and you'll probably notice a marked improvement in your pet's ability. That great leap forward is due to the combination of the short twenty-minute training sessions combined with days off.

Command 17. "Leave It"

You can use "leave it" to keep your dog from snatching pizza off the dinner table, sticking its curious nose into a visitor's crotch, or even growling at a dog in the distance. "Leave it" tells your pet to drop its current sensory focus in favor of paying attention to you. Most often "leave it" is used when your pet is putting its nose where it is unwelcome.

Reflex training is the primary method, but modeling can also be used. Introduce the command by approaching your dog with a treat held in your hand, fingers closed around it, and saying, "Leave it." As you can well imagine, your pet will pay more attention to the food than the new vocabulary and will sniff your hand. Bump it on the nose with an emphatic "leave it." Be sure your hand completely covers the treat lest the pet get even a taste, which is incentive to try again.

Now repeat this procedure. Give the "leave it" command in plenty of time for your dog to avoid contact, but if it reaches out to your hand, again bump its nose with a firm "leave it."

When your dog turns its head to the side at your command, it is beginning to get it. If it turns away from your hand — even slightly — as you give the command, praise lavishly.

When you feel confident your dog understands "leave it," set a treat on a table or the floor within its reach. When it notices or focuses on the temptation, say, "Leave it." Praise if your pup or dog turns away, correct with a nose bump or a jerk on the choke chain if it doesn't. Repeat this style of training with different temptations in different settings to help your pet generalize.

Command 18. "Go to Bed"

Unsurprisingly, this command is usually associated with sleep time. "Go to bed" is also a good way to corral a bouncy puppy or get your dog out from underfoot when you're preparing Christmas dinner for twenty or facing similar domestic turmoil. When your pet is fully trained to it, it will trot off to bed from anywhere in your home.

"Go to bed" can be taught only after "stay" and "down" have been learned. Also, you need to teach your dog what bed is. Take your pet to its sleeping place — presumably a piece of carpet or a bona fide dog bed — and pat it, repeating "bed" as you do so. This targeting associates the word with the object. It also will likely induce your pet to step onto the bed. When it does, give the "down-stay." Praise your pup or dog for lying there, then let it up with a "release" or "come here."

Repeat this procedure, only add the words "go to bed" after "down." Unless the "down" has been a problem, most canines learn this command very fast. In the unlikely event that your pet has trouble, model the command by placing it on the bed and physically downing it.

When the pup or dog shows that it is connecting the command with actually getting on the bed and lying down, position your pet two feet away and give the command. Walk with your pet to the bed and praise it for getting there and lying down. Now, from the same distance, point to the bed and say, "Go to bed," letting your pet move unaided to its sleeping place. When your pet is successful at this, gradually increase the distance until you can send your pet to bed from across the room and, later, from the other side of the house or apartment.

Day Nine

More often than you might expect, dogs learn commands on the first or second try. Be assured that by today your pet knows the first week's work. This is a good time to watch for a common mistake: repeating a known command over and over. Initially you repeat the command to get your pet to make the association. But now, with the association established, you want your pet to obey on the first command. Too often people forget to break away from this initial training methodology, or they get into the unintentional habit of giving a command before they have the dog's full attention and then repeating it again and again. This routine teaches the dog that a command is to be obeyed only after it is said three or more times. Pay attention to what you're doing. Get your dog's full attention before you give the command, then give it but once and require compliance.

Command 19. "Up"

Jumping up is a common problem behavior in canines. Many folks say, "Down," to get their pet out of their faces and back on the ground, but this confuses the dog, who rightfully takes "down" to mean prone. "Off" is the right command, but it can be taught only when the dog is up on something it can get off of. Thus "up" should be taught before "off," and it has useful applications of its own, such as getting your dog to put its front legs on the bed for a good-night kiss.

"Up" tells your pet to put its front paws at the spot you indicate by targeting. ("Up" differs from "jump on" in chapter 10, which tells your pet to put all four paws on a surface.) To teach "up," simply tap any surface, such as a countertop or your chest, while giving the command. Repeat this procedure until the dog or pup figures out what you want, which will likely happen quickly. If your dog is reticent, you may need to model the behavior by raising its forepaws. As always, praise, encourage, and entice whether your dog completed the "up" itself or you had to finish the move by modeling. The praise forms the association and makes it stick.

Command 20. "Off"

As you have likely deduced, "off" is taught from the "up" position. This command belongs in every dog owner's bag of behavioral tricks. It tells your pet to remove itself from whatever it happens to be on: a living-room chair, the front seat of the car, or your aging mother's lap, to name a few possibilities. Also, "off" is used to end "up" as well as the "my lap" in chapter 10.

You can shape "off" simply by waiting till you pet tires in the "up" position, then say, "off" as it gets down. Or you can use targeting, by moving back from your "up" pet and patting your leg to encourage it toward you. Modeling works too. Nudge your dog's paws from the "up" position while saying, "Off," to build the association. If you are sitting or standing with your pet's paws in your lap or on your midsection, simply stand up or move while saying, "Off." No matter which approach you use, praise your dog or

pup when it completes the "off," whether on its own or with your help.

Day Ten

If your pet is failing to obey some of the earlier commands, the time has come to correct with more energy. Physical corrections should be used only when your pet is ignoring your authority. If you have been training carefully and reinforcing properly, noncompliance with the early commands is by now almost certainly an authority issue. You need to let your pet know this is unacceptable. The next time you give a command and your dog fails to respond immediately, correct with a firmly authoritarian "no!," then give the command again the moment the animal looks to you. Chances are that your pet will recognize that you have asserted authority and will respond. If it doesn't respond, use a choke chain jerk-and-release. Be firm enough that your pet looks to you the instant the correction ends. If you don't get that look — which signals that the dog is following your lead — correct harder right away. When your pet does respond, praise immediately and give the command again.

Command 21. "Stand"

I use "stand" on rainy days to wipe off Timmy's, Hoja's, and Keila's feet before they come inside, and it comes in useful for grooming. "Stand" also simplifies a veterinary exam by holding the dog still in a standing position and allowing the vet ready access to its whole body.

Modeling with a bit of reflex training and targeting is the easiest approach. If your dog is lying down or sitting when you begin, pat your leg to entice the dog into a standing position while you give the command. Give the "stand" command as you put your hand under the dog's belly. This is a sensitive spot in the canine body, and your hand there will likely stop by reflex any tendency to sit. Keep repeating the "stand" command to associate the word with the position.

To get the most from this command, you'll want to add "stay" once you get the "stand" concept firmly in your pet's head. "Stand-stay" lets you hold the dog in place while you towel it dry and wipe each of its feet, for example, eliminating rainy-day wrestling matches. If you train this enough and praise your dog appropriately, it will begin lifting its feet on its own as you reach out to wipe them.

Command 22. "Car"

This command is useful for any dog owner who puts his or her dog in a vehicle. It means simply "get in the car," but if you want your dog to take a particular spot inside your automobile, add that requirement to the training.

If you taught "out" with a point and your pet is adept at this command, teaching "car" is as easy as leading your leashed dog or puppy to the vehicle, opening the door,

and pointing inside as you give the command. If your pet hesitates, pat the floorboards or seat to focus its attention. Should this fail, climb in yourself, pat your leg or the seat enthusiastically, and give the command. With a reticent or shy dog, you may have to use treats or enthusiastic praise to invite your pet to you. If this doesn't work — and it may not with a canine who has experienced car sickness — model "car" by giving the command as you pick your pet up and place it inside. Then use the "wait" command to keep the dog in the vehicle while you and any other passengers board.

Call your pet out with a "come here" or "release," whichever works best for you. Most dogs are so enthusiastic about joining you that they will bound out on their own. This poses a danger in heavy traffic, and it is a problem too if you want to leave your pet inside the car or put its leash on before getting out. In either case, use the "wait" command. Because exiting a vehicle can be very dangerous to canine life and limb, I recommend you practice it over and over with absolute insistence on your pet's obedience.

Day Eleven

You have probably noticed that you're not doing all the training yourself. By and large, you are setting up situations that allow your pet to figure things out for itself. It's a sophisticated form of trial and error, and it encourages a dog or puppy to think things through and become accountable for more than just psychomotor skills. Also, you'll find that the relationship with your pet is changing. Now you don't have to work so hard to get your dog's attention. It is starting to look to you for direction and awaiting your commands.

Command 23. "Speak"

This command can be useful for self-protection since a deep-throated bark or growl on the "speak" command is often enough to keep a would-be attacker at bay. It also helps deal with excessive barking by giving you some degree of control over your pet's vocalization.

"Speak" is extremely easy to teach to a dog who is assertive or a natural barker. Reflex training is the best route. Try acting silly, jumping around and moving enthusiastically, while saying, "Speak," and your pet will probably synchronize by barking. Praise builds the association between "speak" and barking.

If you have a less assertive pet who is intimidated by your silliness and withdraws into silence, the problem is trickier and will require good intuitive work on your part. Find a situation where your pet barks on its own, such as strangers coming to the door. When your dog barks, say, "Speak," and praise. Even though your pet is barking in response to some stimulus other than the command, repetition backed by reinforcement will build the association.

Day Twelve

Time to wrap up this basic stage of training. Focus on past lessons, then move on to the final must-have command.

Command 24. "Quiet"

This command is the flip side of "speak." It tells your dog to abide by your desire for silence. It is a good way to stop a dog from barking inappropriately, at cats, other dogs, the veterinarian, or your dinner guests, for example.

You are the one to define what inappropriate is. Many dogs bark when someone pulls into the driveway or approaches the front door. You may want your dog to continue this as a way of warning you of strangers, but also to be silent when the visitor is a friend. If so, you can let your dog know which visitors are acceptable by saying, "It's okay," before you give the "quiet" command.

"Quiet" is easiest to teach with your pet on-leash, and the approach depends on your dog's attitude toward barking. One method is to use "speak," and after your pet barks several times, say, "Quiet," in a quick snappy voice. This is an association-training exercise. Your use of a new word in a new tone will probably quiet your dog for a moment as it tries to puzzle out your meaning. Right then, in that first instant of quiet, you praise, teaching your pet to associate "quiet" with no barking. Repeat this routine to build the association.

Some dogs are quiet during the day, but bark enthusiastically — and annoyingly — at night, usually in the backyard and off-leash. This requires a different tack. When your pet starts barking, say, "Quiet," loudly and quickly, with unmistakable authority. Since the dog is off-leash and at a distance, you need to get its attention. Use the command forcefully, to surprise your pet into momentary silence, then praise its compliance and add some other positive reinforcement, like calling it to you for a treat to prevent it from going back to barking. Keep up this routine, and the association of "quiet" with no barking will develop.

An incessant barker is an even tougher nut to crack. Usually a setup is required, of the sort I discussed in chapter 6, with Fred and Din, his bark-at-strangers German shepherd. Fred had a friend come over, and he used verbal and physical correction to stop Din from barking. But note something important here. The correction wasn't used to quiet Din; it was employed to get her to pay attention to Fred. Correction required Din to follow Fred's lead and figure out what he wanted. Praise is important, too, in handling such problems. Be sure to praise your barking dog the moment it falls "quiet."

Chapter Ten

Optional and Purposeful Commands

Twenty More

*L*IKE you, your dog develops its sense of worth from feeling productive and useful. But unlike you, your pet cannot set its own goals. Instead, you have to set goals for it. You need to be sensitive to your pet's level of accomplishment and increase its performance slowly and carefully, so that it derives satisfaction from continually doing better. As you work more and more with your puppy or dog, ask for a bit extra each time. Expect it to come quicker, stay longer, and release from greater and greater distances, for example. But be gradual. Don't ask for sudden and massive breakthroughs. If your dog will stay for two minutes, don't suddenly increase the success time to half an hour. The dog will only fail, frustrating both you and your animal. Instead, demand five minutes, then seven, then nine. In a while, the "stay" will extend to half an hour, and both you and your dog will be happy campers.

Dogs become what you expect. If you set your dog up to fail, it will. But if you structure its training to succeed, it will come through. In truth, if you want a happy, well-adjusted, obedient dog, you can create one.

The commands in this chapter allow you to advance this process and further your interaction with your pet. Some of these commands require more precision, and others demand sophisticated social interactions or directional behavior. Since you can't sit your dog down and explain in words what this is all about, you will have to be more precise and sophisticated yourself. Typically, precise commands require precise training, which will demand that you set firm limits and be ready to correct instantaneously.

Dogs demonstrate their brilliance when they learn how to respond to commands without knowing what the words mean. But they also demonstrate their brilliance when they figure out how to do only what is required. If you do not demand that your pet respond to the first verbal cue, for example, and instead repeat the command several times before demanding compliance, your pet will await your third or fourth utterance, perhaps even a more forceful tone of voice, before it does what is needed. That's not stupid; that's

very smart. And it is your task to avail yourself of canine brilliance, by requiring that your pet do what you command, and by training in such a way that your pet knows clearly what must be done.

Actually your dog has been training you all along too. Consider one of those times when your pet sidles up against your leg — a form of targeting — and you reach down reflexively and scratch its rump. Your pet smiles and wiggles its bottom in happy response. That's positive reinforcement for you — surely unconscious on the part of the canine, who has never read a book on operant conditioning, but effective nonetheless. And your pet will help you generalize, by sidling up to you not only when you're out back on the patio but also when you're watching TV or sitting at your desk paying bills. The same sidling up, the same rump-scratching, the same happy smile and wiggling in response.

It's quite remarkable really. Dogs train us without reading books, working from their insides, while we read books on training and find out that what we need has been inside us all along. No wonder canines and humans need each other.

In training these precise commands, you need to demand precision from your pet and to ensure that you are doing the training, not your pet. The payoff can be great. As your dog becomes more adept, its sense of self-esteem and personal responsibility grows. You'll benefit too, because your leadership will deepen and feel more satisfying.

Walking, Jogging, and Running

"Let's go" is a pleasantly imprecise command that lets your puppy or dog range about on a slack leash. By contrast, the two commands taught here teach the dog to assume and hold an exact physical position relative to your moving body. Since these commands require precision, mental concentration, and a long attention span, they shouldn't be attempted before your pet is six months old. With some dogs, a year of age is necessary. Let your dog be your guide; the more focused and precise it is, the earlier you can start.

Command 1. "Heel"

This command keeps the dog at your side when you are walking, jogging, or running. "Heel" requires it to stay on your left, its shoulder parallel to your knee (Figs. 1 and 2). "Heel" keeps your pet from getting in your way and requires that it pay attention to what you are doing and physically synchronize with you.

"Heel" is taught with targeting methods much like "let's go," but with much greater precision. Association training and correction are employed to tell your pet it is in the wrong spot. Start with your leashed pet on your left, and target your leg at canine eye level, right where you want your pet's head to be, when you say, "Heel." If your pet lines up facing backward or sideways — an

Fig. 1. "Heel"

Fig. 2. "Heel"

obviously awkward way to walk — reverse its position by taking a step back with your left leg, which draws your pet in the same direction, then moving forward. This maneuver and the targeting provided by your movement will turn your dog around to face forward against your left leg. Walk forward quickly and confidently. Don't be obvious about watching your dog to see if it keeps the correct position since that takes away from your pet's responsibility for staying where it is and distracts it from doing what you want. Instead, encourage your dog to follow you by patting the side of your left leg while you walk, repeating the "heel" command. Keep your voice enthusiastic and energetic, and praise the dog every time it gets into the correct position. If your pet moves out of position, target insistently.

Two things to watch out for. First, don't rely on the leash to hold your dog in position. If you tense the leash, the dog will pull against it, effectively taking you for a walk, not the other way around. Also, by holding the leash tight, you're building resistance in the dog and communicating distrust that it will hold the correct position on its own. Second, *never, never, never, never* adjust your body to bring your pet into position. If you do so, you are teaching your pet that you will move toward it. Instead, you want to teach it to move toward you.

Anytime your dog wanders out of position, turn quickly and walk rapidly in the direction opposite to the one in which it is heading. Correct at the same time, with a sharp noise or a body bump or a snap of the choke chain if required. Praise as soon as your pet resumes the "heel" position.

Once the dog has associated "heel" with the correct position,

gradually reduce the number of times you give the command when you are walking. Finally, say it only once, when you first step out.

In addition to staying alongside you, the "heel" command requires your pet to sit automatically when you stop. Once you have the dog heeling consistently, begin giving the "sit" command each time you halt. If your dog acts confused, show what you want just as you did in teaching "sit" (pages 185–186). When it does sit, praise it. Continue giving the "sit" command at every stop until it is obeying consistently. Then omit the verbal command, and praise your pet lavishly when it sits without being told to.

"Heel" requires your pet to walk at your left side even if you are moving backward. To teach your pet to walk backward with you, give the "heel" command followed by "back" and walk backward. Praise for backing; correct if your pet doesn't. Continue this until your pet gets the idea, then drop the "back" command.

In practicing the "heel," vary your pace so your pet learns to pay attention to you. Be aware of unconscious patterning. It's easy to slip into a habit of going slow first, then fast, or vice versa, training the dog less to heel than to walk slow first, then fast, or vice versa. Keep your pace unpredictable, so your dog is obeying you and the command, not an inadvertent pattern it has picked up.

Also, do not allow your dog on

"heel" to sniff the ground. Use the "leave it" command to keep its nose up and its focus on you.

Command 2. "Side"

This is the flip side to "heel," positioning your dog on the right instead of the left (Fig. 1). It is taught exactly the same as "heel" except, obviously, that the dog changes sides. Remember, too, to change the choke chain during the initial teaching phase (see pages 175–176).

From the "heel" position, give the "side" command and pat your right leg to target. If that doesn't bring your dog all the way around your body, pat the front of your left leg, then the front of the right, then the side of the right, to move your pet around in stages. When your pet gets to the right and faces backward, step back on your right leg, drawing your dog along, then step forward. The movement of your leg creates another moving target and invites your pet to synchronize with you. Step forward with the "side" command and continue targeting and correcting as needed to teach precision.

"Side" can be useful for safety reasons, particularly for walking along narrow, busy streets. If necessity forces you to walk with traffic instead of against it, a dog on "heel" will be on your left closer to the cars. Drivers approaching from the rear may not see your pet, increasing the risk of an accident. Use "side" to bring the dog around to your right, away from passing vehicles.

Fig. 1. "Side"

Retrieving

Play retrieves can be started with puppies, but I recommend postponing formal retrieve training until between six months and one year of age. The retrieve demands a long attention span and good concentration.

To teach the retrieve, you will need a wooden dumbbell of the sort sold at pet stores. Buy one of a size that fits easily in your dog's mouth. Its bulbous ends should extend just beyond the sides of the jaws without rubbing against the lips. Do not let the dog use the dumbbell as a toy. Reserve it for training, and only training.

From a technical point of view, there are three ways of teaching the retrieve. The first is based primarily on modeling, the second combines association training and targeting, and the third employs reflex learning. For most dog owners, I recommend some combination of modeling, association training, and targeting because it provides marvelous insight into the working of dog mind. Reflex learning, though, is a good fallback in situations where quick learning of the retrieve is a must. I discuss all three basic approaches here. Mix and match as best suits you. If you stop making headway, try a different approach and see how it works.

Commands 3–5. "Get It," "Hold," and "Give"

These three commands are taught in sequence since they move one into the other in performing the retrieve.

Method 1: Modeling. Begin when your dog is both calm and alert. The first task is to familiarize the animal with the dumbbell and to associate that object with the command. Put your dog at your side, sitting in the "heel" position. Gently open the dog's mouth, then lay the dumbbell in the jaw so that it rests behind the long canine teeth. As you do this, say, "Get it."

Some dogs object to having their mouths opened. If your dog is one of these animals, don't fight it. Instead, place a hand over the muzzle, so the thumb is on one side of the jaws and the fingers on the other, then press in with thumb and middle finger behind the canine teeth. If the animal clamps its jaw shut, push the corners of the upper lip against the canines. This causes slight discomfort and, in an effort to escape the sensation, the dog will relax its jaws and open its mouth, allowing you to slide the dumbbell into place.

Now, close the dog's mouth around the dumbbell with your hands, one hand over the muzzle and the other under the lower jaw. Use this lower hand to scratch and massage the dog's chin and muzzle and say, "Hold." At the same time stroke the sides of the lower jaw. Use your other hand to massage the muzzle and nose, speaking in a gently praiseful tone and repeating the "hold" command. Your pet will associate the dumbbell with these pleasant sensations of touch and praise and will come to hold the dumbbell willingly.

The dumbbell will taste and feel strange to your dog at first, so don't expect it to hold this new and alien object for more than ten or twenty seconds in the beginning. As the dog becomes accustomed to it, you can extend the time.

To prevent your pet from chewing the dumbbell, be sure to place it on the small teeth behind the canines. Should you place it on the

Fig. 1. "Get it"

Fig. 2. "Get it"

Fig. 3. "Get it"

Fig. 4. "Hold"

Fig. 5. "Give"

molars farther back in the mouth, your pet will chew it reflexively — precisely the lesson you don't want to give.

After several repetitions, say, "Hold," but don't support the lower jaw. If the dog begins to open its mouth to drop the dumbbell, bump it under the chin. Be swift about correcting; don't let the dog actually drop the dumbbell. If your dog never gets the chance to drop it, it won't learn that letting it fall is an option. Praise your dog as soon it regains a firm grip on the dumbbell.

Praise your dog for holding the dumbbell in its mouth, whether it does so easily or only with coaxing. Be low-key in your praise. If your pet becomes too excited, it may pull away from the dumbbell and drop it.

A tidy "give" finishes the retrieve routine and allow your dog to let go. It is important that the dog not release the dumbbell until you tell it to, and also that the object be released into your hands, not somewhere else.

When your dog has kept the dumbbell in its mouth for about twenty to thirty seconds, take hold of the dumbbell, and say, "Give." Be sure you have a good grip on the dumbbell, to reinforce in the dog's mind that its task is to give the object to you, not simply let it drop. Praise the dog as soon as it releases the dumbbell into your hands.

If your pet refuses to let go, work the index finger of one hand into the dog's mouth or press the upper lip against the teeth while keeping

hold of the dumbbell with the other hand. The dog won't like the feeling, and it will open its mouth to escape the discomfort. When it does, praise for a successful "give."

As you practice the "get it" command, you are also teaching the dog to open its mouth for the dumbbell on the command alone. When your dog begins to open its mouth to take the dumbbell willingly, without any help from you, hold it about an inch away from the mouth. This encourages your dog to reach out for the dumbbell on the "get it" prompt. If your pet hesitates about moving its head forward, go back to placing the dumbbell in its mouth and praising it for that action. Then try holding the dumbbell out in front again.

As soon as your dog is willingly reaching out an inch for the dumbbell, extend the distance to two or three inches. When the dog achieves success at this distance, extend it still farther. Place the dumbbell five or six inches in front of the dog's face, but below the level of its chin. This teaches the animal to bend its neck as it retrieves. Each time you give the "get it" command, move the dumbbell a bit lower, praising the dog for each success. Move the dumbbell from side to side as well, to encourage your pet to follow it with its eyes, and say, "Look," a command we will discuss further.

Now it's time to teach the dog to retrieve the dumbbell from the ground on "get it," a move that for some unknown reason is a big step for canines. Hold the dumbbell on the ground in your hand when you say, "Get it." For most dogs you'll need to target this transitional stage by keeping your hand on the dumbbell. After your pet succeeds in retrieving the held dumbbell from the ground, simply touch the dumbbell with your fingertips and give the command. Then remove your hand completely and point to the dumbbell from an inch away. With subsequent repetitions, you can gradually draw your hand away entirely and place the dumbbell on the ground at greater and greater distances from the dog (Figs. 1–5, page 205).

Fig. 6. "Get it"

Method 2: Association Training and Targeting. Association training is a delightful way to teach because it lets the dog discover, through trial and error and without correction, what you want.

Have a bag of treats at hand. You want the dog to know the goodies are there and it will have to perform to get them. Sit with your legs under your chair and your dog right in front, facing you. Hold one end of the dumbbell horizontally in one hand, and with the index finger of the other tap the dumbbell (Fig. 6). When your pet leans forward and touches the dumbbell with its nose, give it a treat (Fig. 7). Have another treat ready because a quick-learner dog may nose the dumbbell again without any targeting. Repeat the targeting, if needed, and say, "Get it," to build the association.

Once you're sure your pet has the idea, require that it touch only the

Fig. 7. "Get it"

Fig. 8. "Get it"

center part of the dumbbell to earn its reward. When that point has been made, move the dumbbell to different spots within arm's reach, first close, then farther away, and also below the level of the chin. Use the "look" command. You'll be amazed by your pet's ability to see the treat in your hand, turn to and touch the dumbbell in the other hand, then turn back to get the treat. The next step is to require your pet to put the dumbbell in its mouth before it receives the treat (Fig. 8, page 207). Here you are upping the ante, requiring more of your pet before it gets the reward. It will respond by trying a variety of approaches. Reward only when it puts its teeth on the dumbbell.

Once your pet is taking the dumbbell in its mouth in response to your command, say, "Hold," while you continue to grip it. Then, as you say, "Give," take the dumbbell out of the dog's mouth. Keep repeating this routine until you see that look in your pet's eyes, the one that indicates it is getting the idea. If you see signs of boredom or lost interest, end on a successful note and pick up where you left off tomorrow.

Once your pet is proficient in taking the dumbbell into its mouth and holding it until the "give" command, let go and require the dog to continue the hold on its own until you say the "give" command. With that lesson taught, move the dumbbell around, starting at different positions and working down toward the floor or ground.

Picking an item up from ground level can be a big step, so keep contact with the dumbbell, targeting it with finger-tapping if necessary. Reward when your pet puts the dumbbell in its mouth. If your pet hesitates or has difficulty, hold the dumbbell in your hands an inch or two off the floor first, then work down to ground level, gradually withdrawing your hand as the training succeeds.

Method 3: Reflex Learning. As you say, "Get it," pinch your dog's ear about a third of the way down the flap from where it attaches to the head. Your pet's mouth will open reflexively, and you can lay the dumbbell in its jaw. Like the prior two methods, this one builds an association between the word and the action, but here the dog has no choice about complying. Once your pet learns to open its mouth voluntarily in response to "get it," continue training with the modeling method.

Command 6. "Look"

This command came up earlier, at the point where you began to move the dumbbell about before saying, "Get it." Obviously the method of teaching is targeting; the movement of the dumbbell attracts the dog's attention, and your praise builds the connection between the dumbbell and the command to "look" as part of the "get it" routine. Soon your dog will associate "look" with the need to look for something moving. Later, you can use "look" in the course of teaching it to retrieve a stationary object that is currently out of sight. Suppose you want your dog to fetch your slippers, which are lying on the floor across the room. Say, "Look," and your dog will begin to cast its eyes about. When they light upon the slippers, say, "That's it," which tells your pet it has the right object. "Get it" will send your pet across the floor to pick up the slippers. Now you need the next command.

Command 7. "Bring It Here"

There's that old bad putdown about somebody having trouble walking and chewing gum at the same time. In fact, all animals, dogs and humans included, have to learn how to do two things at once. Now is the point to teach your dog how to complete two actions simultaneously: holding the dumbbell in its mouth, and walking.

Modeling usually works best. Face your dog while it is holding the dumbbell, and firmly grip the muzzle and the chin from the side, keeping the dumbbell in place. As you do this, take one step backward and say, "Bring it here." If the pup hesitates, pat your leg with your free hand to encourage it to move in your direction. Praise the pup the moment it steps toward you.

Keep hold of the dumbbell to prevent it from falling. If the dog starts to let go of the dumbbell as it comes to you, correct with a bump under the chin — just as in teaching the "hold."

Use lots of encouragement. Remember that this business of doing two things at once is uncharted territory for your dog, and it may well find the command difficult. Keep your animal motivated, and praise for every little success.

Repeat this training process until the dog can hold the dumbbell and walk toward you. Then gradually remove your hand from its mouth, to train the dog to hold on its own, without help from you. Next, move farther away and tell the pup to "bring it here." Slowly increase the distance the dog must walk to get to you. Then increase the dog's pace, enticing your pet to break into a trot and finally into a run by backing up quickly. Stay on guard. If in the excitement of coming to you your dog seems to be about to drop the dumbbell, give a swift bump under the chin to correct. Keep it in mind that this command is best taught if you can prevent the dog from ever dropping the dumbbell and getting the notion that letting it go is possible.

Homework: Perfecting the Retrieve

Retrieving entails a complicated series of actions, each of which must be done correctly, in the right order, and on the proper command. It takes a good deal of practice to train a dog — even a Labrador, Chesapeake, or golden, in whom retrieving is inborn — to retrieve consistently and well. Practice the retrieve often, and practice patience too. Avoid frustration, lest your dog become frustrated as well. Keep working on the basics, and as your pet becomes more adept, increase your demands on its performance — greater distances, longer holds, quicker gives.

Once the dog is skilled at looking for, retrieving, holding, bringing the dumbbell to you, and giving, and is performing the whole routine successfully, you can work on variations by substituting other objects for the dumbbell. Start with medium-sized firm items your dog can grasp easily, such as a length of dowel, rolled paper, or thick leather workgloves. If your dog works well with these substitutes, you can try more difficult objects, both smaller and larger, like a set of keys, balled-up socks, or the newspaper. Keys, for example, are tricky not only because of their size, but also because of their strange cold feel in the dog's mouth, which makes them less inviting. For safety's sake, avoid training the dog to retrieve any objects that could be accidentally and detrimentally swallowed — like coins, spools of thread, nails, or clothespins.

Variations on the Retrieve

Command 8. "Drop It"

This command is like "give," except that the dog deposits the object somewhere other than in your hands. "Drop it" is taught like "give" with one significant change: When you say, "Drop it," don't take hold of the dumbbell with your hands. Instead, the dog is to let the dumbbell fall to the floor. However, because past training has taught it to keep holding, it may not want to drop the dumbbell. You may need to encourage your pet by putting your finger in its mouth and pushing the dumbbell out or opening its jaws so the dumbbell falls free.

Confusion will likely result. In learning "hold" and "give," the dog was corrected for dropping the dumbbell. Now it is being asked to do just that. Use loads of praise to help the dog understand that, yes, you do want it to let go of the dumbbell completely, but only on the "drop it" command.

When your dog understands the difference between "give" and "drop it," you can start using the "drop it" command when the pup has its head over a wastebasket, recycling bin, laundry hamper, or some other receptacle. This will accustom the dog to putting things into containers. Next, as with "give," you can substitute soft safe items to teach "drop it" with objects other than the dumbbell.

Command 9. "Tug"

This play command tells the dog to pull on something it has retrieved. I have used it to train dogs to open and shut doors. You may want to use it in play to engage in a tug of war. "Tug" builds on the canine predatory instinct, and you will see this behavior when dogs play with each other.

Use an old sock, towel, or a length of thick rope to teach "tug," not a dumbbell or some other hard object. Drag the sock along the ground and give the "get it" command, motivating your dog to grab the end of the sock. If your pet seems hesitant, incite its instinctive reaction to movement. Flick the sock back and forth on the ground, or wave it in the air a few inches off the ground, just as you would in playing with a kitten.

When your dog grabs the sock, let go of it, and reward by letting your pet play with it for a few seconds. Then take hold of the sock and pull gently while you say, "Tug." Keep this up until your pet acts determined to get the sock away from you and pulls back. Let go as you say, "Tug," again, so your dog enjoys its success in addition to your praise.

Once the dog is associating "tug" with seizing the sock, hold on for a few seconds after your pet grasps it rather than letting go immediately. Repeat the "tug" command as you hold on. Most likely, the dog will keep its hold, too. Praise it for doing so. Hold on to the sock for progressively longer periods. As the dog learns that it is okay to pull against you, add resistance, forcing it to pull harder and harder. Just be sure not to apply so much force that you hurt your pet's soft mouth tissues or teeth.

"Tug" is one of many games you can enjoy with your dog, but be sure to maintain your leadership. Don't allow your pet to become inappropriately aggressive, bite, or growl. If that happens, take command with "settle," "no!," or a physical correction as required.

Command 10. "Get Your Leash"

Once you have your dog retrieving on command, you can teach it to bring you specific objects, like its leash when it's walk time. "Get your leash" is a delightful command, because you can feel the joy in your dog as it struts proudly to you, leash in mouth.

Start by using the leash in place of the dumbbell with the "get it" command, adding "leash." After a few repetitions, put the leash on the ground, then give the "get it" command along with "leash." If your dog has difficulty retrieving from ground level, use gradual approximations, starting at chin level and working down, just as with the dumbbell.

Next, attach the leash to your pet's collar and say, "Get your leash." A dog proficient at the retrieve will willingly pick up the loose portion of the leash. If it hesitates or seems confused, model the correct action.

The third step is to detach the leash from the collar and lay it on the floor or ground next to some other item. Say, "Get your leash." If your dog goes for the wrong item, correct and say, "Look," and, "Leash." The instant your dog sets its eyes on the leash, say, "That's it," followed immediately by the "get your leash" command. Once your pet has the leash in its mouth, reinforce its action with "hold" and "bring it here." In time and with practice, "get your leash" will include an understood "hold" and "bring it here" and you won't need to repeat these commands each time.

Once this whole routine is down pat, put the leash in a permanent location and show it to your pet. Now train your dog to retrieve the leash from its permanent spot and bring it to you. When you begin, stay close to your pet, but as it succeeds, move away incrementally.

In the course of training, you will need to praise to let your pet know it's doing what you want. But once it understands that getting the leash means a walk outside, you won't need to praise. The walk alone will be the reward, and your pet will have achieved a measure of both responsibility and self-motivation.

Command 11. "Take It to [Name]"

This command is similar to "bring it here" except that it tells your dog to carry an object to a named recipient other than yourself. It can be very useful.

To teach the command, you use the dumbbell and commands already trained. First, tell your dog to "get it" and then "hold" the dumbbell. Next, command your dog to "take it to" someone it knows by name. Cue the dog by pointing to the person you have named — say, your roommate Sarah, who should be only a few feet away at this initial stage. Sarah must encourage the dog to come, tell it to "give" the dumbbell into her hands, and praise the

dog for obeying all three commands. With success, increase the distance between your pet and Sarah.

After your dog has followed this routine a couple or three times, try some new item, like a rolled newspaper or a length of dowel. As you make this transition to new items, give your dog extra praise for responding correctly.

This command can be used for work or play, or for work that becomes play. One friend of mine used it to send a tube of sunscreen via golden retriever to her husband, who was lounging on an inner tube in the middle of a small lake and turning pink. After the dog delivered the sunscreen, the husband sent it swimming back to his wife on shore with the same "take it to" command. The dog enjoyed the whole thing as much as the people.

Social Interactions

These skills can be taught at any age, but real precision shouldn't be expected before your pet reaches six months old.

Command 12. "Shake Hands"

This command gives your pup or dog a well-mannered way to say hello. Your guests will appreciate a pet who offers its paw in greeting much more than an animal who jumps all over them. There are two basic approaches to teaching "shake hands."

Method 1: Targeting. With your pup or dog in the sitting position, put your hand out in the place where you want it to put its paw and say, "Shake hands." (You may have to begin close to the ground, then raise your hand gradually higher as you repeat the training.) Since targeting usually draws the dog's head, your pet may try to sniff your extended hand. Respond with "no!" Snap your fingers or clap your hands to induce your pet to volunteer its paw. Some will, in which case praise. Some won't, in which case try the next approach.

Method 2: Reflex Learning and Modeling. Again, face your sitting pet. Tap the inside of the pastern — the ankle area in a human — on the dog's right or left foreleg as you say, "Shake hands." The tapping will bother your dog, so it will try to move its leg away from the irritation. The instant it moves its paw off the ground, take the paw in your hand and gently move it in the up-and-down shaking motion, praising your pet all the while.

Repeat this routine several times, then refrain from tapping to see whether your dog will raise the paw on its own with the spoken command alone. As always, use praise for any approximation of the right action. Continue encouraging and praising until the dog can raise its paw and place it in your hand on the command alone.

In encouraging your pup to raise its paw, don't pull on the leg in a way that pushes the animal off balance. Should the dog resist lifting its paw, shift its weight onto the opposite leg first. For example, if you are facing your pup with your left hand outstretched to receive its left paw, push on its left shoulder with your right hand. This moves the dog's body weight onto its right foreleg, freeing the left paw.

Command 13. "Kiss"

This command is a must for dog owners who love physical contact with their pets. I recommend it because it helps nourish the fundamental physical relationship between human and canine.

The "kiss" is in fact a quick lick across the cheek. If you watch dogs interacting with each other, you'll see them lick muzzles as a sign of affection and connection. The kiss is an adaptation of this instinctive canine behavior.

There are four ways to teach the "kiss" command. The first is to target by giving the command when you are nose-to-nose with your pet. Smile and smack your lips together to make a kissing sound. Typically, pups and dogs respond to this sound with their own quick lick. As soon as your pup kisses you, praise. It enjoys the kiss for its own sake (remember: dogs relish touch), but the praise associates its own pleasure with the further satisfaction of pleasing you (Figs. 1 and 2, page 214).

The second method entails reflex learning, by giving the command and blowing into the puppy's or

Fig. 1. "Kiss"

Fig. 2. "Kiss"

dog's nostrils gently. Again, your dog will likely respond by kissing. Again, praise as soon as the kiss is planted on your cheek. I read once that this method works with grizzly bears too, but it's much safer with dogs.

If these two methods don't work, try the third. Give the command and make high-pitched, puppyish sounds. Again, praise as soon as the kiss is forthcoming.

Finally, if all else fails, dab peanut butter on your cheek. Give the "kiss" command and offer the peanut-buttered cheek to the pup. Few dogs on this earth can resist peanut butter, and when it licks your appetizing cheek, add praise to the pleasant sensation of the food. If you do happen to be training a grizzly simultaneously with your dog, don't use the peanut butter method with the bear. You might end up as lunch.

Command 14. "My Lap"

As I have said over and over, the affective domain is the center of your dog-training mentality. The stomach is the obvious realm where those gut feelings reside, and nothing is more soothing than a warm body pressed up against your own belly. That's what "my lap" can do. If you have a large dog, "my lap" puts its legs in your lap and the head and shoulders under your chin, a great vantage point for gathering your dog up in your arms to give and get one of the greatest hugs anywhere in the universe. Small dogs and puppies respond to "my lap," too, jumping up and settling in with their whole bodies. It feels wonderful.

To teach the command, sit in a chair with your pup or dog on the floor either in front of you or at a right angle. Attract your pet's attention by patting the side of your lap farthest from your dog as you say, "My lap." (If you've taught the "up" command, use that with "my lap" added.) The targeting motion and sound will arouse the dog's curiosity, drawing it to get up on your lap, and tapping the side of your lap away from your pet shows it precisely where you want it to be (Fig. 1). When it gets there, scratch its chest — which will send your pet to paradise. After it has completed the command several times, stop patting your lap and rely on the command alone. As training progresses, have the pup or dog remain in the "my lap" position for longer and longer periods. To get your pet out of your lap, use the "off" command from chapter 9 and follow with praise (Figs. 2 and 3).

Some dogs, particularly big ones, may respond with more exuberance than you want and try to crawl all the way into your lap. To stop this, correct with "no!" if your pet puts more than its paws and upper body on you.

Command 15. "Go to [Name]"

Since this command is taught with the dog off-leash, be sure you are in a safe and secure setting. Also, teach this to your pet only when it is consistent in obeying "come here."

You need a partner and your pet's favorite treats. Have your partner stand about six feet away from you and the pup or dog, with the treats held inconspicuously in the hand. Give your dog the "go to" command, adding your partner's name and targeting by stepping forward

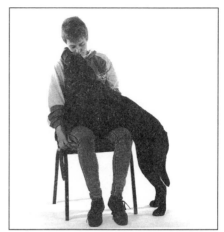

Fig. 1. "My lap"

Fig. 2. "My lap"

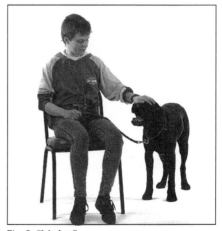

Fig. 3. "My lap"

and pointing the direction it is to walk. We'll again use Sarah as your partner's name. As soon as you say, "Go to Sarah," step toward her, and point. Sarah should crouch in a welcoming position and enthusiastically call your pet by name to "come here." Let Sarah do the necessary encouraging to attract the dog to her. If you try enticing the dog, it will only confuse it and turn it back to you — the exact opposite of this command's intent.

When the dog reaches Sarah, she should welcome it with praise and a treat. Next, repeat the training, only have Sarah send your pet your way as you encourage it to come to you. Then send it back to Sarah, but skip the step forward in her direction. Once your pet is successful, have Sarah remain standing when you send it. After that is working, tell your partner not to encourage your pet as it carries out the command, but to praise only when the animal completes the action. Taper the use of treats, and finally omit them altogether.

Once your pet is doing all of this well, increase the distance between you and your partner. If your pet displays confusion at any time, reinforce your message by going back to the first steps in the training — stepping forward in Sarah's direction, or having her crouch and offer encouragement, for example. Move on to exercises where your partner is out of sight and calls to your pet in order to teach your dog to hunt for the person it is seeking.

When this is all working well, in-troduce a new partner and command your pet to "go to" him or her. After you get the command working well with the new partner, bring both partners in at once and send your dog to one by name and then to the other. Encourage your pet with "that's it" when it moves toward the right person, and have your partners praise when your pet gets the "go to" right. If your pet goes to the wrong person, correct with a gentle "no." Since motivation induces the dog to complete the "go to" command, too much correction will discourage it.

When your dog has the command down, you can turn it into a game. Stand in a circle with two or three family members and send your pet around the circle from one to another, varying the order and praising the dog for every success. Make it fun. Be enthusiastic and encouraging, so you, your family, and your dog all have a good time.

Command 16. "Say Hello"

This command requires your dog to put its head in your lap to be stroked and petted. "Say hello" is like "my lap," but less of the dog — the head only, rather than the entire upper body — winds up in the lap. If "my lap" suits your needs, you may want to skip "say hello." Still, if you'd like to be able to set up low-key physical interactions with your pet, this is a useful command.

Puppies in particular are constantly curious and want to investigate what is going on around them, yet this command tells them to put their heads in one place for several minutes. As a result, you have to be patient and calm to teach this command.

So does the dog. Don't try to teach "say hello" when your pet is excited. Start only when it is already quiet and relaxed. Sit in a chair with your pet on the floor sitting or standing at a right angle to your legs. Give the "say hello" command. Target your pet's head by patting the side of your lap nearer the dog with one hand while laying the other hand on your pet's neck, just behind the ears, and gently push the head toward your body. The targeting on the side of the lap near the dog indicates you want only its head since there isn't room enough for the rest of its body. If this method doesn't work, you can model what you want by taking hold of the head gently and moving it into your lap.

When the head comes to rest in your lap, entice your dog to keep it there. Use your lap hand to stroke the muzzle, cranium, and ears while talking in a soothing, peaceful voice — all of which the dog will enjoy mightily — and repeating the "say hello" command to build the association. After it has kept its head in your lap for a short while, give the "release" command and praise quietly.

Following several repetitions of this procedure, stop targeting or modeling. Once the pup or dog obeys without enticement, take the hand away from its neck as well. If it reacts with confusion, put the hand back on its neck, but use no pressure

to push its head forward. Your pet will likely come into your lap on its own because the head-stroking feels good.

Now practice "say hello" for longer and longer periods of stroking. Then try teaching the command from the opposite side. Once the animal has these variations down pat, you can also teach it to "say hello" to someone else by combining the "go to [name]" command with "say hello." This is a wonderful command for use in social therapy work in a nursing home or other institutional setting.

Grooming

You'll find these commands make the tasks of brushing and combing much easier. They give you easy control of your pet and help turn grooming into both a pleasurable experience and a lesson in your leadership. You can use them too in the veterinarian's office, where they can eliminate exam table wrestling matches at checkup and vaccination time.

Like the social commands, these can be taught at any age, but precision should not be expected before six months. Also, gear performance to your pet's physical ability. Even an agile three-month-old puppy can't jump onto a three-foot-high table, for example.

Command 17. "Jump On"

This command tells your dog to leap gracefully and carefully onto a table or bench and plant all four feet there. It saves you from having to lift a big dog onto a grooming table.

Make sure the table or bench you use to teach this command is low enough for your pet to jump on easily, or put a chair next to it as a step up. With your pet at your side on-leash, walk up to the table (or chair, then table) and target by patting it with the flat of your hand while saying, "Jump on," with enthusiasm and energy. If you can step on the table safely, get up there yourself and encourage the dog to join you. Use an excited voice to overcome fear or apprehension in your pet. You can also entice it onto the table with a food treat.

As soon as it starts to jump up, even if it does nothing more than put its front paws on the table, praise ecstatically. Praise helps overcome fear and says your pet is doing the right thing. Encourage it to get up the rest of the way, and praise further when its hind legs reach the table.

If your pet balks or is reluctant to jump, model what you want by placing its front paws on the table while repeating the "jump on" command. When your pup will put its front paws on the table unassisted, repeat the command while you lift its rump up onto the table. Once all four paws are up, praise your pet. Repeat this process until the pup jumps onto the table without assistance or demonstration. Be sure to praise for each success.

Some dogs won't jump up even after being shown what to do. If that happens, first check to make sure the table or bench isn't so high the dog can't reach it in one bound. If it is in range, move away and, with your pet at your side, run toward the table enthusiastically. When you reach it, step to the side close enough to leave no room for your pet to squeeze past and simultaneously pat the table enthusiastically. The dog will have no place to go but the table, and its momentum will carry it up and on. Praise for success and to instill confidence.

At first, don't expect your pet to remain on the table for long. Gradually you can extend the time. Also, you can raise the height of the table if your pet is growing, in either size and confidence, always being sure to remain within the limits of safety.

To get your pet back onto the ground, use the "off" command from chapter 9. If the animal seems confused, pat the ground with your hand as you say, "Off." Be sure to praise your pet for obeying "off" as well as "jump on."

Command 18. "Turn Around"

Another command useful in grooming, this one tells your dog to turn halfway about and bring the other side of its body within your reach.

Put the dog up on a table or bench with "jump on," then tell it to remain in place for grooming with "stand" and "stay" — which require it to be still. Groom your dog, both to relax it and to get it accustomed to being groomed when it is off the ground. After you finish one side of its body, don't walk around the table to do the other side. Instead, teach the "turn around" command.

Target by tapping the tabletop to your pet's rear, and say, "Turn around." Curious about the sound and movement of your hand, it will turn to investigate. Praise and encourage it to turn farther. Be careful, though, not to so excite your pet that it falls off the table in its eagerness.

If the dog shows it is unsure what you want, step in the direction you want it to go. It will try to follow you by turning. Praise, and keep an eye peeled lest it fall or jump. Repeat these steps, and as your pet gets the point of "turn around," do less and less to target, relying more and more on the spoken command alone.

Command 19. "Roll Over"

Every command has a purpose; "roll over" has three. First, it puts your pet in a good posture for grooming its belly or applying flea powder.

Second, "roll over" teaches your pet to trust you. Being belly-up puts a canine in a highly vulnerable position. Once it learns that it can show its belly to you and not be hurt, it will come to trust that you will not cause it injury or put it in harm's way.

Third, in rolling over, your pet learns to submit to you. Rolling onto the back is a canine way of acquiesc-

ing to dominant individuals. When your pet rolls over for you, it is physically accepting you as leader of the pack.

Because your pet is so vulnerable in the belly-up position, you must be particularly careful not to display anger or frustration in teaching "roll over." If you do vent hostile emotion, you will confirm your pet's fear that exposing its belly is dangerous. That won't help the relationship, and it won't help in teaching the command either.

Also, although "roll over" is logically connected with the "sit" and "down" commands, teach it separately. If all three are taught together, your pet will learn them as one sequence and fail to respond to each as a separate and distinct command.

To teach "roll over," start with your puppy or dog in the "down" position. If its head and shoulders are upright, push against the shoulder to lay it out flat, then pick up one of its legs to scratch the side of the belly, repeating "roll over" all the while. Loving the stimulation, the dog will likely roll onto its side to expose more of its belly. As it turns over, continue to say, "Roll over." When it gets onto its side, reward it with praise.

Once your pet performs this part of the command consistently, entice it to roll all the way over onto its back by continuing to scratch its belly even after it rolls onto its side. Most pups and dogs enjoy the feeling so much that they will surrender to it and go onto their backs voluntarily.

Some dogs need a bit more encouragement. If continuing to scratch the belly doesn't do the trick, gently roll your pet onto its back. Be casual, not forceful, and act reassuring rather than threatening. As you roll your pet over, give the command, and praise when it gets onto its back, as if it had gotten there by itself. After several repetitions of this maneuver, your pet will learn to associate the rolling-over action with your praise and will go onto its back unaided.

Directions

These commands can be taught at any age, but puppies don't have the attention span to work at a distance from you. As they get older, their ability to retain the concept even outside your presence increases and higher performance can be expected.

Command 20. "Go to Your Room/Kennel"

So your Uncle Miltie is visiting and, truth be told, he's a downtown kind of guy who dislikes dogs. This command can save the day, because it allows you to send your pet to its room or kennel when Uncle Miltie walks through the front door, keeping the animal out from under foot all the time your dog-despising relative is in the house. If you follow "go to your room" with the "wait" command, your dog can spend the time in its room, playing or sleeping, without bothering your guest. If you use the "go to your kennel" variant, you can send your dog to the backyard kennel or to its crate.

Teaching this command for either "room" or "kennel" is essentially the same. Let's start with "room," which should be the specific room where your pup or dog spends the night.

Place your pet on a leash at your side, and walk briskly toward the room. Stop sharply at the threshold, say, "Go to your room," and let the pup's or dog's momentum carry it in. If you've taught "out," you can reinforce the movement by giving that command as you point the dog over the threshold. Praise as your pet moves through the doorway. Be careful not the jerk the leash accidentally and pull your pet back to you, contradicting your command.

When you repeat this routine, your pet may anticipate and stop when you do. Target by sweeping your arm forward, encouraging the dog to move into the room and pointing the direction you want it to go.

Once the pup has figured out that "go to your room" means to cross into the room, begin sending the dog in while you stand a foot away from the doorway, then increase the distance to a few feet. Remember not to jerk the leash back toward you. Praise your pet every time it enters the room.

When your pup is going to its

room consistently, take the leash off the pup and give the command, first close to the room, then progressively farther away. Don't expect the dog to remain in the room, however, unless you give a "wait" command once it is inside.

"Go to your kennel" is taught the same way, using the outdoor kennel or the crate as the destination. Start with the pup on the leash, then graduate to removing the leash and giving the command from greater and greater distances.

This command exists for your convenience and, at times, for your dog's safety. *Never, never, never* give it in anger nor use it as punishment.

Remember: Anything done in anger is a punishment that only exacerbates the problem.

Graduation Day

Well, you've made it. If you have faithfully followed the curriculum through, you will now have trained your dog to obey forty-four separate commands. That is an impressive repertoire. And your pet isn't the only one who has accomplished much. You have done quite a good piece of work, pursuing a program that can be demanding and challenging. Congratulations — to the both of you.

Part Four

Home and Health

*I*NTRODUCING *a puppy or dog into your family is very much like bringing a newborn child home. Everything changes. Routines and relationships shift to accommodate the new family member. Likewise, the newcomer starts to learn how the family works and what his or her role is to be. With neither child nor new pet is the task simple. But if you know what to expect, and if you are ready to shoulder the responsibility of your new pet's emotional and physical health, you will reap the rewards of the relationship much sooner and more deeply.*

The first chapter in this section covers the socialization and handling of a puppy or new dog. The basic tasks of achieving a sense of security in your leadership and learning the rules of the house apply to older animals just as much as to younger ones.

The second chapter details the best method of ensuring your dog's health — prevention. Maintaining canine health involves much more than good veterinary medicine. It entails attending to, and cultivating, the relationship between you and your animal. Caring for your dog's health needs helps you stay in touch with your pet at the basic, physical level that is central to a rewarding relationship.

Chapter Eleven

Bringing the Puppy or New Dog Home

*F*IRST off, don't expect too much. Although you can teach an old dog new tricks, you can't teach a puppy more than it's capable of learning. It is, for example, physically impossible to train a seven-week-old puppy to wait until it gets outside to eliminate. At that young age, a puppy has no control of bowel and bladder. Housebreaking cannot start until eight weeks of age, when the puppy just begins to develop a rudimentary capacity to control urination and defecation. Trying to housebreak the pup sooner will only confuse the animal and frustrate you.

Part of the issue is physical capacity; a puppy can be taught to do only what it is capable of doing. Also, puppies, very much like small children, need to learn how to learn.

Learning is itself a skill acquired through training. That's why the training curriculum in chapter 9 starts with simple commands, ones younger dogs can learn quickly and successfully. This early training teaches dogs not only the individual commands but also the how and why of learning — which gives them a better foundation for the more difficult or precise tasks in chapter 10.

In addition, puppies pass through a number of critical learning stages that can affect the rest of their lives, for better or worse. In these stages, puppies are wide open to certain kinds of stimuli and may be overwhelmed, even traumatized, if hit with too much too soon.

Items to Have on Hand

Life with your new pet will go more easily if you have the necessary tools of the trade on hand before it comes through the front door.

- *An adjustable nylon or leather collar.* It is a good idea to get your dog used to a collar early on. It should fit snugly, so that it doesn't slip off by itself or catch or snag on backyard bushes or living-room furniture. By the same token it should not fit so tightly that it chokes. Since puppies grow very fast, check the fit frequently. You'll probably go through two or three progressively larger collars before your dog reaches full size.
- *Dog license.* Check with your city or county to determine local laws. In many areas, a pup doesn't have to be licensed before it is four to six months of age and can be inoculated against rabies. After you get a license, affix it to the dog's collar. You may also want to add an ID medallion to ensure the return of your dog in case it gets lost.
- *Leash.* Get one that is two and a half to six feet long, an inch or more wide, and made of leather, cotton, polyester, nylon, or similar material thick enough to feel comfortable in your hand. The leash gives you control of the dog, even when it is some distance from your body. A thick leash will protect your hands against rope burn in case the dog lunges away from you — not an issue with puppies, but a major consideration when the dog gets bigger and stronger. Personally, I prefer a short leash since there's less to get tangled up in. A retractable leash is also useful, since it lets your pet out to explore on its own but still under your control.
- *A crate.* Crates aren't cruel; dogs find them secure and comfortable (see pages 51–52). A crate provides your puppy with a protected haven and a safe method of travel in a car, and, as we will see, it can be a great help in nighttime toilet training. But never, never, never use

confinement in the crate as punishment.

- *A dog bed.* Your puppy will need a comfortable place to sleep, preferably close to your own bed; you'll want something that's easy to clean. Early on, a simple cardboard box lined with towels will serve the purpose nicely. Later, when the puppy has adjusted fully to its new home, a braided cotton rug makes a good bed. Cleaning is easy; just shake the rug out and vacuum underneath for any dirt that slipped through the seams. If your puppy or dog must sleep on concrete, be sure to raise its bedding up off the floor on a pallet. Many commercial dog beds are filled with materials that help control fleas.

- *A pooper scooper.* This handy device will let you clean up your own yard, a city street, or any other spot where your dog eliminates. That's good manners and, as we shall see, an aid in housebreaking.

- *Grooming brush, flea comb, and toenail clippers.* Canines require grooming; what's more, they love it. Chapter 12 provides complete instructions.

- *Food and water bowls.* Choose ones the correct size for the quantities of food and water your pet needs. As it grows, you may have to move up to larger sizes. Straight-sided stainless steel bowls work well because they are well balanced and hard to tip over, don't chip or break, and can be cleaned easily. Water-loving dogs like retrievers are famous for playing in their drinking water. For them a weighted bucket like the ones used to water horses is a good choice. Just be sure it's not too tall for a puppy to reach into. An automatic waterer — a pressure-sensitive device that attaches to water spigots and releases water when the dog licks it — is a convenient way to provide water when your pup is outdoors. It will quickly learn how to use the device.

- *Food.* A good-quality puppy food is a must, and adult dogs also need balanced nutrition. Ask your vet to recommend a diet suited to your pup's or dog's breed, activity level, and predisposition to such genetic conditions as hip dysplasia.

- *Toys.* Hard rubber or plastic chew toys and lengths of thick cotton rope are excellent playthings and teething aids. Balls should be at least three inches in diameter to prevent accidental swallowing and made of a material that won't tear off in chunks even under assault from sharp canine teeth.

The First Two Days

When you bring your puppy home, give it the comfort and physical contact it needs to feel secure, but don't

Let the puppy be your guide; allow it to invite you into body contact.

overdo social interaction. Let the puppy be your guide; allow it to invite you into body contact. Puppies require a great deal of sleep and constant handling prevents them from dropping off. Also, the puppy needs time and leisure to explore its new surroundings and check things out. Show the puppy around your home, indoors and outdoors. Let the dog gets its bearings before it begins interacting heavily with people.

Your primary responsibility during the first two days with a new puppy or dog is to respond to its needs, show the animal quiet love, and instill a sense of security by protecting it against trauma and injury. The puppy needs to learn to trust you and its environment. You need to be aware of where and how harm can come to the pup and take measures to prevent it.

Cats and Other Dogs

If dogs already live in your house, be sure they're leashed when the puppy or new dog enters the home. Be ready to protect the puppy if an older dog is seriously threatened and appears likely to hurt it. Should an older dog exhibit aggression, correct it immediately. Send the clear message that hostility toward the newcomer will not be tolerated.

Jealousy is a more likely reaction than aggression. Older dogs react to a new puppy or dog as elder siblings do to a new brother or sister. They fear they themselves will be displaced, and this insecurity leads to jealousy. You can use the same approach parents do when they bring a baby home. Bend over backward to give your current pets attention, so they don't feel displaced. Be sure to spend at least as much time with your pets as you always have, and more if possible. And give your current pets the sense that the new pet belongs to them too.

In most cases, it is best to let dogs get to know each other on their own, without restriction. Turn them out in a fenced area and leave them alone. By staying uninvolved you minimize jealousy and maximize the opportunity for interaction between the animals. A display fight may well occur, with various postures, barks, growls, and barings of teeth, all of which are ways canines work out hierarchy. Don't intervene unless one dog or the other is being hurt. In that case, stop the fight immediately.

Often an older dog will become a new puppy's mentor, taking the little one under its wing and showing it the ups, downs, ins, and outs of living with you. You may discover your older animal teaching the puppy how to use a favorite toy or giving it the cook's tour of the backyard.

Should your puppy be frightened by an older dog, don't coddle it. That will only reinforce its fear. Instead, talk to the puppy in a confident, upbeat voice and act as if nothing unusual has happened. This guideline applies anytime the new puppy is frightened. Help the pup overcome the fear by making the incident ordinary rather than reinforcing the fear through misdirected sympathy.

Cats and puppies in the same household usually work things out, but the pup may be scratched a few times before an accord is reached. You can limit the damage by having the cat's claws clipped before the puppy arrives.

Food, Water, and Sleep

Choose a place to feed and water your puppy and put its bowls there. This helps create a sense of security in the animal. Likewise, give it an established sleeping place, preferably next to your own bed. The nighttime connection adds to the puppy's relationship with you, and proximity during sleep will make housebreaking easier.

Puppy-proofing

It is important to puppy-proof your home as a way of protecting your dog's physical and psychological health. You can avoid a great deal of risk by confining the puppy in a crate when you need to leave it unattended for brief periods of time, like popping down to the grocery for bread, milk, and kibble. The crate gives the pup a strong feeling of safety, and it will protect your furniture and other possessions against housebreaking accidents and chewing. Don't, however, confine a puppy to a crate for an extended period since lengthy isolation can be traumatic.

If you must leave the puppy unsupervised, alone, and uncrated, unplug all electrical appliances and place the cords out of reach. Cords are attractive chewing objects, and a fatal shock can result from biting through insulation. Pups have also been know to pull things down on themselves, like toasters and irons, by pouncing on the cord in play.

It's good to keep telephone cords out of reach too. There's no shock danger, but a falling phone can break bones. Likewise, flip up the ends of low-hanging tablecloths. The pup may tug on them and pull everything off the table and onto itself, which can be hard on both your Irish crystal candlesticks and the animal. Securely fasten all closet and cupboard doors to keep the dog away from shoes, tennis rackets, and sports gloves. Place books and other potential chewables on shelves beyond the pup's reach.

In chapter 12, you'll find a list of household and garden poisons, including ornamental and wild plants. Review it and check over your house and yard to be sure anything and everything that can poison the puppy is securely out of eating and chewing range. At the same time, inspect any outdoor area where the puppy plays. Gates should be secured and locked, and the fence must fit snugly against the ground, leaving no gaps through which the dog can wiggle out. You'd be surprised just how small an opening a puppy can squeeze through. Provide your pet with water and shelter when it is outdoors; puppies can overheat, chill, or dehydrate quickly.

A sliding glass door is as big a hazard to a dog as to a human. The puppy may not see the glass, particularly if it is very clean, and run into it. If you have a glass door, keep the screen pulled in front or put stickers on the glass at canine eye level to increase visibility and lessen the risk of collision.

Rules of the House

Following a couple days of let's-get-acquainted, you can begin to draw your puppy more actively into your life and household. This is the time to start teaching the rules by which the dog will live its life in the family, rules that define your new pet's role and give it a sense of safety and belonging.

The first rule is love. Much as with a child, you want to give the dog the deep-rooted feeling that it is loved unconditionally. This rule is in large measure taught physically, by holding, touching, hugging, and — if you are of a mind — kissing the puppy. After the first two days have elapsed and the puppy has settled into its new home, it will be open and receptive to your affection. Bestow it lavishly.

When you pick up your puppy, lift carefully and carry securely. Cradle the chest of the puppy in the palm of your hand and then hold the animal against your body, where it will feel safe and secure. Don't try to carry a dog tucked under your arm. It's too easy for a puppy to squirm free and take a frightening, even fatal, fall.

As soon as you settle on a name for your pup, use it. Teaching the dog its name is the most basic lesson of training (see pages 178–179). In training the dog to respond to its name, you are teaching it to pay attention whenever the name is spoken — the first step in all the training to follow. Use a confident upbeat tone in your voice when you call out the dog's name, and praise it when it responds. The puppy will get the idea in no time.

A word to the wise: In choosing a name, avoid words that rhyme with commands. The similarity can confuse the pup. "Kit" is too much like "sit" for a dog to distinguish; "Neil" is nearly the same sound as "heel."

Right from the beginning, you can use the "no!" command to correct the puppy against chewing, biting, and jumping on people. Unless you want your house and furniture decorated with tooth marks, the pup must learn that chewing anything besides its own food and toys is unacceptable. When you catch the pup chewing something unacceptable, say, "No!," in a firm voice appropriate to the infraction and the pup's temperament, and take the item in question away. If this correction doesn't get through, give the pup a firm tap under its chin or use another of the correction methods described in chapter 7. You need to decide which correction will stop the problem behavior, without delivering so harsh a message that the puppy is traumatized. Take particular care to correct appropriately, and remember to end each correction with praise.

It is also very important not to show anger when you are correcting the puppy. This will likely be its first lesson in how correction works. You are not trying to instill fear; correction is not the same thing as domestic terrorism. It is clear, objective information: "Don't do that."

Biting, like chewing, needs to be stopped right from the pup's earliest days in your family. Pups bite instinctively; you need to let them know that biting humans is simply, purely, and absolutely unacceptable. Correct the pup for biting — even those playful little puppy nips — every time it happens. Use the same discipline for jumping on people. That behavior may be cute in a puppy, but in an adult Saint Bernard it is a health hazard. Again, use an appropriate correction and push the puppy to floor level, praising it as soon as it gets down.

The first rule is love; the second is consistency. As you create the rules of the house for your new pet, enforce them the same way each and every time. The animal will be nothing but confused if you correct it for jumping up, while your spouse, child, or roommate rewards it for the same behavior. Draw your whole family into the training process and enlist everyone's cooperation in consistency.

The Fun and Frolic of Housebreaking

Certainly no aspect of training a young dog or puppy occasions greater apprehension than housebreaking. In truth, though, if you approach housebreaking consistently, with a good understanding of dog mind, the task is simple, straightforward, and practically painless.

Housebreaking may also be required of newly acquired older dogs, particularly if they have been kenneled before they come to you. Follow the same steps as with pups, but you can expect an older dog, which already has physical control, to get the idea much faster — unless it has learned it's okay to relieve itself in the house. In that case, you'll need to start over, just as with a puppy.

"Better Go Now"

"Catch them doing something right" is a dictum from personnel management that applies equally to training dogs. Praising a pup for doing something correctly is even more important than correcting it when it does something wrong. Housebreaking is a prime example.

Although a puppy lacks the physical capacity to control its bowel and bladder until it is four to six months of age, you can lay the foundation for housebreaking by ensuring that the animal urinates and defecates only outdoors from its first day in your home. Since the puppy has no voluntary control of its body, it's up to you to get the animal outside before it eliminates. You need to pay close attention to the puppy and lead it outdoors as soon as it evidences any readiness to urinate or defecate.

Here are some of the clues to watch for. Take your pup outside immediately:

- when it wakes up in the morning;
- when it awakens from a nap;
- after a bath;
- after drinking water;
- after eating;
- after playing or exercising;
- when the puppy begins to search and sniff;
- when it begins to turn in small circles;
- when it starts to squat;
- when it appears nervous or stressed;
- when it looks restless or uncomfortable, whines, or cries in distress.

Get the pup outside the instant you spot any of these signs. If the pup appears particularly distressed and is a distance from the door, carry it out rather than let it walk on its own. Remember: It's not physically capable of waiting around till you finish that cup of coffee or type the next paragraph into the computer. Also, it's good practice to take the pup outdoors at regular intervals during the day to give it ample opportunity to relieve itself.

When you get your pet outside, give the "better go now" command (see page 181). The point is to link the command with the act of eliminating. Stay with the pup; if you wander off somewhere, your pup will follow, forgetting why it came outside in the first place and defeating the purpose of the training. As soon as the pup eliminates, praise it lavishly and happily.

The pup can be trained not only to defecate outside, but also to eliminate in a particular area — which can make the work of cleaning up that much easier. Faithfully place your pup in the same small area whenever you take it outside to eliminate, since the smell of past toileting prompts the canine urge to defecate and urinate. As usual, give the "better go now" command and praise the pup for success. Then clean up the feces immediately. Old feces are a canine turn-off, and your pet will avoid the designated toileting area if it is littered with the fly-specked remains of prior visits.

With luck — that is, if you antici-pate every time the pup needs to eliminate and get it outside in time — your pup will never relieve itself in the house simply because it has not learned that it may. But, then, luck can go bad.

Accidents Do Happen

If the pup does eliminate indoors, you need to correct it and eliminate the evidence of the accident — which can lead to further accidents. Here are the steps I recommend:

- Stay calm. This is an accident, not a personal attack founded on an intention to disobey you. It is an error and only an error. Calmness is required of you to correct the dog and make the correction stick.
- Don't call your dog to you, lest it associate its name with correction. Instead, take the puppy to the site of the accident and point to the evidence. Make sure the puppy knows what you're pointing to. I do not recommend, however, shoving the dog's nose into the feces. You would find this treatment brutal and abusive; so will your dog.
- As soon as the puppy figures out what you're pointing to, correct it with a firm "no!" or a bump under the chin on its own. The correction depends upon the pup's temperament (see pages 131–138). Be unemotional and gentle, but firm nonetheless.

- Take the feces and the puppy outside. If the pup has urinated, soak up some of the urine in a paper towel. Deposit the feces or urine-soaked towel in the yard, and be sure the puppy sees and smells it there.
- Once the puppy pays attention to the waste, praise it lavishly, as if it had succeeded at eliminating outside on its own. The praise creates a pleasant association with eliminating outside, a strong contrast to the unpleasant association of correction with eliminating inside.
- Spend a few minutes with the pup doing something it likes — roughhousing, chasing a tennis ball, whatever. This positive interaction overcomes any lingering insecurity in the puppy that it has been rejected because of the mishap.
- Thoroughly clean the site of the accident inside. If any traces of scent remain, the puppy will be drawn to return to the spot and eliminate there yet again. To counteract and remove the smell, use one of the commercial products that eliminates the smell and quickens biodegradation. These products are available at pet shops.

Help Me Make It through the Night

Many housebreaking problems occur at night, when sleep may prevent you from hearing your puppy's pre-elimination restlessness or sniffing. There are measures you can take to cut down the chances of mishap: offer the pup no food or drink after dinnertime, and either confine the dog to a small area close to your bed or place it in its crate while you're asleep.

If your pup neither eats nor drinks after about 5 or 6 P.M., and if you take it outside to eliminate several times before you go to bed, the pup will start the night with little in its bladder or bowel. The pup should be able to sleep for several hours before needing to relieve itself. Use common sense with this approach, though. If the weather is hot or the pup has played hard, don't deprive it of water. Instead, use an alarm to get yourself up and the puppy outside every few hours during the night.

Confining the dog to a small area near your bed or to a crate takes advantage of the animal's inborn disinclination to soil its own sleeping place. A confined pup or dog will most likely raise a considerable ruckus before it resorts to eliminating where it sleeps, and its agitation is likely to wake you before an accident happens. But don't lounge around in bed for a few more moments of shut-eye before responding to your pup; it needs attention, now! Be aware, too, that this method is not foolproof. If the pup does eliminate in bed or crate, it will likely do so again — simply because it has learned that it may.

As the relationship between you and the dog deepens, nighttime urination becomes less and less of a problem. Not that the dog has any reduced need to urinate; instead, you will become so attuned to the animal that you will awaken spontaneously whenever it needs to go outside and relieve itself. By the time your pup is an adult, chances are it will merely stare at you and you will wake up. The bond between animal and human grows so deep that communication passes right through sleep.

The Blessing of Housebreaking

Perhaps *blessing* is too strong or too religious a word; maybe I should settle for something like *opportunity*. But I mean *blessing,* which refers to the passing of goodness between two beings. That can happen during housebreaking. Although dealing with matters as basic as feces and urine may seem unpleasant at best, you are giving your pup an equally basic lesson in trusting your leadership and love. In the course of careful and consistent housebreaking, the pup comes to realize that you are attending to its physical needs as well as establishing the boundaries and rules of the house. In other words, you are the leader and the pup is safe in your hands. The pup is also learning that communicating with you, by indicating when it has to eliminate, is effective. The dog begins to sense that it can tell you what it needs and you will provide it. The lesson is an important one, central not only to training in the

narrow sense of learning commands but in the wider context of deepening your relationship with your pet through communication.

Introducing the New and the Unexpected

If a flying saucer settled in your backyard and little green-skinned beings with bobbing antennae and lavender eyes waddled down the unloading ramp on seven-toed feet, would you walk right up and offer your hand, or would you run in fear to the nearest bomb shelter? Pups face similar choices repeatedly during their early time in your family. They come from a different, canine world. Many of the things you take for granted in your house and other life settings they may find frightening, threatening, or, perhaps, interesting and inviting. To include your dog fully in your life, you'll want to introduce it to the sights, sounds, smells, and situations of your world.

Whiz, Bang, Clunk, and Zzzzz

As your pup explores your house and seeks its place in your family, expose it to household sounds. Be gentle; overeagerness can frighten the animal. Make sure your puppy's around when you turn on the dishwasher, for example. Nonchalance can dismiss fear. Be involved in petting or playing with your pup when the dishwasher starts, or give the pup a food treat. Continue the petting, playing, or treat as if nothing unusual has happened — because, in fact, nothing has; the dishwasher goes on every day, puppy or no. If the pup reacts to the sound by jumping away, let the animal go. Don't try to reassure the pup by telling it everything is okay. The pup doesn't understand what you're saying anyway, and it will instead pick up the concern in your voice, which will reinforce its fear. Rather, entice the pup back into playing or petting. In time, it will see that you accept the sound as ordinary and, synchronizing with you, it will likewise accept it as ordinary.

Howdy, Stranger

A key aspect of the pup's early emotional development, particularly between eight and twelve weeks, is socialization, the process by which an animal learns who belongs to its primary group. It is at this point that dogs learn to trust or distrust humans, particularly people they don't know.

Teach your pup to accept strangers on its own turf, where it feels safe and secure. Encourage the dog to be friendly. If the pup shows fear, don't coddle it. Instead, entice the pup into the social setting or, alternatively, ignore the dog and enjoy your visitors. Soon enough the dog will realize you're having a good time and it will want to join the action, thereby overcoming the fear on its own.

Visitors also provide an opportunity to train the dog in good manners. If it jumps up on your guests,

bites during play, or displays aggression, correct it, matching the intensity of the correction to the infraction. And when the pup is well behaved — staying off guests, refraining from biting, and acting fun and playful — praise it lavishly.

Grooming

Puppies, like all dogs, long to be touched. They love grooming when it is done carefully and well. Introduce your puppy to grooming with a soft brush and gentle strokes; remember, even a Great Dane starts out small and sensitive. Follow the instructions in chapter 12 on grooming, and be sure to touch and inspect the pup's whole body — feet, ears, tail, even the anus and genitals. Early contact, and the pleasure associated with it, will teach the dog to let you touch its whole body and will also reinforce your role as the animal's leader and protector.

Take Walks

Once it is settled into your home, introduce your pet to the neighborhood and the other localities that make up your life. Chapter 9 provides basic guidelines on walking the wider world with your canine.

Terrible Twos

Dogs, like humans, pass through a difficult developmental stage from about eleven to fourteen months of age, a period often called the terrible twos. As they pass into their second year of life, dogs are something like

Introduce your pet to the neighborhood and the other localities that make up your life.

two-year-old children, who are well known for stamping their feet, shouting "No!," and mounting temper tantrums in embarrassing settings like grocery stores, airport lobbies, and family reunions. But dogs reaching one year of age are actually less like toddlers than adolescents. Teenage boys and girls rebel against their parents and other authorities. Dogs between eleven and fourteen months do the same thing. They re-

sist and challenge, and just when you think you have them in hand, they resist and challenge yet again, even more cleverly.

Your goal during this difficult period of dog life is to maintain leadership. You're something like a father or mother whose sixteen-year-old has taken up motorcycles, rock and roll, late hours, and disreputable friends. You must have faith that the child will soon wise up and enroll at

MIT to study engineering. The situation is much the same with your dog at this stage. It will try, repeatedly and persistently, to topple you as leader of the pack. Don't let it win. Remember: Your dog is not seeking to become the leader, but to reassure itself that you still have the mettle to be top dog. Make sure your pet gets this message clearly. And understand that this stage is a necessary part of the animal's development.

This is a good time to review the material about challenge and resistance and how to deal with it, presented in chapter 8. As for training, review and practice the commands you have taught your dog. It is less important to teach new things during the terrible twos than to consolidate past training and solidify the team relationship between you and your dog — with you as the leader, and your dog as the follower.

Chapter Twelve
Keeping Your Pet Healthy

*I*N dealing with your continuing responsibility for canine health, keep in mind a central and critical fact: Dogs can't talk. When your dog is hurting, it has no ability to come up to you and say, "Master, this cramping sensation in my large intestine has been bothering me for the past two days. I really think I need to see the doctor." Nor will your dog remind you when the time comes for its annual checkup and vaccinations. Instead, it is up to you to establish and maintain a good program of preventive health care and to learn the signs of ill health in your dog.

This information is intended to give you an overview of canine health, not to substitute for regular veterinary attention. Indeed, the first step toward keeping your dog healthy and happy is choosing a veterinarian you like and trust.

A Doctor for Your Pet

It is important to choose a veterinarian you can trust. In many ways, selecting a doctor for your dog is like picking out a doctor for yourself. You want someone with good technical skills, of course. But you also want an individual you can talk to, who makes you feel comfortable, and who will answer your questions.

Veterinarians, like all professionals, vary in what they do and how they do it. Your best guide to selecting a veterinarian is word of mouth. Ask friends and neighbors which veterinarians they use, how they like them, what their experience has been with other doctors. Then visit a recommended veterinarian and see how your like him or her. In the end, your own instinct is your best guide. If a particular doctor feels right to you, stick with him or her. And if you don't like what you see, hear, or feel, then shop around until you find a professional who gives you the necessary sense of comfort and confidence.

There are a number of things you should expect from your veterinarian. He or she should operate a clean, well-equipped facility that includes X-ray apparatus, a laboratory, a well-stocked pharmacy, and separate operating and examining rooms — and he or she should be willing to let your examine the premises. Be sure to look at the office's overnight accommodations for surgical recovery and to check for automatic fire-protection equipment like sprinklers.

As a professional, your veterinarian should have academic credentials, license, and code of practice posted. Support staff should be polite, knowledgeable, and helpful. When you ask about prices and fees, answers should be straight and truthful.

Observe the way the veterinarian deals with your dog. He or she should display apparent affection for animals, and should also act with confidence and concern. Expect the veterinarian to be professional, polite, and personable. Nobody, and no dog, needs a surly curmudgeon. When you ask a question, expect an answer.

A good veterinarian will be willing to teach you basic skills like administering oral medications, putting drops in eyes and ears, taking your dog's temperature, cleaning ears and teeth, trimming toenails, and selecting the right diet for your dog's age, medical condition, and lifestyle. Instructions for home care should always be explicit and understandable. The veterinarian should have some arrangement for emergency care outside office hours. Ask for an emergency phone number in case the need arises.

Like all relationships, your interaction with your veterinarian is a two-way street. There are a number of important things you can do to make the relationship work well.

Always call in advance for an appointment, and explain why the doctor needs to see your dog (is this a routine checkup, or is the animal exhibiting symptoms?). If office staff request urine or fecal samples, or if you are asked to record information like the animal's temperature, activity level, or urination schedule, be sure to gather all the needed information before you arrive.

About calling ahead: This rule applies even in case of emergency. Your dog will receive better care if your veterinarian knows about the emergency in advance and can prepare for your arrival.

Be sure you're on time for your appointment. A veterinary office can be a very busy place, and showing up late won't do you, the doctor, or your dog any good. When you arrive, have your dog on-leash and keep it on-leash until the veterinarian or an aide asks you to remove it.

If the veterinarian prescribes medications, ask for specific instructions on how to administer them. And be sure you're clear on all the doctor's instructions for home care. If you don't understand something, ask for — and expect — clarification. Don't be intimidated by the stethoscope, the white coat, and the professional demeanor. If you don't understand, or if something disturbs you, say so.

Most veterinarians expect to be paid at the time services are rendered. Be prepared to pay unless you have made credit or billing arrangements in advance.

Don't Cure — Prevent!

It's bad enough that all too often we humans take our own good health for granted. You may be following what you know to be a bad health practice, like smoking, but if you feel good now, it's easy to keep on engaging in that bad practice — until it catches up with you, in the form of a health emergency or a chronic disease. The same logic applies to your pet — except that you, as the owner, are responsible for selecting and maintaining good-health practices for your dog.

Preventing health problems is vastly wiser than waiting for them to develop and then taking a sick or hurt dog to the vet. For one thing, it costs far less to prevent disease and injury than to treat it after it happens. For another, prevention saves you unnecessary emotional turmoil and your dog unnecessary pain.

There's another benefit to prevention: It bolsters the relationship between you and your dog. Remember that a dog needs a sense of security and safety in order to be happy. Prevention adds to that sense, by showing the dog that you care and that you are making its world secure and safe.

Diet

There is no one diet for all dogs. Nutrition requirements vary significantly with age, weight, breed, health, environment, physical activity, and breeding status.

Puppies in particular require a high-quality diet, important because adequate nutrition is critical to development of body and brain. Since they are growing very fast, puppies need more protein and fat per pound of body weight than adult dogs. The best choice is a puppy chow from a reputable manufacturer. Ask your breeder or veterinarian to recommend a brand name and how often and how much to feed your pet. Your vet also will keep an eye on your dog's weight as it achieves adulthood and can tell you whether more or less food is required. The same goes for monitoring your pet's weight as an adult.

Put table scraps down the garbage disposal, not in your dog's food bowl. If you feed your dog principally on scraps, you have no assurance that it is receiving the balanced nutrition it needs. Also, dogs do best on a consistent diet, and scraps vary from day to day, possibly putting your dog's digestive system in a state of continuous shock.

Bones also pose problems. Cooked bones are dry and brittle, and a dog's strong jaws can break them into sharp-tipped splinters that may penetrate the gums, stomach, or intestines, always painfully and sometimes fatally. If you want to treat your dog to a bone, use only a large beef knuckle bone that has first been parboiled to kill bacteria and then allowed to cool. Let the dog have the bone for brief periods of no more than fifteen minutes at a time. Should the dog consume too much of the bone at one feeding,

the bone material can become impacted in the intestines and require surgical removal.

Intestinal impaction is the drawback to rawhide bones as well. When chewed and swallowed, rawhide can form a solid mass that clogs the intestines. In extreme cases, surgery is needed.

The best solution to the bone dilemma is the nylon bones available at most pet stores. They are safe and dogs take to them as readily as the real thing.

Also, don't feed your pet raw meat or fish or fluid cow's milk. Raw meat and fish may contain bacteria that can cause serious food poisoning. Cow's milk may cause intestinal disturbances. If you want to give your dog dairy products, use cultured items, such as yogurt or cottage cheese.

Once you have your dog on a particular diet, don't change it suddenly. Shifting from dry to moist or semimoist food, for example, or even changing from one brand to another, can shock the dog's digestive system. The result is often painful and violent diarrhea. If you need to change dog foods, do so gradually. Mix the new food in with the old over a period of days, slowly increasing the proportion of the new food until you are feeding only the new diet. This gives the dog's digestive system time to adjust.

Make sure your dog has access to a water supply at all times, except during housebreaking training. Since dry dog foods contain less liquid than moist foods, dogs fed dry foods usually need more water than those on moist diets. To prevent bloat — a life-threatening buildup of extreme amounts of gas in the intestines — don't allow your dog to drink a large quantity of water right after a big meal of dry dog food.

Never let your dog drink from toilet bowls, irrigation canals, the ocean, or open water sources like streams and lakes, since they contain salts, chemicals, and pathogens harmful to the dog. When you go out for a long walk or hike, carry water for your dog just as you do for yourself.

A change of water source can upset a dog's digestive system just like a change in food supply. For example, going from a well to treated municipal water can cause diarrhea. If you are traveling or moving with your dog, take along some water from home and mix it in with the new water source, decreasing the proportion of water from home over several days so the dog can adjust gradually.

Make a habit of noticing how much water your dog consumes in a typical day. An increase in water consumption can indicate kidney problems, and a decrease can signal a urinary tract infection. In either case, a sudden change in thirst is a sign of possible illness and should prompt a call to your veterinarian.

Exercise

Dogs, like people, need to work out. Exercise helps prevent obesity and constipation, strengthens the muscular system and lessens the risk of joint injuries, and adds to an overall sense of well-being. Exercise is an excellent way to add to your relationship with your dog, too, since you two can share the pleasure of walking, swimming, or playing catch together.

Dogs, like people, need to work up to strenuous exercise. Sometimes owners assume that since the ancestors of the dog used to run down big game over long distances, they can just leash up their pets and lope off for a twenty-miler. It doesn't work that way any more for dogs than for humans. Let the dog build up over time to higher and higher levels of exercise, and remember that short but regular workout sessions are better than irregular bursts of strenuous activity.

Also be aware that dogs are as affected by altitude as people are. Many of the sporting breeds love to backpack, but be sure to set an easy pace the first day or two so the animal can become acclimated. Anytime you are breathing hard in thin air, so is your dog.

Swimming is excellent exercise for dogs as well as people, and some breeds, like retrievers, relish getting into the water. Still, be sure to introduce your dog to the water carefully. Never, under any circumstances, throw a dog in. Even though dogs do know how to swim, they can easily panic and drown. Instead, get into the water yourself and encourage the dog to follow you.

If you swim your dog in the ocean, be sure to choose a safe beach with no undertow. Obviously, too, don't let it swim if the swells are running heavy and strong. After swimming in salt water, the dog should be rinsed off to remove salt from its coat.

Rinsing is also a good idea after a dog swims in a pool, to get rid of the chlorine. If your dog does swim in a pool, be sure you're there when it gets into the water. Never allow an unsupervised dog around a pool. If it falls in and can't figure how to get out, it will paddle around until it succumbs to exhaustion and drowns.

Some breeds require a great deal of exercise, the equivalent of walking ten miles a day, while others can get by on as little as a mile. By no means do big dogs always require longer and harder workouts than small dogs. Instead, you have to set your exercise regimen to the needs of your dog.

The best gauge of the adequacy of your dog's exercise level is the way it behaves after working out. If the dog goes down for a long hard sleep after exercise, it probably had too much. A short nap is about right. And a dog that doesn't act tired at all is probably getting too little exercise for its own good.

Exercise level and capacity vary with age. Puppies usually play vigorously with each other and exercise themselves. Energetic as they seem, though, pups tire fast, need a great deal of sleep, and lack stamina. If you take your puppy out for a long walk, be prepared to carry it part of the way. At the other end of the life cycle, old dogs, especially those with heart or joint problems, need no more than mild exercise, and only when temperatures are neither too hot or too cold.

A hot day can cause hyperthermia, or heat stroke, as well as feet burned by hot asphalt or pavement. When temperatures and humidity are high, cut back on exercise. Also be sure to give the animal plenty of water to prevent dehydration.

The opposite effect, hypothermia, or decreased body temperature, can also affect dogs. Most at risk are sporting breeds that love to swim and retrieve and will keep it up no matter how cold the water. Be aware that a long swim in cold water can spell trouble for your dog.

Grooming

There is more to grooming than making your dog look like a showstopper. For one thing, good grooming pays benefits to the dog apart from mere appearance. A dog who is clean and comfortable feels cared for. Grooming is like massage, too, in that it helps the dog's circulation and relaxes the animal. And the sensual bond created between owner and pet in grooming, as you enjoy the feel of the dog's body and it enjoys your touch, helps cultivate the relationship between the two of you. Grooming likewise gives you knowledge of the dog's body, allowing you to spot changes that may be the first signs of disease, parasites, or injury.

Bathing

How often you bathe your dog depends on how your dog lives. A country dog who rolls in dirt and runs in the fields will need bathing more often than a city dog who gets its exercise on a leash in the park. The rule of thumb is to bathe a dog when it looks, feels, or smells dirty. In no case, though, should a dog be bathed more often than once a week, lest natural oils be stripped from the skin and coat, leaving them dry and irritated. Also, avoid bathing if the dog appears sick or might become chilled.

Use a shampoo designed for dogs; most human shampoos are too harsh for canine skin. Wash the whole body, including the tail and belly, and keep the shampoo out of the dog's eyes. Rinse the coat clear, since any remaining residue can irritate the skin.

After bathing, dry the dog with towels, especially around the ears. You can use a hair dryer if you prefer; introduce it to the animal carefully to keep from frightening your pet. Until the dog dries completely in the air, you may want to confine it to the house or a clean part of your yard. After a bath, dogs instinctively want to roll in something smelly and can quickly undo your work.

Should your dog encounter a skunk or roll in a skunk spray, ordinary bathing will do precious little to defeat that burning-tire stink.

Wash the dog instead in tomato juice, vinegar and water, or baking soda and water.

Combing and Brushing

Every dog needs — and will enjoy — a daily combing and brushing. The basic routine is to comb the dog first, then brush it, following the lay of its coat. Be gentle; you want your dog to wag its tail in anticipation of being groomed, not run off in fear.

The type of comb and brush you need depends on your dog's coat: smooth (beagles and dachshunds), medium-length (golden retrievers and Irish setters), long (Lhasa apsos and Tibetan terriers), double-coated (Siberian huskies and Samoyeds), or curly (poodles and Airedales). Ask your veterinarian, breeder, or pet store owner for advice on the best tools. You can also ask them to recommend a professional for the special grooming some breeds require, like clipping for poodles or stripping for terriers, if you don't want to do it yourself.

If you encounter tangles, knots, or burrs while combing, use your fingers to remove them. Stubborn ones may have to be cut out with a scissors; be careful not to nip the dog's skin as you cut. A little baby or cooking oil or petroleum jelly can help remove burrs and stickers. Paint and pitch in the coat can be removed with nail polish remover, but don't let it come into contact with the skin.

As you brush your dog, run your

hands over its entire body. This keeps your pet used to being touched, and it also allows you to check for lumps, rashes, ticks, fleas, or flea dirt — the sandlike grit fleas leave behind after biting a dog.

Ears

As part of the daily grooming routine, check your dog's ears. They should be clean and free of odor. If the ears are dirty — but not infected — clean them with mineral oil or rubbing alcohol on a cotton ball or swab. Do not use hydrogen peroxide and do not put anything, such as a swab, deep into the ear canal. You might puncture the eardrum.

If the ear feels hot to the touch, looks red and irritated, gives off a brown waxy discharge, or smells musty, it is probably infected. Dogs who have long ears and like to swim are particularly prone to infections caused by moisture trapped inside the ear canal. Trimming the hair around the ear entrance and flap may help minimize infection.

Your dog may signal ear trouble by pawing at its ear, shaking its head, or rubbing the side of the head against furniture, walls, or the ground. One cause of such distress may be a foxtail or other object that has slipped out of sight down the L-shaped ear canal. If you suspect a foxtail, gently squeeze the lower portion of the ear canal. You will find it below the ear, toward the back of the jaw, at about the same level as the dog's eyeball. If the dog flinches in pain, a foxtail, infection,

or ear mite infestation is likely.

Don't try to remove a foxtail or treat an infection yourself. That should be done by the veterinarian. And have the problem dealt with promptly. Untreated infections can impair hearing or cause deafness. Also, a dog with a continuing ear trouble may develop a hematoma — a bloody swelling in the ear flap from broken blood vessels — from constantly pawing at the ear. Hematomas also require veterinary attention, including possible surgery, to stop bleeding and prevent scarring.

Eyes

Inspect the eyes as well as the ears daily. They should look alert, clear, and bright. Matter that gathers in the corners of the eyes can be removed with a soft cloth, and dirt, insects, or foreign objects in the eye can be rinsed out with a sterile eyewash.

If the eyes look cloudy or inflamed, tear or blink excessively, remain closed, or give off a discharge, they are infected or injured. Another sign of eye trouble is the dog's third eyelid, which is normally visible only during sleep. If it can be seen when your dog is awake, or if it appears inflamed and covers the entire eye, the dog should be examined by a veterinarian. Likewise, a dog who is bumping into things and having apparent trouble with its vision needs immediate medical attention.

Eye problems always need to be treated without delay. Proper and timely attention can often reverse damage, but delay can lead to vision impairment or blindness. Also, a dog with an eye problem may paw at its eye, which will cause further injury.

As many dogs age, they develop cataracts, which give the eye a milky color. Also, some breeds suffer from eyelid malformations. In St. Bernards, golden retrievers, Labrador retrievers, and some setters, the eyelids may grow inward and rub against the eyeball, a condition known as entropion. The opposite condition, seen most commonly in spaniels and hounds, entails eyelid growth too far from the eyeball and is called ectropion. Both entropion and ectropion can be corrected surgically.

Feet and Nails

Feet, like eyes and ears, should be checked daily. Inspect the pads for cuts, burns, or raw spots. Burrs may lodge in the crevice surrounding the large center, or communal, footpad. Feel for them with your fingers. Also examine the webbed areas between the paws for dirt, burrs, foxtails, ice crystals during winter, and other foreign objects. If your dog has a long coat and is an outdoor enthusiast, trimming the hair between its toes may help prevent the accumulation of potential irritants.

Dogs don't groom themselves like cats, so anytime you see your dog licking and chewing its feet, it has a problem that requires inspection. Limping or refusing to place weight on a foot is also a sign of trouble. Dogs may chew sore feet to the point of self-mutilation. You can help prevent this by dealing with foot irritations as soon as they appear.

Typically, a dog's toenails have to be trimmed every two to four weeks, depending on the nails' rate of growth and the dog's lifestyle. Animals that spend a great deal of time on cement wear their nails down and require less frequent trimming. Nails that are too long impede movement. A dog should walk on its feet, not its toenails. If the toenails click when the dog crosses a hard surface, they are too long.

Always use a pair of canine nail clippers for trimming, not ordinary scissors. The nails are very strong, and the wrong tool will leave the nails a ragged mess and the dog an unhappy camper. Pull the hair back from the nail, and look at it from the side. The blood vessel that runs into the nail usually ends at the point where the nail starts to curve downward. Trim the hook off the end of the nail, bringing the nail about even with the pad. In puppies, you can leave the nail a little longer, about a quarter to a half of an inch beyond the pad. In both puppies and adult dogs, be sure to trim the dewclaw on the inside surface of the lower leg above the foot.

If you are unsure where the blood vessel ends, clip away a small bit of the nail at a time, or use an emery board. When a speck of blood emerges at the end of the nail, you've gone far enough. Regular nail trimming keeps the blood vessel from growing longer and farther into the nail.

If you should cut too close to the quick, simply apply direct pressure to the cut with a clean cloth or gauze pad or hold a styptic pencil against the end of the blood vessel. When the bleeding stops, apply disinfectant.

Some dogs resist having their nails trimmed. Try doing it after a long exercise session, when the dog is tired and its resistance is lowered. Or relax your dog first by giving it a massage.

The Mouth

As part of your daily grooming routine, examine your pet's mouth and brush its teeth. Start with the gums, which should be the color of pink bubblegum. Whitish gums indicate shock, blue gums signal insufficient blood supply, and yellow or orange gums mean hepatitis. Blue spots on the tongue indicate liver failure.

A dog's breath should smell clean. If it doesn't, something is wrong. A sickly sweet smell on the breath is a symptom of diabetes, and severe halitosis in older dogs indicates kidney failure. The most common cause of bad dog breath is the buildup of tartar and plaque on the teeth or an oral infection.

Some 60 percent of dogs over age six have dental problems, most commonly periodontal disease caused by accumulating tartar and plaque. The gums inflame and the support structure of the teeth gradually erodes, making the teeth loose and painful. The resulting infection also releases a steady stream of bacteria into the dog's system.

Your veterinarian can provide you with a special toothbrush and toothpaste to remove tartar and plaque. Or you can use a piece of gauze dipped in baking soda to clean the dog's teeth and gums. A teaspoon makes a good homestyle scraper for peeling off crusted tartar near the gumline.

Dogs may also suffer from tooth abscesses and cavities. Modern veterinarians can correct these and other dental problems with extractions, fillings, gum surgery, even root canals. These procedures are expensive, and you may be able to avoid them by cleaning your pet's teeth and gums regularly and having your vet scale and polish the teeth yearly. The brushing dislodges food particles and bacteria that cause plaque, while the scaling and polishing removes what plaque does accumulate.

Puppies lose their baby teeth between two and six months of age, and the forty-two adult teeth appear. The eruption of the permanent teeth is painful, and puppies will chew almost anything to ease the discomfort. A nylon bone is a good teething aid. If the baby teeth still remain in the puppy's mouth at eight months of age, consult with your veterinarian about the need to pull them to allow the adult teeth to come in properly.

The Stool

While inspecting the feces is probably the most unsavory part of grooming, it is important. The condition of the stool can tell you a great deal about what is happening within your dog's invisible insides.

A healthy dog's stool is firm and well-formed. If it is bloody, has the consistency of pancake batter, or looks watery and runny, something is wrong. Remember that a change in water source or dog food can cause diarrhea.

It is important, too, to pay attention to the frequency of defecation and urination in your pet. A sudden increase or decrease may be a sign of infection or other disease. Call your veterinarian and report the changes you have observed.

Immunization

Thanks to veterinary medical technology, the six most serious transmittable canine diseases can now be prevented by simple immunization. As long as you start the immunization schedule on time and keep it up thereafter, your dog should never suffer from rabies, distemper, hepatitis, leptospirosis, parainfluenza, or parvovirus.

When puppies are born, they usually inherit their mother's immunities. Thus, a pup born to a female immunized against distemper is itself probably immune to the disease. This immunity, however, diminishes within the first several weeks after birth, and that is when immunization should begin.

Vaccines contain disease-causing microorganisms, usually in a killed or weakened state to keep the vaccine itself from causing disease. When the vaccine is injected, the dog's immune system reacts against the microorganisms, producing antibodies that confer immunity to the disease.

A single vaccine known as DHLPP protects dogs against distemper, hepatitis, leptospirosis, parainfluenza, and parvovirus. Typically, the first injection is given when the pup is six weeks of age, then repeated at eight, twelve, and sixteen weeks. An additional parvovirus booster is given at eighteen weeks. Thereafter, dogs should receive DHLPP boosters every year.

Rabies requires a separate vaccination. Usually the first injection is given at four to six months of age, then the dog receives a booster every one to three years, depending on where you live and the kind of vaccine used. Many states and counties require current rabies immunization in order to get a dog license.

Until your puppy has completed the series of vaccinations at about sixteen to eighteen weeks of age, keep it away from strays or other dogs you fear may not be immunized. If the immunization series is incomplete, the animal may not be completely protected and could be exposed to serious illness.

Vaccination is a significant responsibility of pet ownership. For one thing, it protects your dog against the prospect of suffering and unnecessary death. Also it's your responsibility to other dogs and dog owners. The six major dog diseases travel so fast and easily that one infected dog who never leaves its yard can sicken all the dogs in the neighborhood. The only effective public health measure against these six key canine diseases is proper immunization of each and every dog.

Parasite Control

Parasites are creatures that live on, in, and at the expense of other animals. Dogs have their share of parasites and the miseries they can cause. As with many canine health issues, it is better to prevent parasite infestations than to treat them after they bloom.

Fleas

Dogs don't scratch and chew for lack of something better to do. They don't chase their tails for fun, either. The cause is usually fleas, which irritate the dog by biting its skin in order to feed on the blood. Fleas tend to congregate above the tail, on the tail itself, and around the anus, areas the dog has trouble reaching with its teeth or feet. It doesn't take many fleas to push a dog into misery. If the dog is allergic to fleas, just one bite is enough to trigger a bout of itching and hair loss.

Sometimes people take fleas on dogs for granted, as if they go together like baseball and peanuts, and do nothing about them. In fact, fleas cause dogs pain and suffering and should be stopped. Fleas are a major cause of canine skin problems, and they can also transmit tapeworms. If a dog swallows a flea that is hosting tapeworm larvae, the larvae will grow into parasitic worms that attach to the dog's intestinal wall.

To stop fleas, you have to treat more than the dog. Fleas in fact devote only about ten percent of their time to tormenting your dog. The other ninety percent is spent in carpets, bedding, drapes, and the backyard breeding and depositing flea eggs. You may kill all the fleas on your dog only to have the eggs hatch out a few weeks later and initiate the infestation all over again. Vacuuming your house often is one of the best defenses against fleas. Change bags regularly, so the eggs don't have time to hatch out in the vacuum cleaner, and dispose of the bags in an airtight container that flea larvae can't escape.

The only way to stop fleas is to develop a regular program of year-round flea control and follow it faithfully. Start by discussing the problem with your veterinarian. He or she can recommend the right products and the right treatment schedule to control fleas on your dog and its surroundings. And don't put it off. It's best to begin flea control on puppies as soon as your veterinarian says it is safe.

All flea control products are toxic (at a minimum, to the fleas!) and must be handled carefully. Some over-the-counter products can actually do more harm than good; certain chemicals and flea collars aggravate skin conditions, for example. Flea collars, in fact, are useless on dogs bigger than a cat because the insecticides don't radiate far enough to kill fleas in their prime congregating areas on the rump and tail.

In using any flea-control product, never exceed recommended dosage or frequency of use. And if you select an over-the-counter product, even one that claims to be nontoxic, check with your vet before using it.

Heartworm

Mosquitoes are more than an unpleasant annoyance to dogs. They can also transmit heartworm, a severe parasitic infestation that results in severe impairment and eventual death.

Mosquitoes frequent warm humid climes, and heartworm in the United States was originally confined to the area east of the Rockies, particularly the Southeast. However, as dogs and their owners have moved around, heartworm has moved with them. Today, heartworm is a risk practically everywhere in the continental United States.

Heartworm is aptly named — it is a worm that lives in the dog's heart. Eggs are injected into the dog's bloodstream from the bite of a host mosquito. The eggs hatch into larvae that then grow into adult heartworms, which take up residence in the left ventricle of the heart within five to eight months. A badly infested dog will have fifty to one hundred and fifty worms strangling its heart and respiratory organs, and these worms are continuously producing more eggs and larvae. Sometimes, dogs infected with heartworms show no symptoms, but may die suddenly. Others have an enlarged abdomen, breathe only with difficulty, and are unable to engage in even mild exercise.

Once a heartworm infestation has begun, it can be stopped only by treatment with an arsenic compound, which is very risky. The better approach is to put the dog on a preventive medication that keeps the larvae from growing into adult heartworms. The rub is that if adult heartworms are already present, the preventive medication can kill the dog. Therefore, the dog must be checked first, with a diagnostic blood test, to see whether it is already infected. If not, the preventive medication can be administered on a regular basis.

Check with your veterinarian about when to begin heartworm screening and medication for your puppy. Thereafter, adult dogs on the preventive medication should be tested for heartworms every one to two years.

Mites

Mites — which aren't insects at all, but arachnids, tiny eight-legged relatives of spiders and ticks — cause both skin and ear problems for dogs. Ear mites are the most common. These tiny parasites enter the ear canal and cause a miserable irritation, setting the dog to scratching and pawing at its ear. Sometimes a mite infestation causes a brown discharge from the ear. Ear mites can be stopped, but they are difficult to eradicate. You must follow your veterinarian's prescribed medication schedule diligently.

In the skin, mites cause mange. Demodectic mange is caused by a mite that lives in the hair follicles of most dogs, but actually causes mange in only a few breeds, usually short-haired dogs. Demodectic mange appears as reddish bald spots, typically on the head and leg, and is difficult to treat.

Fortunately, demodectic mange can't be transmitted to humans. Unfortunately, sarcoptic mange can. This mite burrows into human skin just as readily as into canine, but it is readily treatable. In the dog, symptoms of sarcoptic mange are hair loss, skin rash, and severe itching.

Ticks

Ticks pose more of a hassle than a hazard to dogs. These parasitic arachnids are common in many parts of the United States in woods and brush, where outdoor dogs pick them up. The adult tick buries its head into the dog's skin and lives off the dog's blood. A severe tick infestation can make a dog anemic, and in rare cases an attached tick paralyzes a dog. Usually the dog regains use of its limbs as soon as the tick is removed.

Attached ticks can be difficult to see, particularly in thick- and long-coated dogs, but they are easy to find by touch. They feel like hard bulbs protruding from the skin and are most likely to be found when you are grooming your dog. The best method of tick removal is to take hold of the tick with a tweezers and pull it out with a twisting motion. Don't worry if the head breaks off in the dog; it will disintegrate soon without harm and be absorbed. After the tick is removed, rub disinfectant on the bite to prevent secondary infection.

The biggest danger in tick removal is exposing yourself to disease. Ticks can carry Rocky Mountain spotted fever and Lyme disease, both serious illnesses in humans. Always use tweezers, not your bare fingers, when you remove a tick. And never crush a tick against naked skin, yours or the dog's. Pathogens in the tick can enter your body even through unbroken skin.

Worms

Different kinds of intestinal worms commonly infest dogs, and they must be treated by a veterinarian. Although over-the-counter worm medications are available, treating the dog for the wrong kind of worm can have serious consequences. If you suspect worms, check with your veterinarian before beginning treatment.

Many puppies are born with roundworms, an intestinal parasite they pick up from their mothers. These worms can also infest adults. Dogs and puppies with roundworms usually have a pot belly, dull coat, and chronic diarrhea, which may contain visible roundworms — they look like pieces of string.

It is important to stop roundworms. For one thing, they don't do the dog any good. For another, they can infest humans, typically through fecal contact. Small children, who spend a great deal of time crawling on the ground and putting things in their mouths, are particularly susceptible.

Puppies should be tested for roundworms at four to six weeks of age, and again at four months. Thereafter, it is a good idea to have your veterinarian examine a stool sample annually to check for roundworms. If they are identified, the worms can be stopped effectively with medication.

Small (less than one inch long) and threadlike, hookworms attach themselves to the dog's intestinal wall and suck blood. In a bad infestation, blood loss is so severe that the dog becomes anemic. Its gums pale, and its stools take on a dark color, tarry consistency, and rank odor from blood leaking into the intestine and mixing with fecal matter.

The larger whipworms, which are typically two to three inches long but so thin they have a whiplike appearance, infest the colon and cause abdominal discomfort, weight loss, diarrhea, and anemia. In some cases, though, whipworm infestation produces no symptoms.

Tapeworms reach about an inch and a half in length. Most dogs get tapeworms from ingesting a flea that contains tapeworm larvae, which emerge from the digested flea, attach to the intestinal wall, and grow into adult worms. Tapeworms are annelid, or segmented worms, and they reproduce by shedding body segments into the dog's feces. Often you can see these segments in the feces or around the dog's anus; they look something like grains of rice — shiny-white and translucent. Usually dogs that have fleas also have tapeworms — and vice versa — so both fleas and worms have to be treated simultaneously. Your veterinarian can prescribe and schedule the right medications and control procedures.

Poison Control

The poisons most dangerous to your dog are the substances you don't know are poisons. Practically everybody realizes that insecticides and herbicides are potentially toxic to dogs and humans alike. But are you aware that chewing the common landscape shrub oleander can kill your dog, as can potato sprouts or snails that have fed on snail bait? Typically, any substance that can kill a human will also kill a dog. But since dogs and humans have different lifestyles and sensory orientations to the world, dogs are vulnerable to certain poisons — like chewed oleander twig — to which humans are rarely exposed and therefore do not recognize as dangerous.

Antifreeze is a good example. Both dogs and cats are attracted to it, but antifreeze can be fatal if ingested. Rat and snail poisons are also dangerous. They are grain-based, as are most dog foods, so a dog may slurp them up just like its favorite kibble, with potentially lethal consequences.

The list that follows will give you an idea of some of the common poisons found around the home, garden, and woods. Use them to inspect your dog's surroundings and ensure that the animal does not have access to toxic materials, foods, or plants.

Household Poisons

- all tobacco products
- bleach
- cleansers and detergents
- foods: apple seeds, apricot pits, cherry pits, chocolate, nutmeg, peach pits, potato eyes, raw fish and meat
- medications for humans
- nail polish and nail polish remover
- paint, including old chipping paint

Shop and Gardening Poisons

- antifreeze
- ant stakes
- battery acid
- gasoline
- kerosene
- motor oil
- rat poisons
- snail and slug baits
- snails and slugs that have eaten bait
- varnish, paint thinner, stripper
- weed killers

House, Garden, and Wild Plants

- household plants: caladium, castor bean, dieffenbachia, dumbcane, elephant's ear, lantana, mistletoe, philodendron, poinsettia, rosary pea
- garden flowers: aconite, autumn crocus, bird of paradise, buttercup, Christmas rose, daffodil bulbs, foxglove, hyacinth bulbs, iris bulbs, jonquil, lily of the valley, narcissus bulbs, nicotiana, tulip bulbs
- ornamental and cultivated shrubs: azaleas, Carolina jasmine, chokecherries, Christmas berry, common privet, English ivy, holly, hydrangea, laburnum, laurel, lupine, marijuana, oleander, rhododendron, wisteria, yellow jasmine
- cultivated vegetables and fruits: avocado, potato, rhubarb, tomato, sorghum
- wild flowers, herbs, and shrubs: arrowgrass, baneberry, bloodroot, cowbane, cowslip, delphinium, field peppergrass, flax, horse nettle, jack-in-the-pulpit, jimsonweed, larkspur, mayapple, mustard, nightshade, poke weed, poison hemlock, skunk cabbage, wild radish, woody aster
- trees: black locust, buckeye, chinaberry, elderberry, horse chestnut, manchineel, mountain mahogany, oaks (and acorns!), wild black cherry, yew

Avoiding Hazards

One of the best ways to keep your dog from suffering unnecessary pain, injury, or disease is to avoid dangerous objects and situations. Some hazards are equally dangerous for humans and dogs, such as hot stoves, open fires, and contaminated surface water. But others, like tennis balls, are benign to you but potentially quite dangerous to your dog. This section runs down some of the obvious — and not so obvious — hazards.

Choke Chain

This necessary training aid can strangle a dog if used improperly. Never leave a choke chain on a dog that is unsupervised or running loose. Also never secure or tie a dog with a rope or long lead tied to a choke chain. It is all too easy for the dog to get into a tangle where it unwittingly hangs or strangles itself.

Cold, Heat, and Bad Weather

Dogs actually don't do any better in bad weather than you do; they just complain about it less. In fact, dogs are bothered by extremes of temperature as well as snow, rain, and intense sun. Sensitivity depends somewhat on breed. Alaskan Eskimo dogs, malamutes, and Siberian huskies originated in Arctic climates and are equipped to handle the cold; the Chihuahua, originally from tropical Mexico, tolerates heat well. Still, don't just assume that long-haired dogs can take the cold and short-haired breeds love the heat. Under the right circumstances, any dog can be chilled into hypothermia or made subject to heat stroke.

Low temperatures are as potentially dangerous to your dog as to you, and its coat is only limited protection. Hypothermia, or overly low body temperature, can result from prolonged exposure to cold. Small and toy breeds are easily chilled owing to their size, and dogs swimming in cold water can become dangerously cold. Take measures to keep your dog warm and dry at all times.

Overheating can occur quite fast in dogs because they lack sweat glands, except in their feet. Instead, they dump excess heat by panting. In a confined spot, like a car parked with the widows up in full sunlight on a hot day, a dog can suffer heat stroke in a matter of minutes. For the short-nosed breeds — who are anatomically inefficient panters — even riding around in a car without air conditioning on a hot day can be unbearable.

Dirty Bowls

You wouldn't eat from a soiled plate or drink from an unwashed glass. Don't make your dog do it either. Unwashed bowls can harbor bacteria and other pathogens. Clean your pet's bowls regularly with hot soapy water, and be sure to rinse away all the soap, which can cause diarrhea.

Dogs on the Loose

Other dogs can provide great company and entertainment for your pet, but beware of stray or unfamiliar animals. They may be carrying disease or parasites, or a fight could break out, leading to injury.

Electrical Cords

Puppies like to chew practically everything, including electrical cords. The results range from painful to fatal, including burns in and around the mouth, shock injury to the brain and heart, intestinal damage from swallowed bits of wire, and fractures and abrasions from falling appliances.

Foxtails

These sharp spiky seeds from several species of wild grass can easily penetrate a dog's ears, nose, eyes, feet, vulva, or penis sheath, burrowing inward and causing serious damage and pain. When foxtail grasses first come to seed, they are green and soft, but the seeds harden as they age, turning brown and sharp. The many small barbed bristles attach to a dog's coat and help work the seed into body fold or orifice.

If you have foxtails growing on your yard or land, the best approach is eradication, either by pulling them up or using an herbicide recommended by a weed control expert or agricultural extension officer. Be sure to confine your dog after weed killer is applied; some herbicides are quite dangerous. If you mow foxtails, don't leave the seeds on the ground. Rake and dispose of them.

Any time you take your dog into the field during the foxtail season, groom and inspect the dog carefully when you get home. Check all body parts where foxtails can enter. And do it promptly; a foxtail can easily bury itself deep enough to require veterinary attention in a matter of hours.

Garbage

Some dogs act as if the greatest fun in the world is knocking over garbage cans and slurping up whatever goodies they find there. Trouble is, garbage is also full of contaminated food, potential poisons, and physical hazards like broken glass and opened tin cans. Keep your dog out of the garbage.

Glass Doors

Animals, like children, sometimes don't see a glass door and plow right into it. Injuries can range from a simple bump on the nose to a severe facial or head laceration from broken glass. Putting stickers on a glass door at the dog's eye level can help, and keeping a screen pulled in front of the glass also makes it more visible.

Hot Cars

Even on a seemingly cool day, a car parked with its windows shut turns quickly into a hot box that can make your dog terribly uncomfortable. When temperatures rise into the eighties or nineties, a closed-up car can soon hit 110°F, more than hot enough to cause brain damage or death in a dog confined inside. Whenever it's warm, don't leave your dog shut up in the car, even for short periods.

Hot Spots

Fireplaces, barbecue grills, stoves, irons, and pots on the stove are every bit as dangerous to dogs as they are to children. Dogs, like children, are curious, and they may burn themselves just by trying to see what's going on with something hot or burning. Dogs have been burned by spilling boiling pots on themselves, usually because they were trying to get close for a good sniff, and singed their mouths trying to steal a chop or steak off the backyard grill. Anytime your dog exhibits interest in something hot, use the "leave it" command (see chapter 9).

Hot Streets

If you've walked barefoot across a sun-baked beach on a blistering hot day, you'll know how a dog feels on asphalt in the summer. Because their feet are shoeless, dogs feel surface temperatures intensely. Beware of hot surfaces, particularly those sitting in the sun, and never ask your dog to walk, sit, lie, or stand on what amounts to a hot plate.

Insects

Mosquitoes can be kept away by using a spray insect repellent of the kind you apply to yourself. Be judicious and use the spray lightly, particularly around the sensitive nose and lips, which are most vulnerable to bites.

Spider bites and bee or wasp stings are most likely when a dog is investigating. Dogs sniff and taste their way through life, which means they are most likely to be bitten or stung on the nose or in the mouth. Keep your dog away from things that may harbor insects, such as rotting fallen fruit and the yellow jackets it attracts.

Livestock

A good swift kick in the head or body can kill or seriously harm a dog. Pets who don't know their way around horses, mules, and cattle should be kept away from them.

Medications

Don't use over-the-counter medicines without checking with your vet first. And don't change prescribed medications without checking, either.

Off-Leash

Keeping your dog on a leash is one of the best ways to protect it. Letting a dog run loose can get you in trouble with the law, since many counties have and enforce strong leash laws. Running loose can also get your dog hit by cars, shot for harassing livestock, poisoned by garbage or contaminated surface water, bitten by other dogs, or stolen by dognappers. At home keep your dog fenced, and away from home keep your pet at your side and on a leash at all times.

Open Windows

Dogs do fall. They love to see what's going on outside, and in their eagerness they may lean out too far and take a tumble. At home, don't leave unscreened windows open, even low ones. Open windows are an invitation to escape and run loose. Secure all screens; a strong dog can push through.

Scents on the wind are a canine turn-on, but dogs should keep their heads inside the car. For one thing, the rushing wind can dry out a dog's sensitive nose, ear, and eye membranes. And flying objects can cause real harm; imagine smacking into a dragonfly at sixty-five miles per hour. Rocks, nails, and other road debris kicked up by other vehicles can also do harm. Small dogs may even lose their balance and fall out of the car through an open window. For safety's sake, keep your dog — all of your dog — inside the vehicle. Open no car window wider than half the width of your dog's chest. Dogs can squeeze through remarkably small openings.

Pickup Beds

Some folks just love to hang a rifle in the rack, put a dog in the back, and tool around in a pickup. It's macho as can be, but it's very dangerous for the dog, which can be tossed out onto the road and into traffic at the least bump. If you must put your dog in the back of a pickup, crate or cross-tie it securely.

Rats

These rodents are prime carriers of the leptospirosis bacterium. If you have them, get rid of them — but avoid rat poison, which your dog may get into, with potentially fatal consequences.

Small Metal Objects

Staples, paper clips, nails, screws, and the like belong on your desk or workbench, not inside your dog — where they can perforate stomach or intestinal walls. Fishhooks, hairpins, bottle caps, razor blades, spools of thread, buttons, straight pins, and sewing needles all pose a risk. Don't put them anywhere your dog can get them.

Swimming Pools

A dog who falls in and can't get out will drown. If you allow your dog into your pool, do so only when you are there to supervise. Otherwise, fence the pool securely and keep the dog from freelance forays in solo swimming.

Tennis Balls

Tennis balls are great for playing catch. They are soft and won't hurt teeth or gums, and they are too large to block the animal's windpipe. The danger arises if a dog chews on a tennis ball and swallows the stringy covering and the rubbery insides, which can choke it. Use tennis balls for catch, but don't let your dog use them as chew toys. Instead, keep tennis balls in a secure place away from your dog between catch sessions.

Toys

Many of those cute little doggy playthings in the pet store are dangerous. Anything painted, small enough to be swallowed whole, or chewable into small pieces is hazardous. Squeak toys are a dog favorite, but they are usually soft and rubbery, easily torn apart and swallowed. Use them only for playing catch, and don't give the dog the opportunity to chew them into swallow-size bits and pieces. The same goes for Frisbees, which can be torn apart and swallowed. Use them only for catch, not for chew toys.

Painted toys are dangerous because the paint contains lead, which, when swallowed, poisons the dog. Wood toys can splinter, piercing the dog's gums, throat, or internal organs.

The only truly safe full-time toys are those made of hard rubber or nylon. When you are selecting balls and other toys, be sure to get a size large enough that it cannot become stuck in the dog's throat and asphyxiate it. Thus, the bigger the dog, the bigger the ball.

Tying a Dog Up

Tying a dog causes all manner of behavior problems, particularly chronic barking and aggression. It is also dangerous to life and limb. Tied dogs can tangle themselves in ropes or chains, and they are likely to be attacked by other dogs, with no way of escaping the assault. Check chapter 3 for safer ways to restrain your animal.

Undisposed Feces

Clean up your dog's toileting area daily. Leaving feces around smells bad, draws flies, and spreads parasites such as roundworms.

Unsanitary Kennels

Dirty dog areas are breeding grounds for bacteria, viruses, fleas, and intestinal parasites. Wash kennels down regularly and be sure to use chlorine bleach after each washing to kill pathogens.

Detecting Ill Health Early

Every dog, no matter how clean its environment or up-to-date its immunization schedule, will someday fall sick or be injured. When that happens, the key is to recognize the trouble as quickly as possible and seek veterinary attention before a small problem grows into a major disaster.

The list that follows gives many of the basic signs of ill health or injury. Be aware of what they are, and if you spot any one of them in your dog, consult with your veterinarian right away.

- abdominal swelling
- appetite increase or decrease
- bloated belly after eating or exercise
- blinking eyes excessively
- blood in stool

- change in appearance
- choking
- constipation
- convulsions
- coughing persistently
- dehydration
- depression or chronic fatigue
- diarrhea
- difficulty in urination or defecation
- dragging leg or legs
- drinking pattern change, marked increase or decrease in water consumed
- dry heaves
- dull coat
- extreme sensitivity to bright lights and/or loud noises
- fever
- foaming at mouth
- gagging
- glassy eyes
- gums other than bright pink
- hair loss in patches
- hearing loss
- inflammation or swelling
- involuntary urination
- labored breathing
- limping
- lumps under skin
- mood changes (irritability, aggressiveness, listlessness)
- offensive odors, from anal glands, mouth, skin, ears
- pain reaction when touched
- paralysis
- pawing at face or ears
- pus-like discharge from eyes, nose, rectum, vagina, or wound
- resistance to movement (e.g., refusal to climb stairs or get into car)
- restlessness
- scratching or biting at body repeatedly and persistently
- seizure or convulsion
- shaking and tilting of head
- shivering
- skin that is stiff and inelastic
- sneezing continuously
- sores that won't heal
- stiffness in joints, limbs, or muscles
- stool changes, particularly appearance and smell
- swelling
- tenderness
- temperature increase or decrease
- ulcers on skin
- unconsciousness
- vision loss or impairment (e.g., dog bumping into walls)
- vomiting
- weakness
- weight gain or loss
- wheezing
- whining, as if in pain
- worms visible in stool

The Importance of Keeping Up

Finally, one of the best steps you can take for your dog's health and welfare is to pay attention to the increasing flow of research findings now making their way into wider knowledge. Only in the past two decades have we begun looking closely at the dog itself as a unique and worthwhile organism. These days, more and more investigators at major universities and research institutions are focusing on canines. Some are studying them from a medical point of view, learning new approaches to veterinary surgery and treatment of canine disease. Others are parsing out the dog's many genetic traits, building a new understanding of the varying contributions made by inheritance and environment to physical and emotional makeup.

This rising wave of research springs from a change in the social role of dogs. Once canines were merely work animals, only as good as they were useful. But as dogs move deeper and deeper into our lives, in part through innovative roles like assistance work, their status in society has changed for the better and made them fit subjects of study. This is to the good. As we know more about dogs, we understand them better.

Do yourself and your pet the favor of staying up on the new knowledge about canines. Your veterinarian can be one source of that information, particularly from the medical and clinical point of view. Take the time to read periodicals and magazines on dogs, and don't be afraid to join a club or network of dog owners — these days you can even find them online, through your computer modem! Learn all we are finding out about these marvelous animals, and you will come to a deeper, healthier, and more rewarding relationship with your own pet.

The Assistance Dog Institute is dedicated to improving the relationship between dogs and individuals with disabilities in a manner that maximizes the capabilities of both. Today there are over sixty programs worldwide involved in training and placing service dogs.

For more information about the Institute's continuing canine research and development work or to send a tax-deductible contribution, please contact:

The Bonnie Bergin Assistance Dog Institute
P.O. Box 2334
Rohnert Park, CA 94927
(707) 585-0300

Index